CHaUTaUQUa

20th Anniversary of the Chautauqua Writers' Center

issue 5

Editors
Jill Gerard
Philip Gerard

Contributing Editors
Diana Hume George
Philip Terman

Advisory Editor
Rebecca Lee

copyright © 2008 Chautauqua Institution

Chautauqua is published each June by Chautauqua Institution, a not-for-profit corporation under section 501 © (3) of the United States Revenue Code. Subscriptions are 20.00 for two years (domestic) and US 18.00 for one year (foreign). Single copies, US 14.95.

The opinions expressed in *Chautauqua* are not necessarily the opinions held by the editors or by Chautauqua Institution.

Acknowledgement is made to copyright holders on pages 383-385.

Chautauqua interns: Teresa Sheehan, Jonathon Smith
Copyeditor: Tom Dunn
Chautauqua Institution Archives Support: Jon Schmitz, Jason Rodriguez
Production Manager: Emily Smith
Cover and Book Design: Kara Norman
Photo Design Support: Corinne Manning

On the cover:
Mott, by Stephen Westfall 2007. Oil and alkyd on canvas, 24" x 24", courtesy of Lennon, Weinberg Gallery, New York.
Fraternizing: Soldiers and Girls, by Dr. H.S. Brasted, courtesy of Chautauqua Institution Archives.

Inside Photos:
"Post Office Clerk," 1907. Photographer unknown.
"Derek Berryman, student painter," 1960. Photographer unknown.
"The Service of Approach," 1909. Photographer unknown.
"Gov. Nelson Rockefeller," 1962. Photographer: Josephine Herrick.
"Ring-Around-The-Rosy," 1913. Photographer unknown.
"The Old Pier Building," taken between 1886-1911. Photographer unknown.
All photos courtesy of Chautauqua Institution Archives.

ISBN 978-0-9791403-7-2

UNCW
CREATIVE WRITING

Produced by The Publishing Laboratory
Department of Creative Writing
University of North Carolina Wilmington
601 South College Road
Wilmington, NC 28403-5938
www.uncw.edu/writers

THE CHAUTAUQUA WRITERS' CENTER is a lively community of writers at all levels of development who cultivate the courage, craft, and vision necessary to grow as artists under the tutelage of nationally recognized authors. Started in 1987, the original core program of eighteen summer workshops, readings, and lectures has grown to include the Chautauqua Writers' Festival, *Chautauqua*, and an active support organization, Chautauqua Readers & Writers.

The Chautauqua Writers' Center is located on the grounds of the historic Chautauqua Institution. For nine weeks each summer Chautauqua offers an extraordinary blend of programming in the arts, education, religion, and recreation. It is at once a community, a renowned center for the performing arts, and a resource for the discussion of the important issues of our time. The Institution comprises 750 acres on the shore of Chautauqua Lake in southwestern New York State. A National Historic District, it attracts 150,000 visitors during a season of more than 2,000 events.

At the Chautauqua Writers' Center, you can choose from one or more of the nine week-long sessions, combining a two-hour writing workshop with a vacation in the Victorian lake-side village. Enjoy the symphony, ballet, theater, pop and chamber music, family-friendly shows, lectures on contemporary issues, sports, beaches and more—all while polishing your writing skills.

For more information about specific workshops, tuition, and housing, visit us on the web: http://writers.ciweb.org.

SHERRA BABCOCK, Director of Education
LESLEY WILLIAMSON, Assistant Director of Education
CLARA SILVERSTEIN, Program Director

contents

The Life in Art

1	PHILIP GERARD *Chautauqua: A Moveable Feast*
4	PHILIP TERMAN *Job Description: Poet*
6	MICHAEL MCFEE *The Recitation*
7	MAGGIE ANDERSON *Art in America* and *The Artist*
11	RICHARD FROST *Cereal*
13	DAN MASTERSON *Clown with Trained Duck*
15	CARL DENNIS *Recall Notice*
17	DINTY W. MOORE *Apparently, Good Men Are Still Hard to Find*
20	WILLIAM HEYEN *On Joyce Carol Oates*
22	JOHN HOPPENTHALER *Recipe* and *Arts & Crafts*
25	BRUCE BENNETT *Calligraphy*
26	KATHLEEN AGUERO *Why I'd Rather Be Nancy Drew* and *Zen Nancy*
28	WILLIAM HEYEN *The Sea*
29	DAN MASTERSON *By the Sea, By the Sea*
31	ALICE B. FOGEL *How to Live: Poetry, Mystery, and the Holy Silence*
41	MICHAEL WATERS *Epistle Sonatas*
42	ALICE B. FOGEL *Aria*
44	RICHARD FROST *Drummer Young* and *Drummer Goes to Hear Harry James*
48	MARILYN ABILDSKOV *Inside*
56	SUSAN KINSOLVING *The Ocularist Said*
57	MICHAEL WATERS *Man in Black*
58	GEORGE LOONEY *Husks*
60	STEPHEN COREY *The Two Gentlemen of Verona* and *Romeo and Juliet*
63	RICK HILLES *Missoula Eclipse*
66	KATHLEEN AGUERO *Competence*
68	GREG KUZMA *Childhood* and *Excerpt from "A Litter of Blossoms"*

Private Lives in Public Life

- 80   Ann Hood *Comfort Food*
- 83   Alan Michael Parker *Peaches or Plums*
- 85   Kristin Kovacic *My Son Asks If I've Ever Worn a Bikini*
- 86   Ann Pancake *Said*
- 91   Philip Terman *Three Card Monte* and *With My Brother at Walden Pond*
- 96   Leslie Rubinkowski *Message*
- 104   Jan Beatty *Long White Sky*
- 106   Nancy Reisman *Another Kiss*
- 123   Mark DeFoe *Are You Out There?* and *I Was Flying and You Were Driving*
- 128   Maura Stanton *Milk Toast*
- 129   Jane McCafferty *Welcome the Demon*
- 135   Diana Hume George *White Girl*
- 149   Laura Kasischke *My Son Makes a Gesture My Mother Used to Make*
- 150   Sara Rath *Naked Ladies*
- 158   George Looney *Loss Has Left the Moon Charred*
- 160   Richard Hoffman *The Wave* and *A Reflection*
- 162   Jane Ciabattari *Mama Godot*
- 168   David Valdes Greenwood *On Father's Day*
- 171   Mark DeFoe *Mantle's Knees: A Kind of American Prayer* and *The Last Days of Amelia Earhart*

Our National Life

- 178   Jim Daniels *Reicarnation of the Peace Sign*
- 180   David Bouchier *The Plastic Horse of Troy*
- 182   Gregory Donovan *Quipu of the Scorched Lord* and *Sarah Henry, Phantom Wife: 1775*
- 187   Joan Connor *Good People*
- 199   Mary Gilliland *Scottish Roots*
- 201   Alan Michael Parker *The Song of Mrs. Hue*
- 203   Michael McFee *Slate Headstones, Charleston, S.C.*
- 205   Peter Fortunato *Good Morning America*
- 207   Geraldine Connolly *When the Surgeon* and *Evening Marina*
- 210   Faith Adiele *A Hunger for the World: The Personal Steps Out With the Political*

216 EMILY BARTON *Eli Miller's Seltzer Delivery Service*
221 MAGGIE ANDERSON *Small Citizens*

THE LIFE OF THE SPIRIT

224 RICHARD HOFFMAN *Winter Psalm*
225 LIZ ROSENBERG *The Saint Who Could Talk to the Damned*
235 ROBERT CORDING *Ossuary, Mt. Athos*
237 ROBIN BECKER *The New Egypt*
238 JEFFREY HARRISON *Household Spirits* and *Visitation*
240 STANLEY PLUMLY *White People, White Bible*
242 ROBERT CORDING *Hedge Crickets Sing: Some Thoughts On Art and Spirituality*
253 PHILIP BRADY *Gilt*
255 CAROL FROST *Man of War*
256 KIRK NESSET *The Dead Know Too Much*

LIFE LESSONS

264 SARAH WILLIS *Swimming With Dolphins*
276 JAN BEATTY *Procession*
278 TODD DAVIS *Golden* and *The Sunflower*
281 RICK HILLES *The Last Blue Light*
283 RICHARD TERRILL *At Himmel's Cottage*
309 GEORGE LOONEY *Some Long Forgotten Sea Chantey*
311 CAROL FROST *To Fishermen*
312 SUSAN GRIMM *The Lungfish Gasps In Its Cocoon of Tears: Adaptation* and *Lake Tahoe Roil*
315 LEE GUTKIND *Dr. Mason*
322 ELAINE TERRANOVA *Meteor*
324 MAURA STANTON *Snow Globe*
326 RON MACLEAN *Last Seen, Hank's Grille*
343 GABRIEL WELSCH *Canticle for Snow* and *What the Deaf Boy Heard*
345 ELAINE TERRANOVA *Casually Vagrant*
347 RICHARD LEHNERT *To the Nights*
349 DAVID LAZAR *Melon Man*
357 MARY GILLILAND *East of the Garden*
358 BRUCE BENNETT *After School*
359 MARGARET GIBSON *Dead Reckoning*
361 ANTHONY DOERR *Butterflies*

364 Contributors' Notes

*It is true of the Nation, as of the individual,
that the greatest doer must also be a great dreamer.*

—Theodore Roosevelt

a moveable feast

Chautauqua: a moveable Feast

Philip Gerard

I. a moveable Feast

Teddy Roosevelt famously called Chautauqua "the most American thing in America." In an age of globalization, defining a national identity may seem anachronistic, and yet the opposite is true: a nation secure in its own identity can look outward to the wider world for culture, art, literature, and ideas, broadening its intellectual and artistic palette, incorporating fresh ideas and aesthetics.

As Booker T. Washington observed about our language, "We don't just borrow words; on occasion, English has pursued other languages down alleyways to beat them unconscious and rifle their pockets for new vocabulary." Lacking all but a few centuries of our own history, we have always been a nation that takes in new ideas, whatever their source, and puts them to good use.

Such a nation is guided by a healthy, true, and accurate idea of who its people are, what they want from their government, and how best to achieve their collective ambitions in a peaceful manner. Such a nation is not governed by fear or blinded by pathological delusions of grandeur.

Thus it is also with personal identity—and nations, after all, are made up of people, each of whom in some small way contributes to that amorphous thing called "the national character." A person who has reached some accurate sense of who he or she is at the core—what beliefs inform his actions, what principles underlie her behavior, what aspirations underlie his ambitions, what knowledge informs her decisions—that person can approach the world with the confidence to try out new ideas, to test principles against experience, to question received wisdom, to interrogate the culture and contribute to its evolution. To listen, and to read—deeply and broadly.

Honest self-knowledge is the foundation on which character builds. And self-knowledge derives from knowledge of the world in all its complexity.

From its founding, Chautauqua has been as much a philosophy and an aesthetic as it is a physical place, a 750-acre village of houses and cottages, theaters, stages, artists' studios, recital halls, practice rooms for musicians, churches, seminar rooms, and lecture halls on the shores of Lake Chautauqua in western New York State. Its soul lies in the American passion for self-improvement—the drive to enrich oneself culturally, artistically, morally, and intellectually. This is the spirit that residents and visitors experience during the nine-week summer season.

It is no exaggeration to say that the founders of Chautauqua, Lewis Miller and John Heyl Vincent, intended to help shape the American character by democratizing the pursuit of knowledge. But they could hardly have anticipated just how influential a force for enlightenment Chautauqua would turn out to be. When it began in 1874, it aimed to provide "vacation learning"—first as a kind of Methodist Sunday school but almost immediately broadening its scope into secular studies of all kinds, especially science, education, and the arts. Nowadays, each season more than 150,000 people attend public events on the grounds and 8,000 students enroll in courses.

Self-improvement was the original impetus for Chautauqua. Ambition in its best sense—not for career advancement or commercial gain, but ambition as a way of completing oneself, to understand, to be better, to live more fully in the culture that nurtures and unites us.

The educational mission has defined Chautauqua from the beginning. It is, after all, the act of teachers *teaching* that ensures the survival of culture, the vibrancy and relevance of its ideas, its aesthetic and history, the continuing refreshment of it with new art and thought, across generations. It's an essential transaction for civilization.

Introduction

Chautauqua, now a world-renowned and revered institution, became a national movement through an ingenious enterprise that was essentially a way to "broad-cast" that transaction, in the sense of a farmer sowing seeds. It did so by means of a very special book club—the Chautauqua Literary and Scientific Circle. The movement—a logical extension of vacation learning—was directed toward women, who could study in their homes and meet with other Chautauquans in any of the 10,000 local "reading circles" around the country. All of them completed a course of prescribed reading and writing about the books they had read.

Graduation—called "Recognition"—was, and still is, held on the grounds of Chautauqua. The graduates are marched under a golden archway, constructed especially for the ceremony, into the Hall of Philosophy, a spacious open-air pavilion resembling a classical Greek temple. There they are formally inducted into the society. In the old days, festivities included numerous sermons and speeches and, as at any other summer camp, always ended with a ceremonial campfire.

A belief in the value of education as an end in itself and as a tool for progress and active citizenship has been a mainstay of American values since the days of the Founders. Legions of immigrants have embraced education with an almost religious zeal. Chautauqua—the place and the movement it created—took that faith in education one step further. Rather than make education separate from life, it sought to integrate it into daily life. People did not have to go to some separate place to learn—they could learn at home. If they chose to travel to Lake Chautauqua, their vacation could incorporate learning. Self-improvement was portable, a moveable feast. Art and ideas and spiritual questing would become a part of the daily routine, a way of living. They would not be an embellishment of life but a practical part of it.

Soon "Chautauquas" traveled to every corner of the nation, often operating under tents during the summer season. Many thrive to this day.

CHAUTAUQUA

II: THE EXEMPLARY LIFE

For more than a hundred and thirty years, Chautauqua Institution has served as a stage, classroom, and pulpit for leading figures of their times, including Ulysses S. Grant, Booker T. Washington, William Jennings Bryan, Alexander Graham Bell, Susan B. Anthony, Helen Keller, Charles Lindbergh, Jonas Salk, and Thomas Edison, who understood both the stuff of dreams and the stuff of the world: "To invent, you need a good imagination and a pile of junk."

In 1918, during the rise of world socialism, John D. Rockefeller lectured on capital and labor. In 1936, with a second world war on the horizon, Franklin Delano Roosevelt delivered his "I Hate War" speech. In between, in 1929, Amelia Earhart landed her aeroplane on fairway 14 of the Chautauqua golf course and delivered her account of being the first woman to fly across the Atlantic to 5,000 spectators at the Amphitheater, then four hours and fifteen minutes after landing, took off again into the wild blue.

Of all the luminaries who have left their stamp upon Chautauqua, Teddy Roosevelt—TR—is in some ways an exemplary figure to keep in mind when contemplating its mission, history, and aspirations. For one thing, he delivered a speech there—as did seven other Presidents. And he spoke to many other "Chautauqua Societies" around the country that had sprung up in emulation of the original, including the Jewish Chautauqua Society of Atlantic City, New Jersey, to whose members he spoke on his favorite subject, Americanism:

> "You are not to be excused if you do not have a high ideal. You are not to be excused if you permit yourself to accept the view that anything that is base or mean or unworthy is to be pardoned; that you are to pass by with a laugh civic corruption or social misdeed. You are to have a high ideal, just as high as you can raise it, but you are to strive to realize it in a practical fashion."

Introduction

That's the American spirit—idealism realized in practice. One could almost say that this is the Chautauqua spirit: don't just admire art, go ahead and make some. Don't just understand democracy, participate in it. If you have faith, then act on it. Notice too that TR didn't hesitate to admonish, to lecture, to educate, even to preach in his own secular fashion. Again, Chautauqua from its inception has been about education.

He embodied many of the best and noblest American virtues and also exemplified important flaws—the very flaws that arise out of our peculiarly American vision of the world. Because he was larger than life in almost everything he undertook, his triumphs are more obvious and his failings more catastrophic. In that way, he is like a Shakespearian figure—not entirely tragic, though surely knowing despair at the end. More the protagonist of one of the historical plays.

He put his own life on the line for his principles. He was the very incarnation of the "can-do" attitude, a champion of the underdog, a believer in progress and the virtues of technology. He was the apostle of self-improvement, physically, intellectually, and spiritually. He began life as a sickly boy in a household divided by the Civil War (his mother's family owned slaves, his father was a Lincoln man) and wound up the epitome of the "strenuous life" of the outdoorsman, leading a country that probably never again will enjoy such unity.

He took on every challenge of his life with spirit and gusto. He was a voracious reader and a best-selling author and a famous naturalist before he became a celebrated political reformer and the hero of San Juan Hill and a legendary president who left the greatest stamp of any individual in history upon the physical landscape of America by creating both the National Park system and the Panama Canal.

But he also struggled with his own racist tendencies and habits. He was perhaps too quick to resort to armed force to back up national prestige—a failing we have not outgrown. He was impatient with complexity and tended to cast the personalities of the world as heroes or villains.

He embodied most of the contradictions of American culture. He was physically brave and a Nobel Peace Prize winner who also helped drum up two wars—the Spanish-American War in 1898 and what was called The Great War, until it was superseded by a greater one and had to be designated simply as World War I, leaving ample latitude to add numerals to denote future wars. The Great War took his beloved favorite son, Quentin, as the second great war took his namesake son, a general who landed on D-Day. Both were renowned for boldness that amounted at times to foolhardiness, in the manner of the father who had trained them.

He was called the "Peacemaker President," but he made his political fortune the day he charged up a hill in a Third World country leading a band of volunteer Rough Riders in a war that seems, in retrospect, unnecessary, even trumped-up. He was a family man who sent all four of his sons off to war and agonized over their fates.

He had unbounded faith in America, as an idea of democracy no less than a place, and yet he founded an American empire that at times ran roughshod over the peoples of less powerful nations.

He placed tremendous trust in Providence, yet experienced a long dark night of the soul after his wife and mother died only hours apart on the same day. He retreated to a ranch in South Dakota and remained inconsolable for almost two years afterward. When he lost the 1912 Presidential election for the Bull Moose party, he again retreated to lick his wounds, this time to South America to visit his son Kermit. I've always found it fitting that his last great adventure—a trip through the Amazon rainforest that nearly killed him—was a journey down the River of Doubt.

III. a season Between Covers

Chautauqua carries on the American experiment as TR—and thousands of others over its long existence—envisioned it. For nine weeks each year, in churches of all denominations, faith wrestles with doubt. Politicians

Introduction

and statesmen stand up in lecture halls or the amphitheater to argue the virtues of their worldviews. Artists, musicians, and actors explore the limits of their crafts in theaters and concert halls while passing on their wisdom to chosen apprentices.

And writers synthesize all of this robust activity of the mind and senses and soul: artfully addressing pop culture, personal trials, family matters, religion and rituals, ethics, history, and social issues, while they ponder the nature and aesthetic aims of their poetry, fiction, and creative nonfiction.

Right from the start, Chautauqua was a place of reading and writing, and over the years the literary arts became a prominent focus, culminating in The Chautauqua Writers' Center—this season celebrating its twentieth anniversary. For two decades, its staff, volunteers, and visiting writers have served fellow writers and readers through workshops, readings, discussions, craft talks, contests, and publication. *Chautauqua* wraps that milestone between covers and anchors a new incarnation of the Center's signature publication. It marks the transformation of *Chautauqua Literary Journal*—in future issues simply *Chautauqua*—into a more deliberate reflection of the remarkable phenomenon that has been such a force in American culture, offering that vision to a national audience.

In crafting this volume, we contacted every writer we could find who served—or will serve this season—on the Center faculty, searching out work that exemplifies the spirit of inquiry and discovery that pervades The Writers' Festival and the subsequent nine weeks—education in the broadest and most inclusive sense. *Chautauqua* tries to capture that spirit.

The prose and poetry is organized into five creative seminars, each focused on an aspect of our lives that is addressed in some fashion onsite by guest speakers and teachers, in lectures, seminars, workshops, performances, and discussions, during the actual Chautauqua season: art, the individual in the community, government, spirituality, and education. If you listen, the poems, stories, and essays speak to one another, commenting and critiquing, playing ideas off one another, taking shared themes in different directions.

The original Chautauqua inspired a national movement of such energy and optimism that even Roosevelt, himself a human dynamo, was impressed by its force. Traveling tent shows imitating the programs presented there brought theater, opera, classical music, art, theological debate, and literature to the hinterlands all across America.

It's hard to imagine a movement of such determined, democratic idealism and faith in education sweeping across, say, autocratic Germany or class-conscious France. There may well be a class system in America—many critics have made cogent arguments—but there also exists a naïve, national optimism that denies it vehemently as a first principle: any little boy—and now any little girl—can grow up to become President. There's no civic problem so intractable it can't be solved by citizens of good will hashing it out in a town meeting. One person, one vote. Politics is meant to be rowdy and disorganized, a regular donnybrook of conflicting opinions. A free press is essential to a democracy. So is freedom of religion and conscience. Every child can be taught—none will be "left behind." Genius is one part inspiration and ninety-nine parts perspiration. All the great ideas of philosophers, the sublime experience of art, the literature of the ages, are available for the taking: a person must simply make the effort.

It's our mythology, a glorious one, if you ask me. My parents were not college graduates. Their parents, mostly, could barely speak English. They left their villages and journeyed thousands of miles to take part in that mythology, whose clearest expression is Chautauqua—where a couple of seasons ago I listened to Elizabeth Von Trapp, granddaughter of the refugees celebrated in *The Sound of Music*, tell family stories and sing "My Favorite Things" as a thousand people sang along. In one remarkable moment, a young folk singer, a terrifying escape from the Nazis, a family legacy, and a canonical Broadway show and movie all

Introduction

melded together in a single experience. It was a complicated, thought-provoking, and joyful moment—as such moments must always be—at once private and communal.

Reading poems and stories and essays is like that—a profoundly individual and private experience but also one that carries a reader into the great stream of literature, a shared experience after all.

So think of this volume as a kind of portable Chautauqua season between covers. The sections reflect, loosely, the general categories of experience addressed during that season, and each category contains its own inherent conflicts. The categories are the invention of the editors, not the writers, a convenient way of playing one writer's vision off another's in the spirit of oblique, artful dialogue.

"Job Description: Poet" is a fitting overture to "The Life in Art"—contributing editor Philip Terman's good-humored and dead-accurate evocation of the place of the poet in a contemporary society which requires a paycheck to validate work. Kathleen Aguero's persona compares her own mundane life to that of fictional girl-heroine Nancy Drew, having fun with the fantasy but also finding some deeper insights into why we need cultural icons and how we choose them. In a series of excerpts from a long heartfelt memoir about his own Chautauqua experience, Greg Kuzma distills the essence of that experience for an artist, and its lasting value.

"Private Lives in Public Life" offers portraits of individuals trying to reconcile their interior reality, the life of the intellect and imagination and soul, with the urge to be a social being and the responsibilities of participating in some larger civic entity—a family, a community, a town. Ann Pancake's short story "Said" investigates a shooting and the urgency of the guilty parties to get their story straight—a near impossibility, with all the conflicting versions. Ann Hood writes eloquently of grief and the small gestures of kindness it inspires in others, who offer the only comfort they can: food.

The issues in "Our National Life" begin with the peace sign, an anachronism made fresh again in a contemporary context in Jim Daniels's lovely meditation, "Reincarnation of the Peace Sign." Joan Connor gives us a new version of an old Irish fairy-tale about the disappearance of Bridget Cleary, a reminder that our national ethos is braided from the strands of many national myths. Faith Adiele addresses the necessary intersection between politics and art in "A Hunger of the World: The Personal Steps Out With the Political."

The writers included under "The Life of the Spirit" are not preachy or dogmatic. They delve into corners of the soul sometimes neglected by mainstream religion, including love and communication beyond the grave in Kirk Nesset's short story "The Dead Know Too Much." In many of the works, belief wrestles with skepticism, as in Richard Hoffman's haunting poem "Winter Psalm."

"Life Lessons" makes an implicit argument: education is central to the human experience. We learn deliberately, we learn accidentally, we learn in spite of stubbornly resisting the lesson, in spite of our comfort in our own ignorance. Education has always been at the heart of the Chautauqua project, so it is fitting that this is a broad and deep section. The lessons are often ambiguous. Sarah Willis writes with deep feeling of an illicit love affair with a dying man, an affair that is both wrong and necessary for both of them, in her short story "Swimming With Dolphins." Sometimes, as in Anthony Doerr's breathtaking essay "Butterflies," the lesson waits in ambush, a kind of miraculous surprise for a traveler alert enough to see it, receptive enough to simply take it in without question or doubt.

We introduce each of the five sections with a short epigraph, quoting a celebrated figure who visited Chautauqua.

We deliberately quote men and women who left an imprint on our culture but who, though they wrote books, were not primarily literary artists. We wanted to emphasize that writing creatively does not happen in a vacuum, that though the writer must retreat to a calm, private space to create his or her art, the world is always roiling like a storm just beyond the garret window, intruding its context into the writer's

Introduction

imagination: politics, social upheavals, wars, celebrations, popular culture, crime and punishment, technology and adventure, loves and losses and family, religion and finances, celebrities and scandals and triumphs of altruism, sports and atrocities and the magnificent and terrible natural world, and, of course, all the other arts: opera, symphonies, paintings, sculptures, dances, plays, and all the rest. The writer's art is constantly communicating with other art forms. The writer's subjects, themes, conventions, style, and aesthetic all derive from a fertile conjunction between the personal imagination and the public world beyond the window.

Likewise we have chosen cover art that reflects a startling contemporary aesthetic overlaid on the traditions of an earlier Chautauqua. Stephen Westfall's lively geometric painting, *Mott*, captures the eye, even as it comments on *Fraternizing: Soldiers and Girls*—the same way that the swimsuited young women have captured the eyes of the soldiers from Fort Niagara who are chatting them up across a picket fence on Heinz Beach in August, 1945. Because the photograph is folded into front and back covers, you can't see the soldiers ogling the young women until you open the book. The surprise presence of the soldiers enlivens the scene, turns it into an encounter—perhaps romantic, maybe a little sad, maybe even a little humorous.

So settle back on a couch or a comfortable patch of grass and spread this book open like a tent to shade your eyes as you immerse yourself in the world of imagination, language, and ideas that lives under its covers. Like the original Chautauquans, you can enjoy vacation learning. For as many minutes or hours as you like, you are part of the Chautauqua Writers' Center.

Good reading,

Philip Gerard
Wilmington, NC

CHauTauQua

20th Anniversary of the Chautauqua Writers' Center

Literature is my Utopia. Here I am not disenfranchised. No barrier of the senses shuts me out from the sweet, gracious discources of my book friends. They talk to me without embarrassment or awkwardness.

—Helen Keller

The Life in Art

Job Description: Poet

Philip Terman

Isn't it my job to loaf and lean at the table,
to nap at inconvenient hours, my shirt
untucked? Aren't I getting paid to speak
inappropriately, to remain silent
when pressed, to avoid meetings?
Would you rather me be punctual?
Would you rather me answer the phone?
When the snow arrives, I'm paid
to stick out my tongue. When
the light bulb shatters, my task
is to describe the dark. Don't expect me
to always return to the same chair
like a dog to the same tin bowl
in the corner of the kennel. I sleep
when others are awake, am awake
when others sleep. Hunger
is the most important ingredient
in my diet. When you point
to a plane, I'm staring at the moon.
When you point to the moon,
I'm digging the earth with my teeth.
I'll sign your petition with my epic.
Don't follow me unless you want
to go somewhere else. Don't
be surprised if I respond
to your chastisement

Philip Terman

with an embrace. Or if I claim
paradise from my dungheap.
Or if I continue to talk long after
the wind has spoken its last elegy.

THE RECITATION

Michael McFee

She stands to speak its lines, then shuts her eyes
against the light that might erase the words
she's worked for two straight weeks to memorize.

What does she see in there, on that black screen?
The poem as script, a private feature film,
shot by lyrical shot and scene by scene?

Her eyelids shiver. She sways forward. We wait.
The poet waits, to hear his dead self live.
She licks dry lips and pulls herself up straight

and then it comes, the title, stanzas, all.
The body really is the greatest poem.
Breath. Throat. Tongue. Teeth. The fall

into fortunate speech filling our ear.
She smiles unblinded at the final phrase:
her eyes are shining. The said world is here.

art in america

Maggie Anderson

Three of us, two poets and one painter,
drive out into clear autumn weather
to gather in some harvest
from the roadside stands
where pumpkins are piled up
like huge orange marbles in the sun
and the gray Hubbard squash
are disguised as blue toy tops among
blueberries and jugs of apple cider.
We have to make our choices,
as in art, calculate the risk
of making them too ordinary, pale,
like a pool ball hit too thin
because we get afraid
when the table's so alive.
We also risk bravado
(too many pumpkins, or too large)
and, since nothing's ever free,
we might have to put things back.
But today, we think we'll
get it right because
we're not alone
and we're laughing,
arguing a bit,
examining the vegetables,
making up our minds, and

CHAUTAUQUA

saying how we think we might
believe in the perfection
of communities of artists,
the common work among us.
What one of us does not get said,
the others will.

THE ARTIST

Maggie Anderson

Tamsen Donner, laying out her linens
in Illinois and packing up the books
for the school she would start in California,
had no way of knowing if any of the children
playing in the red dust by the wagons might
be an artist. But eight-year-old Patty Reed
sitting on the wagon tongue talking
to her doll, knew even then what would be
required of her on the trail. She knew
it would be her own flat insistence
and determination—"God has not
brought us this far to let us perish
now"—that would keep the armed men
of the Relief Party to the task of bearing
famished children on their backs through
waist-deep snow. Patty Reed knew
to pack up a satchel to carry out with her,
as she'd seen her mother and Tamsen Donner
do, before they left the States. She knew
enough to hide it from the practical men,
risking their lives to take her down
the mountains. She carried it with her,
underneath her clothing, through the High
Sierra snows, away from the yellow light
of the fire at Alder Creek, where the dried
flesh she had eaten was the mule she had ridden

CHAUTAUQUA

through the Wasatch. She carried out three things:
a small glass saltcellar, her black-eyed doll,
a lock of her dead grandmother's hair.
When Patty Reed was safe at last in the warm
camp in the foothills, she lifted up her thin
dress and unwrapped her little bundle. The men
moved away from her and said nothing, as,
past her hunger, she brought out these things
of beauty and of memory, and began to play.

Cereal

Richard Frost

The little boy, fifty years ago, thinks that his cereal
from Battle Creek, Michigan, is somehow the serial
he likes to be scared by at Saturday matinees,
and the cowboys' checkered tablecloth is the same
as the Ralston cereal box with its red and white squares.
Words flicker and gallop like *Gun Battlers of Grim Creek*—
disappear, reappear, black hats, white hats,
white puffs of smoke, rifle fire, pistol fire.
The herd tumbles over the bank. Heard they robbed the bank!
Words have little smells, tastes. *Saw horses. Sea horses. Shoe trees.*
Shoo fly. Button your fly. Defense stamps. Offense, fence.
One nation invisible. Hot dog. Dogfight. Planes. Cross the plains.
Hangar. Clothes hanger. Pea. Pee. P. Polite. Light pole.
Today the ex-little boy learns that in Battle Creek
they turned to the breakfast cereal business,
invented grape nuts, early in the twentieth century
because the demand for animal feed was diminishing.
That's what makes him remember cereal and serial,
etc., and how one thing leads to another.
The grown man thinks now that maybe he has lost something,
that maybe now he's so sure of his words, that they mean
what they mean, that they *are* those same things,
that he's lost the feel, the texture, the little aromas
of words. *Baseball, bowl, bowel.* He doesn't really *hear*
the words, because they always mean something.
So the man goes around saying *train, traaain,*

CHAUTAUQUA

training, rain, aviary. He walks his dog
and says *tree, three, three tree houses, mouse*.
He is so happy! He wraps his tongue
around the words. He tastes them. People look at him.
He gets out of his car and says *look, walk, watch,
town, window, wind, windshield wiper*.
He gets back into his car and turns on the wipers,
which scuff and squeal because it isn't raining.
He remembers the little song of the windshield wipers.
Saduffa, saduffa. More and more comes back.
He is a little boy again, sitting between his parents,
whose conversation makes no sense to him. *Pamphlet. Ambassador.
He loves them. Superintendent. Arbitrary*. He's going home.
You think he's likely to function well in this world?
You think he will? Would you bet your beans on him?
The cop is probably walking toward him right now.
He'll have trouble understanding anything seriously.
Serially. See? *Certainly. Central. Circle. Creek. Cereal.*

CLOWN WITH TRAINED DUCK

Dan Masterson

After Everett Shinn's Painting

Mildred, the Barnabus-Bailey Carnival duck, performed her swan song yesterday in Toad Suck Hollow, Arkansas. The deceased, famous for her disdain of audiences and her sashaying waddle to the strains of "Flat Foot Floogy with A Floy Floy," was accompanied by Arnold the Clown, always second fiddle to his top-banana partner, on a flight home last night to the seclusion of their residence on Long Island.
—The Amagansett News, December 12, 2002

Arnold got the billing, but Mildred
Got the crowd. Arnold didn't like it
For crying out loud would put her
In a dither & get her dander up
While Arnold tried to salvage
Whatever she'd disrupt. By now,
They'd done it all, played every
Carny town. She'd flip flop up
The ladder, but refuse to come back
Down. She'd sit there in a piffle

That the limelight seemed to bring
While Arnold blew his flugel
Horn & tried to dance & sing.
But she'd just dilly-dally & watch
Him like a hawk, her eagle eye

CHAUTAUQUA

Squinting as he'd beg & walk
The walk. He'd try to raise her
Hackles with his brand of flim
Flam yak, but she'd let it slide
Just like water off her back.

Razamatz, zippidydoo, the whole
Kit 'n' caboodle made no dent
Whatsoever on Mildred's bird-brain
Noodle. & then, all of a sudden, she
Flies the coop right into a yokel's
Face, sending sad-sack Arnold
Off on a wild goose chase: lickety
Split, alakazam, shivaree-boo
They go. But Mildred, no spring
Chicken, is laid out like feathery

Snow. As always, Arnold is kneeling
Shedding buckets of crocodile tears,
& Mildred is playing the possum
As she's done for all these years.
But when Arnold ruffles her feathers
& gives her a peck on her brow,
She doesn't rise to the moment
For the roar of her final bow.

Recall Notice
Carl Dennis

He's one of those teachers who decides one morning
That his approach to the novel or play
He's taught for decades is a little biased,
And resolves, in the name of justice,
To right the balance. Now he's ashamed
To recall his unmannerly hauling of royal Lear
Before the court of a sophomore classroom,
His pronouncing the old man not merely headstrong,
Hungry for praise, and prone to rage,
But flagrantly ignorant of world,
Confident he can cede his kingdom
And still retain his kingly authority.

Yes, it's all true, he admits,
But isn't it also true that the king
Deserves to be praised as well,
After the arrogance of Act One,
For shaking his feeble fist in the face of calamity
And asking aloud what can be made
Of the nothing he's left with,
Or the next to nothing?

Other teachers may be as willing as this one
To correct themselves for the sake of truth.
But how many would worry about the students
They taught the old view? How many would dream
As he does of recalling the notebooks filled in class

CHAUTAUQUA

For some serious alterations in focus and tone?
Or if not the notes of all, then those of the few
Who paid attention and remembered the class
Long afterwards. Rebecca Bryce, say,
Who sat near the front twenty years ago,
Head bent, taking every word down,
While most of the others studied the rain
Soaking the hemlocks outside the window.

To her he'd be happy to send a note
Expressing the hope no lecture of his
Berating Lear for believing the praise
Lavished on him in Act One is sincere
Left her suspicious of friendly overtures,
Reluctant to let her guard down for a moment.
And he hopes that none of his pious commending
Of Lear's belated humility and contrition
Induced her to suffer injustice tamely.

From her it would be a pleasure to hear
That his worry is more than a little ridiculous,
His claim to an influence
He never came close to possessing.
Let her think of him as a fool,
The kind of fool, if he could choose one,
That Lear becomes at the end,
Oblivious to the issue of kingly authority.
Let the kingdom he's lost stay lost
While he chats with Cordelia.
Let those who would do him a service
Patrol the perimeter of his cottage,
Turning messengers from the court away.

Apparently, Good Men Are Still Hard to Find

Dinty W. Moore

For three days, nothing rises or converges near the sprawling white house that Flannery O'Connor shared with her widowed mother and two maiden aunts during most of her teenage years. As best I can tell, the old house on West Green Street, in Milledgeville, is abandoned—not in disrepair, but unoccupied, and vacant.

The O'Connor mansion is right next door to the Old Governor's Mansion, where I'm staying, a guest of Georgia State College and University. The school was called Georgia State College for Women when Ms. O'Connor attended, right before she lit out for Iowa City. William Tecumseh Sherman spent some time here as well, occupying Milledgeville in 1864 during his fiery march through the South. Milledgeville was the Capital in those days.

I'm staying in the Governor's third-floor master bedroom, the room Sherman no doubt occupied during his brief stay. Not much of a Civil War buff, I find the view of O'Connor's childhood home from my window to be the bigger thrill. The house is impressive: tall columns framing a grand entranceway, majestic windows, a stone wall enclosing a generous, though badly-overgrown, double lot.

Each night of my stay, I read myself to sleep from O'Connor's collection, *A Good Man Is Hard to Find*. I love the whole book, especially the title story. Few works of short fiction are bleaker, yet with her ear for dialogue and characters like Red Sammy Butts, a man whose stomach hung over his pants "like a sack of meal swaying under his shirt," I find myself laughing out loud. She does that to me.

O'Connor even mentions Sherman at one point, with a small aside about family silver hidden behind a secret panel. Hidden from Sherman's troops.

CHAUTAUQUA

I find myself checking out my bedroom window at odd hours, staring into the O'Connor home and the overgrown backyard. Hoping for ghosts.

ON MY FOURTH MORNING, I linger near the property line separating the grounds of the Governor's Mansion from Miss Flannery's backyard. The large, flat, waxy leaves on one of the family's many trees have caught my eye, and I've moved in for a closer look.

Then I notice a car parked in the meandering driveway—surprise enough—until I see a small white-haired woman in a straw hat approaching from the back steps. Her dog, a feisty black lab, is standing in a patch of ivy, ripping a McDonald's bag into shreds.

"He is so bad," the woman says. "Can you believe he pulled that bag right out of my car?"

Momentarily embarrassed, I apologize for hanging over the wall, pulling on the waxy leaves. "I was just admiring the house," I explain.

"This was Flannery O'Connor's home," the woman offers. She examines me closely from under her wide straw brim.

"I know," I answer. "I know who lived here."

THE WOMAN INTRODUCES HERSELF as Louise Florencourt.

"I am Miss Flannery's cousin," she explains. "We were contemporaries."

That makes Miss Florencourt roughly seventy-five years old. Had Flannery not died of lupus in 1964, she would be the same age as this cousin, perhaps living again on West Green Street, perhaps still turning out books.

"Do you like the house?" Miss Florencourt asks me, her sharp eyes seeming to record my every reaction.

"I do," I say.

She seems pleased, explains that she is the caretaker of this house, and of Andalusia as well, the O'Connor family farm on the outskirts of town, home of the famous peacocks.

"I'd like to invite you in," she says, gesturing to the back porch, "but it is such a mess."

"Oh, I don't...."

"It's so hard to find a proper contractor," she interjects quickly. "I had a good one a few years ago, but the man just disappeared."

"The house needs work?" I ask.

"I had a second man just this past year, but it didn't end happily," her eyes twinkle, "for either of us."

The dog finishes ingesting whatever flavor the fast food bag held for him and comes over to stand by his owner's feet. Miss Florencourt reaches down to skritch his ear.

"There's so much to be done," she says. "Maybe in ten years, if I'm still alive, and you visit, I can invite you in. Maybe then."

For the moment, I'm struck dumb. I am just this close to a tour of Flannery O'Connor's childhood home, it seems. This close, and I have no idea what to say. Should I press the issue, offer to fix a few things myself? Impress Miss Louise with my knowledge of her cousin's writings? Appeal to the dog?

But there is not time.

Miss Florencourt smiles her gentle smile, as if she could read my very thoughts, then reaches down to hitch a leash to her errant pooch.

"Not today," she repeats. "Not until everything is back in shape." She looks up at the big house, shakes her head. "It's so hard to get a man to come in. Just so hard to get proper work done."

On Joyce Carol Oates

William Heyen

A few weeks ago I dreamed that we all lived within a totalitarian regime, that I'd been arrested and ordered, as a kind of Kafkaesque trial, right then, unprepared as I was, to write down within a specified time, the titles of as many Joyce Carol Oates books as I could. *Schnell*, a voice said. The ones I could not name would disappear from existence.

I started weeping, for even though I had read most, and, given time, would probably be able to name even the earliest Vanguard Press novels and LSU books of poetry, even a dozen limited editions, even though I knew *On Boxing* and her book on George Bellows and the names of most Rosamond Smith mysteries and her children's books and her books for teen-agers and the major books that had kept me in thrall—*Them* and *Bellefleur* and *Blonde* and *American Appetites* and many others from Dutton and Ecco and elsewhere—and of course I could not forget those books special to my heart that she seemed to create all at once in a trance, so seamless were they, *Black Water* and *Broke Heart Blues* and *We Were the Mulvaneys* and *The Falls* and others—and even though I knew the names of most of her books of stories, could even picture their jackets, and of plays, and of criticism, and even books she'd edited, *still* I knew that I would not be able to name everything, that my friend would lose some of her work, that her family would be decimated, and I would not forgive myself for this.

But then Joyce herself was there. I saw her in my dream as her husband Ray had described her in a letter when, in 1999, she read at the Aran Islands Literary Festival in Ireland. Ray wrote: "The reading was at a 2,000-year-old stone fort on the highest, windswept point of Inishmore, with local youths dressed as Druids on the battlements waving torches. It was here that Joyce read from her new novel, the wind tearing at her hair and the pages of her manuscript." Now Joyce said in my dream, "Never just you mind, there are more, there will always be more." This was the clearest audition from any of my dreams, ever, Joyce Carol Oates saying, "Never just you mind, there are more, there will always be more." She was grateful for all of her books that I'd saved—this must all have to do with my need to collect (and, in fact, I've always felt the unnecessary need to protect Joyce), but she was completely absorbed in what she was writing now, in sustaining the generative force of the present as the wind, that wind of time, tore at her and her manuscript. The "never just you mind" was a clue to the intuitive—never just of the *mind*—and unconscious sources of art that had somehow always consoled and sustained her, that would console and sustain us, in our perilous time and place, if anything would.

Joyce Carol Oates's ever-unfolding *oeuvre*, whatever her present story or subject, is an embodiment, an em*book*ment of astonishing psychic health, and is certainly already complex enough and capacious enough to welcome us and future readers—never just *you*, mind!—for always.

Recipe

John Hoppenthaler

I'm the one working the kitchen, making stock
from chicken wing tips I'd saved in the freezer,
some bouillon cubes, the picked-over carcass

of last Sunday's dinner. A gallon of spring water,
celery stalks, a few cloves of garlic for luck &
health, a handful each of sliced carrot & sweet Vidalia
to deepen the color & keep you, dear, rooted

to earth. I'm the one straining out sediment
with a Chinois, golden liquid pooling there,
filling the bottom of your mother's favorite bowl,

the one setting broth in the fridge to chill,
scraping off next morning's greasy patina of fat
from the surface—it's been winter here forever!
I'm the one simmering, steaming, ladling soup

over wild rice in your finest kiln-fired crockery,
Chef de Cuisine of intense flavor, of this *oh so
nice* homemade & homely midday decadence.

aRTS & CRaFTS

John Hoppenthaler

More interesting to me were notches and chevrons,
quarter moons snipped free from folded sheets
of construction paper, not the colored "snowflakes"

themselves, taped later to classroom windows
or tacked onto bulletin boards. And bulletin,

indeed, portent of the hardest winter, memorandum
to ominous skies stretching their pall over Clarkstown.
I swept confetti from my desktop and stuffed it

down into corduroy pockets until recess
when I sat alone, crown rung of the monkey bars,

and hurled fistfuls of magic into oak leaves
that swirled, then stalled, then scurried across
the playground blacktop. Small matter,

but still, surly Miss Cruz yelled me down, made me
gather what scraps I could trap under sneakers,

and marched me inside to copy onto loose-leaf
page forty-three of Webster's dictionary. Words
took on their meanings then, risen from

CHAUTAUQUA

that schoolboy spell. Winter passed
as well, curling flakes replaced in December

with sloppy cutouts of Christmas trees and Menorahs.
More interesting to me, though, were snow angels
lucky fifth graders were spiriting just outside,

jacketed bodies so easily occupying the chilly
spaces their legs and wings had scissored wide.

Calligraphy

Bruce Bennett

Ad Maiorem Gloriam

He peered with pleasure at the tiny sign,
a skill it took him all those years to learn.
Noted its graceful curve, the way the line
wavered, but then grew strong at its return.
He wondered whether he too would grow strong
and finish with a flourish, work well done,
God's good and faithful servant. What went wrong?
Why couldn't he simply labor with the sun,
the way he once did, then call it a day?
Why was he subject now to stabs of doubt,
unanswerable questions? Who could say?
He scrutinized his work again. Without
it, nothing mattered; that alone he knew.
Through it he lived, whatever else was true.

WHY I'D RATHER BE NANCY DREW

Kathleen Aguero

NANCY'S TO DO LIST

Ask jeweler to trace origin of stolen bracelet (might be a clue).

Remember to rescue drowning girl who just happens to be niece of missing heiress.

Practice back-hand.

Pack pastel party frock for visit with chum at the lake.

Bind Hannah's sprained ankle.

Go to party with Ned but make him hide in the bushes to eavesdrop.

Help Dad pack for trip, then escape from attic, sneak down hidden staircase, knock gun from crook's hand.

Climb over wall to evade man trailing me.

MY TO DO LIST

Call Visa to report credit card stolen (might just be misplaced).

Remember to pick up Betsy's friend Sally after school. Mention to her mother, who just happens to be sister of head of foundation, that I've submitted grant application.

Do back exercises.

Buy cheap scarf at Walgreens to cover stains on silk blouse so I can wear to the Johnson's party tonight.

Take Mom to orthopedist to check on sprained ankle.

Make casserole for Johnson's party. Try to find out if Ned already got grant I applied for.

Help Timmy pack for overnight, then get warm clothes out of attic, vacuum stairs, knock ice off porch roof.

Bang head against wall.

zen nancy

Kathleen Aguero

The roadster's on blocks.
She walks most everywhere
or takes the bus. What curiosity
she feels is inner, quiet.
The mysteries she solved, so innocent
they hardly seem crimes at all. She laughs
at her logical mind. She was an icon
for a certain type but that girl
keeps getting younger and Nancy's sleuthing
more difficult cases these days:
the code of the aurora borealis,
the trail of the horseshoe crab, the sound
of stone, the color of air,
the vast and clueless sky.

The Sea

William Heyen

I couldn't see which titles, but they were mine,
boxes of them piled six boxes high, or ten,
or three, the piles tottering, the bottom boxes wet.
I knew my books would suffer, despite their root-

bound overhang, for this was the time of hurricanes,
but I still thought to save them, me with my broken hip,
maybe carry them, or some, maybe at least
a few boxes, a box or two, to higher ground,

so bent my knees properly, but couldn't quite
grip the cardboard to pile a small box onto
a larger one to carry two, then couldn't even rescue one.
Poetry had already slipped into where compost

becomes the sea, that brine oversoul that now
seeped around the boxes & my bare ankles
as I tried to lift armfuls of orphans to my bosom
to awaken where I'd been before I wrote them.

BY THE SEA, BY THE SEA

Dan Masterson

Based on Delvaux's *The Village of the Mermaids*, 1942

This morning, one of our companie looking over board saw a mermaid ... a Sea came and overturned her. From the Navill upward, her backe and breasts were like a woman's ... her skin very white; and long haire hanging down behinde, of colour blacke; in her going down they saw her tayle, which was like the tayle of a Porposse and speckled like a Macrell.
—Henry Hudson, 71 degrees north in the Barrents Sea, near Norway, June 15, 1608

Waiting for rain, they dream of tidal waves
That will sweep them back into the sea, but
For now, they sit on their spindle-leg chairs
In front of their owners' sheds, the fishermen,
Armed with keepnets, who caught them in frolic
Too close to shore, who now dress them in gowns
Draped to the ground, concealing their broken

Caudal fins, which flop as legs from knees,
Rendering them useless, unless in bed, & useless
As a means of escape when the masters carry
The mermaids to the seaside for their midnight
Immersion which allows them to survive on land,
To feed the men's fantasies. But there are plans
Afoot. Mer legend reminds us that some earn powers

CHAUTAUQUA

From the deep through long silence & meditation
& lack of motion, & as you would see, if allowed
To visit their passageway, each is aspiring to be
The one who frees her sisters & sends their captors,
Cruel & coarse, to a watery grave. The mermaids are
Caned for their lack of passion & their annoying
Quiet & their failure to communicate. Yet, they sit

Wholly within themselves, their backs raw from
Floggings, their folded hands sending signals on
The sly: names of family safe beneath the sea,
Prayers addressed to gods in unison, sacred images
Hung in air by fingers signing in the slightest way,
Casting shadows from one to the next, barely moving
Against the sun. & soon: a day a week a month,

some afternoon, one of them will unfold her hands,
Disturbing the air about her, churning it to frenzy,
A mist that will darken to storm, caudal fins
Regenerating in great thrust on the heaving wave
That engulfs fishermen destined to drown, their
Remains allowed to surface as nothing more
Than brackish waste befouling a stern & empty sea.

HOW TO LIVE: POETRY, MYSTERY, & THE HOLY SILENCE

Alice B. Fogel

Adapted from a lecture given at Chautauqua through the Writers' Center, Summer 1999

"Only mystery enables us to live," the poet Lorca might have said if he had been asked to expound upon "how poetry helps people to live their lives." That was the theme put to the panelists at the American Poetry Review's twenty-fifth anniversary celebration. (As it is, he said it in another arena.) And I think he would have been more to the point, because, after all, what do we mean when we talk about poetry in the context of "how to live," particularly in a time when life itself on this earth is so threatened? Do we mean its art or its language, which reveal humanity's truths? Profound universal emotions? Connections to ourselves, each other, to the world and its others, or between things?

I think we mean all these essential, elemental aspects of poetry, something that together might be what Lorca called the Duende: the inexplicable power and inspiration of mystery that overcomes us as we become present to the very fact of existence. It comes to us from all of nature, and from the arts and sciences whose source is a sense of wonder at being part of nature, and in all these cases the vessel that holds us in thrall is silence. What we experience there that enables us to live, and might, finally, save our lives, is godliness.

Silence. Poetry. God. Let me define my terms.

Silence: a condition of surrounding quietude and internal peace, a slowing down of time and pace, that allows us to receive higher or retrieve deeper states of being and connectedness. Silence is not an absence of sense or senses, is not emptiness, nothingness, or any other sort of lack.

I mean that condition that finally lets us shut out static, tension, logic, petty argument, daily hustle and bustle, and other mundane, trivial, even destructive mental miscellany, and permits us to feel in rhythm with a more profoundly meaningful, universal, life- or soul-enhancing beingness. Holiness, in that what is most sacred is Life. Silence gives us a necessary, if oxymoronic state of simultaneous alertness and rest, of stimulating entrancement, through which love, ideas, images, or emotions can freely flow.

Poetry: ditto.

God: hmmm.

(As a personal note, I should say that when I talk about God I don't picture a being of any kind, certainly not one that resembles any man, and in fact nothing that could be represented figuratively in sculpture or painting, although sculpture, painting, music—and silence, and poetry, to name a few possibilities—often do represent godliness, or what is holy. For me, what is holy, what embodies God, is Life. But I don't think the specific aspects of how we envision what God means to us will interfere with what I'm exploring here, if we leave room for subjective interpretations or variations.)

I am after something in the imagination, the presence of mind, the cognition, that makes us human but not merely human, so that we stop to consider the habitually unconsidered. A trillium opening miles from here under a fern, unwitnessed. Stars emerging through retreating light at night. The steady streaming of fluids in our bodies. Death and survival. The wherewithal to be as if beside that trillium, and know the simple truth, wonder and brevity of its life so like your own, doing nothing more practical than blooming.

So when I talk about silence and poetry and their connections with each other and with the mystical, I am talking about things that take us out of our overblown but cramped egos, our small, isolated, busy, self-obsessed, economics-centered selves—and most of us do like those little vacations, really. They give us a chance to feel a fuller range and more complicated—or more simple—mixture of emotion than we may normally allow ourselves, perhaps because in such states we are less cluttered with fear. Simultaneously, we feel more significant—every star, every trillium, is a miracle, so I must be too—and more acceptingly dispensable. So marvelously much more significance is here than merely me. There is some kind of order to it all, it seems then (as there is in poetry's holding of its contents), that does make the pain—as Wordsworth believed—bearable, the way ritual supports believers. Such a silent condition is an accessible gift that we don't often enough take.

And yet it requires some gumption, not to mention courage, to resist filling in silent spaces. And it takes some time spent with silences to learn how full they already are.

> Leonard Cohen's poem, "Gift":
>   You tell me that silence
> is nearer to peace than poems
> but if for my gift
> I brought you silence
> (for I know silence)
> you would say
>   this is not silence
> this is another poem
> and you would hand it back to me

Some quality in poetry is the same as that in certain silences, and causes the same effect, if we listen well. When William Carlos Williams said that we might not get the news from poems, though men die every day "for lack of what is found there," he was referring to that same necessity in life for mystery, for listening to silence. Because isn't our sense of life itself the most existential, if not religious, metaphor of all—the temporary embodiment of spirit? And what human art forms do, too, is embody spirit, lend matter to the ephemeral (or vice versa)—in ways that momentarily stay time.

Now, we all know that poetry's medium is words but don't be fooled by that "fact" into thinking that poetry is made of words. As Cohen is saying, it isn't. "Pure poetry," Russell Edson agrees, "is silence. [It is] almost a nonlanguage art." True poetry waits in that right brain along with images, sensory gatherings, associations, spatial impressions and all the rest—and only casts its line across into the lake on the left to fish for language to express all that. If you read it only for the words, it will not awaken your silences and mystify you wonderfully, but will only frustrate you in its seemingly mad illogic and leaps. And that is because the ideas and subjects didn't come from words but from all those other elements that sprang from the author's silence.

Look at how poetry appears to us, and why. Poetry has always consisted of rhythmic, "broken" lines surrounded by blankness, unlike prose which fills all available space to the margins on all sides (sounds like our lives on the average day). Or, if prose is a lawn, I see poetry as a tree, its roots below ground, its trunk here before us on earth, its limbs reaching toward the cosmos. Poetry's irregular lines are branches extending into air, appearing almost to be supported by the air around them. Sometimes they are brocaded with leaves, birds, blossoms and fruit, other times more streamlined and plain, but in any case they are separated by air the way that bricks are separated—or is it joined?—by mortar. So the silences supporting the words of poetry are also significant, necessary, meaningful, integral to their containment and form, as well as their rich themes, which are life's themes: loss, beauty, death, renewal, grief, love, the holy.

Increasingly, poets have been employing even more blankness in their poems—unfinished sentences, listed fragments of thought, non sequiturs, spaces within a single line—sometimes in place of punctuation or even words, sometimes not—and also ellipses, dashes, and multiple colons creating series of phrases like room after room after room in a kind of railroad car effect. Assuming these are intelligent choices and not ineptitude at finishing a thought or just plain laziness on the part of the author, what might be the reasons for these odd and purposeful grammatical alterations?

Alice B. Fogel

In the foreword to Amy Clampitt's *Collected Poems*, the poet Mary Jo Salter calls Clampitt's use of spaces "a visual hint both at God's silence and at poetry's limitations." I'm going to argue with this as oversimplification, or even reverse simplification. We know from the Old Testament that God's silence was a concession, an acknowledgment that certain kinds of authority, of voicing, could be overwhelming, dangerous, even deadly to mere humans. I don't think a true poet's spaces or silences are limitations, any more than the biblical God's decision in favor of silence is God's limitation. Both may appear as boundaries, though in fact they are more likely a mocking of the stultifying boundaries of expected logic in lesser beings. I think Clampitt's use of space, like Jorie Graham's precipitous breaks or Emily Dickinson's famous dashes, are the poets' nods to vastly different forms of knowing. They appear as a kind of pacing, the breathing or the held breath, the sound of one ear listening to the inner, wordless spaces linked to "the other world," as the ancient mystical poet Rumi would put it—and we'll get back to him later.

Silences are thresholds, and we have to ask ourselves how comfortable we are with transitions, crossings over, with standing between, hovering like an impending question mark without answer or, as Keats put it, without "any irritable reaching after fact." A little death between breaths, like that moment of purity after exhalation and before inhaling again. How much do we love the fertile potential of such uncertainty, as opposed to the accomplished sense of completion? Where we fall on these scales might tell us how much we can stand poetry, not to mention silence and mystery.

But thresholds are between somethings, as negative space lies between solids. Think of those optical illusions such as the faces which are also the sides of twin vases or urns. The space defines the solid as the solid defines the open space. They depend upon each other like the brick and mortar. So language—not just poetry's but all language—is born of primeval silence and returns to it. And in the presentation of the poem, just as words shape thought, the blank spaces shape the considerations between formed thought, the moments of waiting for the approaching, anticipated light to dawn. Meaningful words give us pause. Poetry's pauses allow time to expand into those spaces and fill with mystery and meaning.

Used in this way, silences create time (timing) and become complex parts of speech like rests in music—utterly necessary parts of the controlled pattern that gives us rhythm, pacing, tone, mood, sense. Musical rests—and poetry's silences—shape time. Music and speech would both be unintelligible, as melody or meaning, without the designed and timed rest. Both music and poetry depend for melody and meaning on the power of omission—call it silence, even God's silence—engendering those leaps that take our hearts with them and make metaphors so effective and so large.

Reading the omission is a challenge like listening to a child's emotional outpouring: You try to hear the sound of the left-out, the between-the-lines plea, the unsaid need. Just because you can't hear that truth doesn't mean it isn't there. Sunlight appears "silent" or invisible, to the eye, though it consists of all the colors in the spectrum. You just can't see them without the intervention of a refractor, nor understand what you are seeing without some knowledge, awareness, effort, or talent for surprise. The unknown is a kingdom! We need to make the effort to listen to what the silences say, though not in so many words.

The Aboriginals of Australia perceive in every plant, rock and curve of land its own vibration and meditation. What we might call barren land is a family of living, unique ancestors singing; where newcomers see "nothing," they see time, relationship, self. In the same way, a city person might go to the country and see an "empty" field. But if he stepped inside the truth of that emptiness, if he emptied himself in order to enter it and let it enter him, he would find that that "empty" field contained easily two dozen kinds of wildflowers, grains and grasses, each with its congregation of bug life. That it throbbed with fluttered wings, rubbed thoraxes, buzzing varieties of bees. What kind of emptiness is that? That small animals burrowed and basked there, that large ones came there for breakfast. That heat and light and weather charged and changed the moisture condensing or evaporating beneath leaves and stems, and mites and earthworms busily bulldozed under them. That he could and probably does regularly eat some of what grows there. It would be a wind-sickled, bird-called, insect-droned, hoof-stepped, leaf- and blade-bustled, living and life-giving "silence" he had teeming there. Empty field indeed.

Nothingness is too often mistaken for what is not heard or taken notice of, instead of what is truly absent. Here is where Rumi comes in. A thirteenth-century dervish mystic, he was ahead of his time in many ways, such as in believing that all religions worshipped at one altar, and that we must keep a soulful balance between the material and spiritual worlds. He also believed that language springs from the "holey" body the way music emerges from the reed flute. The "empty" reed is in fact full of a mystically and physically exchanged air that is the essential, shaped, ancient and ever-renewed breath of life. He advocated that we empty (open) ourselves daily in such a way as to let that kind of spirit enter and be let loose through us—and he wrote a lot of poetry. Rumi ended 500 odes with "khamush"—silence. His translator, Coleman Barks, says, "language and music are possible only because we're empty, hollow, and separated from the source." It is that separation that makes the reed moan for its home, and that makes us want to make art that gives us the silence that is God—or that other world within ours, our true home, the holy—calling.

Many poems are variations on that silence, or translations of it. "A white flower grows in the quietness. / Let your tongue become that flower." That is Rumi saying our words can only come from a time of silence at the source before they can really ring true and natural. Writing about the poetry of Mark Jarman, Charles Simic invokes the "silence of holiness, the silence of the answers in the quest of holiness . . . the silence that wells up between the words of poems." Those silences are not stubborn refusal; they are the answers, the meanings themselves, the pain and the healing in one. Jarman himself has said that in writing, he "wanted to crack open the silence of heaven and force a divine presence from divine absence," which reminds me of Annie Dillard's young man trying to teach a stone to talk. Isn't it ourselves we thus "crack open"? Is God, or the spiritual world, absent or merely silent? Silent, or merely unheard by our closed or oblivious ears? Is silence the same as absence? Are we really listening? Perhaps the divine presence is like a spice in the sauce of life, unidentifiable as a separate taste, but detectable in the success of the overall flavor. If so, is that spice's presence a concealment or an inclusion?

The poem is a pregnant silence that gives birth to its own source, archetypal. The poem is a closed box, which, when attended to, opens and speaks, lets loose spirits, objects, thought, association and memory, experience—and all across millennia, race, and tongue. Robert Frost said that poetry is the "philosophical attempt to say matter in terms of spirit, or spirit in terms of matter" in order to "make final unity." Like the reed flute, we are always longing to get back to the "empty" field, even while we cling to our over-full distractions. One way to achieve "final unity" in manageable doses is through metaphor, that seamless joining of seemingly disparate parts, bringing to us the otherwise unattainable. And poetry's form mimics our simultaneous yearning and holding back in its counterpoint between words and silences, the etched marks and the spaces.

Sentences themselves may be informative, musical, sent by meaning toward meaning, but in poetry we spread and terrace them with spaces. It is important to read poetry honoring the shape of it, its layers of branches and air. In poetry, the meaning of a line is dependant (literally) upon the break that sets it free; its future impends as its break is mended and its meaning reformed by subsequent lines that lead us onward and send us back. Poetry should be read with those pauses at the ends of lines or within the lines felt in the mouth and heard in the ear.

Alice B. Fogel

They signify because those silent breakages and breaths have more to say beyond sentencing. They are the spaces between the bars, a pairing more life-enhancing, and more complexly anguishing, than mere walls. Here we see beyond the measured cell to the greater imagined yonder. Silence inserted this way into otherwise grammatical sentences, or in place of the predicate, can produce prolonged moments of mystery, in deeply dramatic states.

Or, if done badly, deeply dull ones: oh, no, there's that speechless void again, the dash unsupported by depth, the ellipsis tapering off into the sunset. So each piece of silence had better be backed and framed by a structure or suggestion of thought, emotion, image or metaphor or it truly won't speak, and will only be a fragment at the dump, not a potsherd at a dig. When done honestly and well, the omission in poetry, whether in the figurative leap or the physical withholding of more words, is "telling," like the treasured presence of a dear friend without the need for comment. Deletion should be less evasive bridle and more evoked bridge, urging us to see with an inner eye the catenation that connects thing to thing and place to place, and, therefore, poet to reader, reader to God. The process of elimination as illumination. The flower blooming out of a crack in the sidewalk. The resting place at the cyclone's eye. This is when the silence that comes before and goes beyond words takes us in, fills us with that song of holy grace that only comes with emptying.

I do not advocate that silence stand in place of intelligent or intelligible thought, in poetry or anywhere else. It is no substitute, and will not instruct if it is not given concrete context, the way matter and spirit co-exist, or as musical silences (rests) counter-inform the shaping of musical melody and time. The suspension of sound is suspenseful, as are the breaking and recreating of pattern in life, in music, and in lines of poetry. Rhythm mimics life's combinations of the familiar and the unexpected; weak and strong beats imitate seasonal fallowness and growth; images repeat, leave, sequence into story; and, like the wind of a first breath, silence can fill us with even greater physical sensation and spiritual inspiration than events or notes or words.

The silent spaces of a poem help us hear the mystical silence ringing in its heart, and they suggest that the echoes of meaning—not only in a poem but always—do not end but only reach beyond our ken. But if we discount them, or choose not to hear them, we are left with the other kind of emptiness, the real nothing kind.

Of course, we could live without poetry. Our capacious spirits would still struggle to inhabit our meager skins. What we can't live without, and must remember in our insanely noise-filled days, is the mystery and silence poetry asks us to hear: the holiness of all that is natural, life-giving, and right. How could we live without its necessary nourishment for our bodies and our souls? How could we live without crossing infinite, infinitesimal, invisible bridges to the holy right here, every remaining day, everywhere, around us?

epistle sonatas
Michael Waters

Salzburg, 1772–1780

Airy, joyous, and brazen with distilled
Brevity, only seventeen survive.
Mozart composed them for the Archbishop,
Who did not want the Mass prolonged with lax,
Unnecessary threnody, but sought
To enliven the gap between the dead
Droning of the Epistle and facile,
Narcotic unreeling of the Gospel.
Good work if you can get it, though Mozart
Wasn't pleased to be bound by tedium.
Te Deum. So he labored winter hours
Over each clipped piece, each note in its nook,
Till the sonatas sparked with vengeful glee,
Polished like enduring, lyrical poems,
Not commonplace hymns or prose poetry.

aRIa

Alice B. Fogel

from *Interval: Poems Based upon Bach's Goldberg Variations
& the Predicament of Embodiment*

All durations have beauty. Or in shaping time
was Bach lost to all but the count, not consonance?
One in the other, carriage and contained,
body and spirit, hitched, indivisible:
From the ground up with fractal scaffolding
he built his arc, this liquid bridge for the daily
practice of sameness, sequence, awaking
change, the brief, the sustained—and the enduring
whole bears as one all notes, as one word might
all said or sung. Where does it come from, the material
of the beautiful? And how aligned or skewed
toward discord, how reasoned with ardor and risk,
how little or much design or dumbfound—
how can we know? Grave, heavenly,
like the illumined face of a god rubbed from stone,
these breaths so wholly numbered and numinous....

Mere miracle of physics? Mathematics' holy writ?
Most musical web of ordered intervals framed
by symmetry, division, multiples—most melancholy
joy: Ten parallel horizons zenithed
toward always, thirty-two limiting longitudes:
A language, a form, a key. God, Johann: When in thrall

Alice B. Fogel

my hands' transparent pentimento arches intimate
to make the passage—to touch you—
your immortal body—it is as if the finite, bound,
has unwound when your *now* becomes now anew,
now mine. As if thresholds allow recrossing: Forever
to be content, a soul at home, with a life like art
more puzzle than plan, more flight than counterweight,
the perfect grid of abiding piers upon which you
superimpose the moving force
of brilliant ephemera . . . .

Drummer Young

Richard Frost

Baltimore, forty years ago—
West Fayette, a corner bar
and my quintet: piano, tenor,
trumpet, bass, drums. I parked
down the street, beside a churchyard,

an iron fence, a tipped stone,
and Poe's grave. Every night
I greeted him, and in five hours
said good night to the bones, the shadows,
the low searching trees. The jazz

went unrecorded, and the man
with the big forehead and baggy eyes
was long since chewed to nothing; yet
I said good night, and in my brain
my music swirled companionably

with the cicadas fiddling in the shadows.
Cold sober, I might have seen a ghost
fenced in the humid summer night,
but here was only the woven mix
of images, the holy noise

Richard Frost

of what I believed was poetry—
the shadows, the leaves, the tipped stone,
the empty vase, my own steps,
the car door, and what seemed
almost there, another fine morning.

Drummer Goes to Hear Harry James
Richard Frost

It is 1947, and the big bands are still there. Drummer
is at the Edgewater Ballroom in San Francisco, standing
at the lip of the stage, eye-level with the pants cuffs
of the sax section. The band, oh, man,
is playing some of the same tunes Drummer knows
from his records. He knows every measure, and he moves
with the musicians, on top of everything. The musicians
know when someone is really listening. They can tell
by the person's eyebrows, which rise with the chord changes.
This is the second set, and Harry James
has actually appeared. He is married to Betty Grable.
He is tall, dark and angular, and he sounds just like Harry James.
Drummer is wearing his powder blue modified zoot suit,
spread collar, Windsor knot. He's in his world.

A man with pomaded hair and a thin black mustache,
a variety of lounge lizard, begins calling out drunkenly,
"Play *Harvest Moon*." He keeps it up, between tunes
 and into the next set. *Harvest Moon* is square,
and Drummer is both amused and embarrassed.
Whenever the guy calls out, Drummer catches the eye
of one of the musicians and winks. Drummer likes
it very much that this person is such a fool.

Drummer stays all evening, into the last set
when Harry James has left, and the band is playing

Richard Frost

for itself as much as the dancers. During an intermission
Drummer has bought one of the musicians a beer
and explained that he is a drummer. Drummer almost believes
he's part of the Harry James orchestra. Then in this last set,
while the drunk is still asking for his tune,
during a ballad medley, the second trumpet
stands and threads *Harvest Moon* like gold
over the Edgewater Ballroom, over the dancers,
and over Drummer's pompadour.

Inside

Marilyn Abildskov

I can't explain why I've become
—k.d. lang

Her life used to be about the music. She studied and went to school and for eight hours every day she played, she practiced, she ran her fingers up and down the keys with diligence and discipline and effort, so much effort, and how could you fail to admire such effort? How could you fail to call such effort *heart*? Yet her heart was not in it, not in the music, not in the life. Her life was *about* the music—she especially loved Chopin—but she was not *in* the music, not even in Chopin.

At home, as a girl in Matsumoto, she was good, one of the best. But here in Tokyo, in college, it was different. There were so many students like her, so many who practiced and played and studied for hours every day. And there were those who did all that and who had something else as well, whose lives were *in* the music and you could hear the difference, she could hear the difference, that small note of confidence, of authority, of something she could not quite articulate or express, something that was not in the music, that was not in her life, something that she knew—for this part she could hear—made all the difference. *All the difference.*

She was unhappy in those days, as a college student studying music at an all-girls' Tokyo school. Unhappy and unhealthy. Her breathing became labored, her body anemic. Sometimes after eating, her fingers flew up to her face. Traveled inside her mouth. Toward the back of her throat. She did not mean them to. They moved of their own accord. Like playing the scales—it was easy, it was rote. Her body's cycle slowed, then halted altogether. Her body had forgotten how to bleed.

Marilyn Abildskov

Her life on the outside continued as normal. She continued practicing eight hours every day, playing the scales, playing those compositions intended to improve her technique. Her boyfriend, a teacher at preparatory school, continued to stop by. Every Wednesday night, he came to her apartment, a small, shoebox of a room in a Tokyo high-rise. Every Wednesday he would come and she would make him dinner and after dinner, they would lie down. And every Wednesday, after dinner, he would enter her and she would remain very very still. Sometimes he cried out and as he did, she would go away. Her body would flatten, take leave of itself, disappear. Her heart would slow and she could feel herself shrinking, disappearing into pale and listless folds of skin.

It continued happening, this diminishing effect, this losing of herself but not in passion, this losing of herself, this watching of the spirit as the spirit evaporates, so now, the only time her body felt well was after he had gone, after he had left her apartment, after all the food was gone, too, after everything had been—*it must be*—expelled, all evidence of pleasure on her body's indifferent behalf, because it was not pleasure, none of it, not the music, not the food, not the man who came on Wednesday nights. It was duty and she hated it. She hated him, the man who entered her but could never be *in* her, no she would never let him in. She would hold herself back. *Men are such animals.* She hated her life. *A life of duty.* This is what it means to be a Japanese woman. She speaks to herself a language laced in fury. *You cannot dream big.*

She gave it up, the music. One Thursday afternoon. She could see no other way. She would not become a concert pianist as she had dreamed. She would not hear the note that would change everything. A shaft of sunlight hit the black polish of her piano at home. She noted the dust, the way the sunlight exposed what she had not noticed before. How beautiful the sunlight was, not despite the dust but because of the dust. She was tired. The sunlight was beautiful. The piano was dusty. She must dust. She must practice, she must play. But she was so tired. She rested her hands for a moment on the keys. She knew these keys better than anything, better than anybody. Better than her own body. She stopped. Shut the piano lid.

She quit. There was no choice now but to move on. She turned to English. Again she studied—*deference, daybreak*—and again she practiced —*package, postpone*—and again she threw herself into the rhythm of a new life—*jealousy, jewel*—this time, a new language, one she had loved like music since she was a child—*buttonhole, coconut, sleepyhead, snowdrift*— one for which she had a certain proclivity toward, one in which she had demonstrated *proficiency*. She threw herself into the language and memorized the vocabulary and studied the grammar and practiced her pronunciation. *Envelope. Etiquette. Hover. Huddle. Practice. Spacious. Sparrow. Narrow. Uproot. Uppermost. Wayward. Whisper.*

And after college, she made English her livelihood, she made it her job. She returned to her hometown, taught at her hometown's highest-ranked high school. She was good to her students, broke the lessons down into manageable parts, encouraged them to study, to move beyond, *Hello, my name is Emi. I like rice.* But to study for what? In case they might travel? She wanted to travel. She wanted to leave. To leave the mountains circling her city, to leave her parents who thought her a failure—she has not married yet, after all; she would never marry— and to leave her job, this school, this room. The teachers' room where everyone was so unfailingly dutiful and polite. *O-saki ni shitsurei shimasu. Gokurosama. O-tsukaresama.*

Sometimes she missed the music. She still loved music, still loved Chopin, still loved his ballads, but rarely did she play them anymore what with her new life, her new job, her schedule and such, all the duties of being an English teacher, all the classes to prepare, all the notebooks to correct, all the *enkai* to go to, those mandatory teachers' parties where the male teachers got drunk and from underneath the table, touched her thigh.

The man from Tokyo, from Wednesday nights, he was gone now, he never called anymore. *Thank goodness for that.* She spent evenings at home, correcting student papers then studying for hours each night on her own, learning the meanings of dozens of new words. She was entering a new level of language, entering a brand new discourse. *Apprehension. Clandestine. Dissonance. Indelible.* She listened to English-language tapes. She joined a conversation group. She found an American teacher, took lessons one-on-one. Her teacher pushed her. The words continued, they piled up. *Nebulous. Odyssey. Palpable. Paradox.*

She battled her shyness, fought against her nature, braced herself from the desire to hide. She was used to hiding, to wrapping herself in the formalities of the language. She knew how to use words like a kimono—to beautify, to cover, to constrict. Instead, she opened herself up one word at a time, loosened the *obi*, attempted to articulate herself. She used the first-person pronoun. She made distinctions—*I prefer beds to futons and rice to bread*—and began to reason, began to elaborate, all in a foreign tongue. She learned more words, more phrases, more subtlety and nuance. And as she studied, her fluency grew. She committed herself to learning the meaning of idioms, those illogical, dreamy ways of expressing thought. She learned what it means to be *between a rock and a hard place* or what *going without saying* suggests. She understood—this one was easy—what it means to *play one's cards close to the chest.*

From the outside, she remained a model of maturity, *as cool as a cucumber*, calm as can be, her skirts long and neatly pressed, her nylons never run, her blouses clean and white and feminine. Her hair was long and black and shiny and thick and she pulled her beautiful Japanese hair into cheerful braids or a single elegant ponytail, one that reached all the way to the middle of her back. But there were changes occurring, shifts from within. Some rhythm inside her had begun to move, and it was to this rhythm inside she was starting to submit.

One day, as she studied prepositions, all the differences between those tiny words like *in* and *on* and *under* and *near*, something happened, something so innocuous that she didn't have reason to get nervous, she didn't have reason to anticipate any trouble, she didn't have reason to cultivate any fear.

CHAUTAUQUA

In the classroom. *On* the desk. *Under* the book. *Near* the woman. There was a tape. A small homemade cassette on which her American teacher had recorded a variety of songs. The songs came from women's voices. And from this variety of women's voices there was one voice in particular that stood out: a voice as clear and compelling and filling as water, a voice that understood what she herself could not begin, through music or English or anything else, to adequately express. That the cravings were constant, relentless, alive. That the cravings of the body were impossible to deny.

She listened. She wept. There was something in this voice she understood. She went to the library to find out more. Checked out books. Read the biographies one by one. Bought every one of this voice's CDs. There was so much to look at, so much to hear. She marveled at the ease of the voice, the ease of the body from which the voice came. There was a picture of the voice gracing the cover of an American magazine called *Vanity Fair*: a beautiful woman dressed in a man's clothes, pinstripe trousers, suspenders, the *works*; the voice sat in a barber's chair; a voluptuous model shaved the voice's smooth man-woman's face. And through her studies, her obsession, she knew: *this* was love, to be inside your life; *this* was love, to wonder so.

After that, she changed. Everything changed. *You changed everything*, she said to her teacher, the one who had so casually, so innocently handed her that tape. *Everything*.

She moved to San Franciso. Walked in the Castro. Watched the people. The men and the women. Especially the women. She had never seen so many beautiful women. So many women and all breathing this same new marvelous air. She studied the large women in their Indian shirts and their flowing skirts. She studied the hard-as-armor women in their t-shirts and biker shorts. She studied the women together and apart and she studied the language and she practiced as she moved through the streets, but now the study was in service of living a larger life, of getting underneath her own skin. She made friends. Classmates now. Other graduate students at her school. She joined a fan club and wrote fan letters to the voice that had, she believed, taught her to live such a life.

She fell in love. Not all at once but one letter at a time. For the first time, now, she understood. The words *head over heels*, they meant something real. She was head over heels in love. She wrote letters every single week. This woman, too, was a fan of the voice. They talked about the voice and their past lives and their present worries and what their future together might mean. Such funny syntax: *their* future. *Two* people. *One* future.

They sent pictures, then met. Entered a new stage of their affair. And now she let this woman go deep. Inside. Her mouth. Her pores. All over her hair. Into private places where no one had ever been before. She understood what it meant, this phrase, *to get under someone's skin.*

She cut her hair. Started wearing pants. Began to travel to places she had never traveled before: to small towns in Alaska, to out-of-the-way places in Canada, to all the places where the voice had ever lived. She made a pilgrimage, she made all kinds of stops, she created a constellation of dot-to-dots, traveling to Nashville, that place where so many voices had sung and Nashville, like others, made her weep. She wondered, is this why a woman travels? To weep over cities that do not belong to her? To make herself over in a foreign place? To learn the language that will give her back her voice?

She was fluent now. Inside.

Just thinking of kimono, she said, *makes me ache.*

YEARS LATER, SHE VISITS her American friend, the one who had been her teacher, the one who gave her that tape. They sit on the floor of a square room of an apartment in a sturdy Midwestern state. It is hot tonight, the hottest it has ever been, and they are wiping their foreheads and drinking wine and getting flushed and remembering how they used to meet in cool Japanese cafes to drink coffee and eat chocolate silk cake.

You changed everything, she tells her friend.

I changed nothing, her friend says. *All I did was hand you a tape.*

She thinks of the day her friend left Japan, how her friend had been crying, how her friend could not be consoled. It was over some man, some distant Japanese man, and her friend, the American, said she couldn't help it, she loved this man though he didn't love her. The friend was *bereft. Beside herself. Sad to the bone.* So many words now to describe one sorry state. She took her friend to a jazz cafe where the two ate cheese toast and drank cafe au lait and then she took her friend to the train station to see her off and she held her friend's hands in hers and clasped them tight. So there they were, two women, two friends, one on a train, ready to leave, the other on the platform staying home, one eager to stay, the other eager to go and both of them stuck. Two women. One with her wild and wavy reddish blonde hair, the other in her straight black braids. And both of them crying now. And all that talk between them over the years and still so many secrets, still so much neither one could say.

Maybe that's why, she remembers thinking, *maybe that's why a woman travels.* For some moment of parting just like this, some scene that's sad and swollen and secret and strong.

Tonight, then, what can she say to her friend? That she had not changed? That her friend had not changed *everything*? She would not lie. She would not look away as she has done in other moments that meant so much. She would look at her friend. She would be direct. In Japan, it is impolite to look someone so directly in the eye; it is impolite to speak so freely of what weighs heavy on the mind. She wants to say so many things, that her desire had been fierce, her desire had been huge: to marry the spirit to the flesh; to begin her real life. There had been necessity—there always is—in doing that. Her life had been at stake, something vital she understood was essential in life. And to save herself meant changing *everything*, and to begin, there had been that voice, there had been that tape.

I'll tell you something I've never told anyone before. She speaks calmly now with a note of authority that those who have been saved once will recognize. Her friend hears the nuance, that small but all-important shift. She smiles to think how far they've come.

When I heard that voice, that voice on the tape, the blood in my body—that is when the blood in my body began to flow.

The Ocularist Said

Susan Kinsolving

A convincing eye comes from attention to detail:
the sunbursts or striations of an individual iris,
or those unique specks of color that appear to be
just dropped in, dabs of interest, as if an artist
took an arbitrary brush of the palette. Ah, those
dark brown eyes flecked with amber, those blue
eyes shaded violet, the green ones edged in russet.

The surrounding sclera too has its tints, white
with subtle shades of yellow age, grey illness, or
the pink of drink. This is why an off-the-shelf eye
looks fake, hokey, and hackneyed. So sit down
please. Try not to blink. In order to paint your eye
I need to think about color and you. Now I must
stare at your one eye while you gaze at my two.

Man in Black

Michael Waters

June Carter Cash, d. May 15, 2003

Why Noah summoned two of each creature
Poses no puzzle to any sentient
Breather. The dove hunched on a knobby branch
Misses his mate, though still coos all morning,
And the fat cat prowls the feather-strewn lawn
As if God lay hidden among fallen
Needles. Six kittens caper behind her.
Inside the house, I allow the lonesome
Sound of Vassar Clements' antique fiddle
To trick the wound into thinking it has
Healed. Always this sense of forward motion
Only to be pulled up short like the hound
Blustering wildly against his taut chain.
No heaven but in the momentary
Glimpse of sunlight on iridescent breast,
Or in the note silked on air as horsehair
Caresses gut, sending forth its blue throb
Into the churchy silence between barks.
When I step outside, I can't remember
Spring—the world's hushed now, anticipating
Waters that will pummel the green earth flat
And the one dove who'll fly off not knowing
If he can find an exposed mountain peak
Or, come nightfall, make it back to the ark.

Johnny Cash, d. September 12, 2003

HUSKS

George Looney

Is memory some chord off a rosined bow
that vibrates the air long after we can hear it?

Music's always been more than what's heard.

Mozart said he played the abandoned husk,
what was left when music shivered into flight.

Go on, forget how the garish clown sang
the saddest aria Mozart ever put down
through the delirium of his father's ghost.

Forget how the clown's pale face burst, an aneurysm
in the klieg's savage circle of light, his raw,
dark mouth swallowing every sorrow in the music.

Forget how its echo trembled along the taut cord
the flat foot of the highwire artist touched
the way the toe of a six-year-old girl tests the water
of the public pool her first trip. Forget how water is
always lit up from within, remembered, how
the cord trembles under the man in silver tights
the klieg light burns into the memory of
everyone, below, too afraid of a fall to applaud.

Time is more a trapeze artist, that pause between
letting go of one hand & grabbing another,

George Looney

that damp slice of gravity cut thin & served up
with gravy & some bitter sprig of herb. The taste
lingers on the tongues of all who gasped
through the pause before breaking into applause.

Music pulled out of taut strings can't compete.

It could be said the clown knows more of the physics
of memory than do the bodies, sleek & covered
in second skins that gleam, blinding, in the spot light.

Time may question itself in mid-air, but memory
is more likely to pile in to a tiny car & drive
in circles, going nowhere, the horn the ghost of
some almost forgotten pleasure. Or the husk
of some dark bit of music, Mozart's *Lacrimosa*, say.

Memory stays closer to the heart, that floor of
packed dirt full of the prints of myriad beasts
of burden. Carry on, memory says. Forget
what flies off. It is what remains, the husk
each heart beat leaves in the chest, that matters.

The air, it vibrates, the past flung through it
in bodies in tights. The clown, though,
the clown beats his chest with a foam rubber hand,
over-sized, that points as if to blame. Now
it points to a sky that could be said to be pain,
or the remnants of an almost silly music culled
from gaudy fiddles. Now it points to his heart.

THE TWO GENTLEMEN OF VERONA

Stephen Corey

i

What they loved: love.
Whom they failed: lovers.

ii

The dollar bill	exhibits the Great Seal,
its floating eye	near a pyramid's peak
seeming always	the purest mystery—
child's terror,	adult's silent question—
its Latin tags	top- and bottom-heavy:
always watching,	they say, or *vigilant*?
Oh no, I say,	that eye is burning love
never sleeping,	loving all it sees,
carried abroad	by each woman, each man.
A loves B, C	loves D then B. D's left,
C fights with A	while B denounces C.
Easy enough,	this plotting out of life.
We have, at last,	just two things: the constant,
the inconstant.	We can each make our lists.
Shakespeare knew this.	Ophelia. Gertrude.
He hammered this.	Desdemona. Iago.
He laughed at this.	Henry the Fifth. Falstaff.
He wept at this.	Cordelia. King Lear.
Coin of the realm,	this flimsy scrim of love.
So contrary...	*go kindle fire with snow*
before you seek	to know the one of two,
the two of one	that spinning off will go.

Romeo and Juliet
Stephen Corey

for Tom

In Burlington, Vermont, the lovers glide
as dancers on the college green, shadowed
by the chapel and the sugar maples
Shakespeare—to his loss—could never write of.
Duck-duck-goosing around the dips and swirls
the full cast patterns in the dusk, R and J—
aren't they that familiar to us all?—
seem blithe and desperate at once. No play
here, even, only prologue to a darkness
houselights dimmed will make to mirror darkness
full by then on the grass sprung back, darkness
making ready inside—as if alive—
to fall on every step a world could take.

We did not enter the then-bright theater,
my cousin, his wife, and I. The offered dance,
suddenly not just the Capulet ball
foreshadowed, but the whole life, seemed enough.
We walked, they not quite thirty, I just past,
through the simpler night the city produced.
I neither saw nor dreamed the single hose
wedged through a back-seat window, heard no voice
failing to rise from a woman alone
in her sweet bitterness of chosen air.
I then heard no one entering the dark

CHAUTAUQUA

garage to gather in the steeped, wrong flower.
I could not sense the world would offer up
its startling, constant promise quite so soon.

Missoula Eclipse

Rick Hilles

Believe the couple who have finished their picnic / and make wet love in the grass . . . Believe in milestones, the day / you left home forever and the cold open way / a world would not let you come in.

Part of the inscription on Richard Hugo's headstone in Missoula, Montana, from his poem "Glen Uig."

If I could live again as just one thing
it would be this early Autumn wind
as it cartwheels the rooftops & avenues
of the Pacific Northwest; the way the air
of orchards vaulted in the mind of Keats
as he brimmed over with his last Odes
dreaming of the mouths his final words
would touch & kiss through any darkness

like a shooting star; the way a starry-eyed
stranger once blew smoke into the night
before offering me her cigarette outside
the 92nd Street Y, where I'd just given
a reading, so that I didn't even notice
sad-faced Jim Wright in a patch of leaves.
And there we were again, Jim weeping
& breathless to tell me he'd stopped drinking

and was in love; and, in a voice reserved
for children (and the very lost) told me

CHAUTAUQUA

he had cancer. I wish we had hightailed it
then into my dream of Rome, the dream
where we are laughing at our dumb luck
and near giddy as we exit the gilded portal
& enter a day too bright to see the Spanish steps,
where, for us, apparently, it is always noon;

I always wanted to take Jim to Rome—
to see the black ink of cuttlefish
and shadows blue the edges of his grin
even if we were just to stand penniless & eye
the sparkling wishes tossed into fountains,
one whose water surrounds a sculpted hull
of a boat that's lost its mast, held in a state
of perpetual sinking as Jim points to the flat

where John Keats died, his friend Severn
at his side, drawing him over and over—
even after his last torment; Jim tells me
about the dream he's having lately
in which Keats appears, practically
flying up and down the Spanish Steps
in inline blades; Jim wants so badly
to grab the frilly garment of the white-

shirted Romantic, who now is naked
to the waist and in black spandex,
in death forever beautiful and ridiculous,
but Jim's afraid to wake us from the dream.
Still, there's a melody under Keats's breath.
It might be from Haydn's "Water Music"
or just the syncopated rhythms of the boat
we ride, Our Fountain of the Sinking Ship.

Rick Hilles

Oh, to be so close to the poet we love
who died at half our age not knowing
what he would become for so many of us,
understandably, makes us a little insane.
Jim asks if I know what it all means
& then he's coming at me like Sonny Liston,
as if the only way affection can be shown
between men like us is with an open fist.

And, forgetting a moment that I am
not even the merest breeze in your living hair,
and that a boneyard in Missoula, Montana,
negates this vision, just now to my dead friend
I'm real as any man who's loved his life,
&, stunned by it, tries to face what he can't take,
when the trees of Rome rattle their silver leaves,
and Jim picks me up, like nothing, in his arms.

competence

Kathleen Aguero

Nancy's sick of being competent,
but she can't quit because someone made her up
and she still earns them money.
A hundred crime victims whimper
like strays in a pound. Mystery
after mystery, formula plots
Nancy can solve in white gloves and a hat.

That one sold so well,
and they write her into another.
Right about now she'd like to change plots
but she can't figure out how to trade in her roadster
for a bucking bronco or a truck
with a rifle underneath the front seat.
She'd like to strip off her clothes
as slowly as daybreak in winter
and tease some crook into her bed. She
has transferable skills but doesn't know
how to describe them. Sometimes she thinks
she'd rather serve coffee in the local diner,
slap a wet rag across tables
so it smudges more than it wipes off.
She'd listen to people's troubles
without having to solve them.
Maybe things would be different
in a bigger city—New York or Rio—

or on a farm so remote only she
ate the vegetables grown there.

Or, just once, could she
be the one to get rescued?

Nancy sighs, opens her mail.
It's the author again:
Next victim—missing heiress.
First clue—empty locket.
Same wardrobe. Same car.

CHILDHOOD

Greg Kuzma

We will build the poem
around some incident
that happened long ago.
Long ago means ten years
to the five-year-old.
Long ago means ten
centuries to the
academician—No poetry
since Chaucer he snorts.
We will build the poem
around a car driving away,
some dirt in a pot,
a few flowers.
Someone in a house is
making supper. She
is making a stew. She
cuts up carrots. You
can hear the meat sizzling,
splashing itself in its own
hot fat. Outside, in the
street, I have just
fallen off my bike.
I taste the cinders and
the leaves. I feel
the cold against my cheek.
Five years later, it is
winter. I am throwing

Greg Kuzma

snowballs with Paul Ruby.
We hate each other.
A snowball hits me in the
face and breaks my glasses.
Later, summer, we sit
on the lawn in front
of his house. We are
finished with swords,
we are finished with cops
and robbers, with "Gray Ghost."
We are playing mumbletypeg,
with a little knife.
One day amidst these years
someone led me over Franklin
Field, past the ball diamond
into the woods
where the giant turtle
lay in a pool of white worms.
Another day I am at the plate
hearing the shouts of the boys
taunting me. I took it
personally. I took everything
personally. I struck out.
I never played again.
In winter I recall
the skating in the park.
They would flood the tennis
courts, take down the fences.
Scratchy music played.
And there was a girl—
Terry Manfrates—whose name
I just remembered today,
with bright red cheeks

CHAUTAUQUA

and clean white teeth.
I did a funny thing.
I never took my skates off
in the shack
like all the others,
but kept them on my feet
all the way home.
It was a two-block walk
on crusted snow,
or if on the sidewalk—
on the points so as not to dull
the blades.
A curious gait—
a boy half frozen
walking on his toes.
Once a girl took pity on me,
her father stopped their car
to give me a ride.
Another time we'd sit
beneath the oak trees
for hours.
Giant acorns, I don't know
what kind, littered the ground.
It was a contest
to find the biggest one.
Some, when they hit the
street, would pop their caps
off. The round of
the shell was dry and
smooth, with a white
film like dried glue for hair.
It was a wondrous thing
to rub them in your hands.

From "A Litter of Blossoms"

Greg Kuzma

Anybody who gives a talk, especially a talk at Chautauqua which has a long and strong tradition for such things, carries a tremendous responsibility, and I was shaken, frightened beyond explanation as I worked on mine. The more I worked on "say what you know," the less I was sure of anything, the more naked I felt myself to be. But the weight of responsibility that comes to those of us who get the chance to do this sort of thing is a sweet weight. In my case, I had almost doubled my burden. Not only was I speaking on what I know, but I was talking about the joy and the wonder of "saying what you know." And what do I know? And how do I know that I know it? This sort of encounter with the naked self is what every writer faces in her daily work, or what every writer hopes to achieve somewhere in her work before she dies. But truth disclosed or faced down in the privacy of one's computer room is very different from making a speech in front of people who are often better-educated, older, and more thoughtful than you ever thought you might be. It was a formidable task, and it was hard for me to take anything else very seriously until I had finished writing my talk, and then, a week later, finished delivering it.

Here was another wonderful dimension of Chautauqua, that this is a place of public occasions. It is a public place. It may well be, for many of us, that place where every summer reside many of the people we would hope to address in our work. The writer, they tell us, always imagines and writes to an ideal reader or audience. Here, as we gather for morning lectures in the amphitheater or at that Women's Club for the weekly poet's talk, the audience is real. The ideal and the real have merged, and when this happens, as it happens so rarely in our culture, the world is made whole.

CHAUTAUQUA

❧

THERE IS EVERYWHERE we went at Chautauqua a sense of a respectful distance. People who come here, maybe all of us, come after all from the broken world. The renewal that comes from retreat, the renewed energy that can be ours in such a magical setting, is very much a quality in this experience. Once, after midweek, we briefly left the grounds to have dinner with friends. Two hours "out in the world." We could not wait to get back inside the gates. The world seemed primitive and haphazard and accidental, exactly, in fact, that world we had been so delightfully describing all week long, but which we now had no immediate desire to live in anymore.

ART AND LIFE? How do they inform each other? Where do they meet? How do they dance? At Chautauqua, they meet as partners—first one leading, then another, then another, each leading and teaching if it can, learning from the others if it can. It is a place for music. A place for a wonderful art-and-craft show where all the work is first-rate: we could have bought anything and been proud to have it in our home. It is a place of the "American Experience." This place awakens us calling on us to be open, opening us, surprising us by how much we are taken seriously, by discovering how much we have to give and to understand so well, to be receptive to so much. Or to use one in terms of the other, as we did when we evaluated the keynoters during the week, Kelly so impassioned, so rhetorical, a little windy maybe, but who could rouse us. Sandel so sane, so reasonable, such dignity and such brilliance of the mind. All sorts of eloquence surrounded us, sometimes in the service of grand ideas, sometimes perhaps more in the service of itself, confirming the possibility of eloquence, where language can rise not only to occasions but beyond occasion, words that inspire through their right rhythms and sounds, to become indelible on the mind, language itself as the currency of being.

The question of who we are always grows more complex. All the various references to America as a young country, or as a country that now, after many failures and many sobering experiences, has lost some of its former brashness and its fresh self-confidence, have always amused me, but now I see how much the story of America is the story too of people in America as they age. As we have more and more behind us, we have more and more to engage or resist. We bring more awareness to our lives, even as, ironically, we have less and less time in which to enjoy what we know or work out our ideas. For many of us, the past is something which must be forgotten or kept locked away, with only highly-select memories admitted to public discussion. But then in Mary Jean's living room at Chautauqua I found myself doing the same thing, leaving the past behind, ignoring confusions I have not been able to comprehend or resolve.

Perhaps some of the great power of Chautauqua for me can be explained in this. I return to the place of my origins, which many of us is the place of our family. But I who have no family still wish to return, and perhaps that longing is even stronger in me. Chautauqua is even part of New York state, which is compelling. Our trips East were always "back to Pennsylvania"—maybe because I was ashamed of Rome, New York, and what had happened there, the dissolution of my family, the death of my brother. Now, after years of healing, the return is both to Erie and Barb's family and to New York, my state, and to both the old and the new that Chautauqua represents. Perhaps such a crude, abstract formula is not sensitive to all the richness here, but Chautauqua clearly becomes a place of renewal in the very heart of what has for so long been suppressed or denied.

That Chautauqua is a place is important, and not just a state of mind or a series of associations or gestures. But that it is both is important. The ideals of Chautauqua are transportable, or they persist in the mind as possibilities for future action. The Chautauqua ideal is explicable, can be discussed and explained, even though it is mysterious and perhaps ultimately beyond knowing fully. That it is perhaps more present, both more felt and more pervasive within the gated community on the shores of Chautauqua Lake makes it seem even more precious. The physical community, the buildings, the summer programs, the events, become the "real" which keeps alive visions of the "ideal" of Chautauqua. Or it is in the inefficient working through of what is humanly possible, what real people can do, what real people can rise to, however disappointing, that forever frustrates the ideal but defines it and which increases our longing. Chautauqua would be a wonderful example to us even if it were a failed community, much like those utopian societies the nineteenth century was so enamored of. If Chautauqua had existed, and lived through its heyday, and then withered, it might still call to us like an ideal and wonderful civilization destroyed by "progress" or human greed or jealousy, or maybe the shifting of the economy of the region or the fortunes of those founding families whose wealth were the wellsprings of its vitality. Such a story would still speak to us, would still make us look deep into history as into our own selves, to review our hopes and to examine upon what foundations we would build our world. But Chautauqua exists. It is both fact and dream. Or it shimmers in the mind between dream-state, heaven and earth, nightscape and landscape, landscape of the mind and the soul and what is possible in the human prospect.

SO POWERFUL IS the idea of Chautauqua that even while Barb and I were there, as we walked its streets and attended its lectures and entertainments, it was magical. It was as if we had become characters in a living play, a brilliant and compassionate play, not only a play of character but a play of ideas, a play about beauty, a play which takes as its province all that might be said on behalf of what we are and the best that we might become. As if we were already doing that shorthand compilation to keep track of this endless cast of rich and unforgettable characters, each who seems to represent some "type," some vision of the universe, some partial explanation of reality. Earlier I have spoken of "Chautauqua moments," which is akin to recalling the great moments of an opera, the great arias, the great duets and choruses. One is tempted, leaving Chautauqua, to treat it as if it were a work of art, some moments ill-defined, some moment undeveloped, some characters not fully expressive, some roles badly acted. This metaphor was very much alive for me when I gave my talk, for instance. I had a powerful sense of obligation, that I had a role to fill, that I could not, for instance, let Mary Jean down in front of the Chautauqua Women's Club, and that I could not also betray myself, or misrepresent myself, whatever I might be, if I could ever determine what that is. That I had a part to play, perhaps not a major part, but which if performed well, with sincerity, and with feeling, and with my whole energy, would contribute to the success of the whole. Is that not the very calling of community? The very center of its necessities? I worried about perspiring. Perspiration is not something often seen at Chautauqua, except maybe on the tennis court. Everyone seems totally composed, even the young men sweeping up little pieces of paper or dead leaves, a la Disneyland, which I witnessed one morning early going to class. Even the young women who wait tables at the Athenaeum Hotel restaurant, certainly the most intellectually alive waitresses I've ever met. We talked to one of them all during lunch, and she became a friend.

One night toward the end of our week, we returned after a panel at the amphitheatre and prepared to retire early as so many Chautauquans do, to be more fresh for the next splendid day. A strange and wonderful music filled the street. All we could think of was someone overly in love with Mozart had her CD cranked well beyond the level we had to come to expect at Chautauqua. Barb was already in her pajamas when we looked down the street and sensed that the music was coming from the plaza park. We got dressed and went down. Under a streetlight in front of the corner restaurant with its outside tables four young musicians had gathered. Two violins, a viola, and a cello. They were playing *Eine Kliene Nachtmusik*, then other quartet pieces. A small crowd was gathered, but the quartet played as if guided by some inner impulse. Though people now and then came forward and put a dollar or two in an open violin case, the children seemed unaware of the audience.

CHAUTAUQUA

We sat on the curb, my arm over Barb's shoulder, even as the beauty of their music radiated out into all the gathered houses; built close together as they are, the houses seemed to draw even closer to each other, and closer to the plaza, as if intent in their listening. As if in the very layout and design of this place we express our great need to be close to each other, however different we may be, however apart we may feel ourselves to be. Never have I heard more beautiful music, nor have I heard such music played by such young people, and so joyously. As packed as Chautauqua is with lectures and concerts and events of all sorts, this event was unscheduled, spontaneous as it were, arising of its own accord from out of the very center of Chautauqua. Most assuredly from the genius of the composers it rose, and from the beautiful and inspired playing of these children who, somehow, have given themselves so entirely to music it rose, and also from the houses and the people and the community and the ideal that is Chautauqua it rose. In a place so beautiful and so fulfilling it seemed almost ordinary, capable of being lost in the endless progression of gorgeous and generous gestures. Or as astonished as we were we also had begun to expect such miracles, though it also seemed too much, some scene in the opera where the composer or director had grown a bit excessive and a bit sentimental, too much perhaps a symbol and a set piece, too much an idealization even of the ideal itself, a consummate moment, a crystallization of meaning into one gorgeous timeless figure of beauty. Later we tried to talk about it in various places, to people who had not been there, and we were greeted with the same sorts of disbelief that must have greeted the wise men or the kings who came in homage long ago.

WE CAME TO SAY upon leaving Chautauqua that everybody there is on their "best behavior." Everybody is just exquisitely "nice." The risk in saying this is to suggest that it's too good to be true. People who think of Chautauqua as an elitist playground or a summer colony for the rich could use such information as ammunition. "These people don't live in the real world!" I can hear them shouting angrily. An emotion—anger—by the way—which we did not see expressed any time during our week. How much then is the "real" of the world all that is hurt or damaged or spoiled in the human story? How much do we accept anger and hatred and violence and despair as part of the human condition, and how much are we then willing to live under such conditions? One of the ongoing declines of our culture certainly has been the erosion of civility. Bringing the secret self forward has been our goal for a long time, and to break down the inhibitions which constrict and restrain us as individuals. In the pursuit of freedom of speech we have set free the demons of the mind, and I have myself contributed to this. Upon the irreverence of one generation the next must build its own irreverence, until as now, there seems nothing left that is sacred or safe from the coarseness of contemporary life. Not the courtesy, not loyalty, not gratitude, not even human life, not the family, not even the person. We have become the barbarians at our own gates, both outside and inside of ourselves.

Barb and I talked at lunch today about my essay. I told her that I found the essay moving more and more toward the idealization of Chautauqua, how one of the unspoken conclusions I find myself approaching is that it is a kind of heaven on earth. I said that I was finding Chautauqua to be the answer to all of America's problems, that the more I think about it the more convinced I become that the answer everyone is seeking resides within us, that it exists now and here, and that it has existed for over a century.

Character is Power.

—Booker T. Washington

Private Lives in Public Life

COMFORT FOOD

Ann Hood

These are the things I remember:

My five-year-old daughter, Grace, loved cucumbers sliced into perfect circles, canned corn, blueberries, any kind of beans, and overly ripe kiwi. A family vacation to southern Italy had left her with a taste for lemons and kumquats. She carried hard, dried salami in a small pink and white gingham purse and liked to go with me to Italian delis for fresh buffalo mozzarella. Her favorite dinner was pasta—*noonies*, we called it, a leftover mispronunciation from her older brother Sam when he was a baby—with butter and freshly grated parmesan cheese. Every day she took the same thing for her school lunch: pre-packaged cheese and crackers, those cucumber rounds, half sour pickles. When her friend Adrian came over for lunch they always ate Campbell's chicken and stars soup, Ritz crackers, and either pomegranate or kiwi.

While I cooked dinner, Sam and Grace both helped me. They layered the potatoes for potatoes au gratin-*cheesy* potatoes in our house; they peeled the apples for apple crisp, the carrots for lentil soup; they shook and shook and shook chicken in a baggie of salted flour for chicken marsala. Grace used to like to press her thumbprint onto peanut butter cookies to flatten them before baking.

These are the things I remember: a fire in our kitchen fireplace, soup simmering on the stove, Sam and Grace bursting in with their cheeks red, their snowsuits wet, dripping snow across the wooden floor to snack on pickles straight from the jar before heading back outside. Or: our first backyard barbecue of the year on a surprisingly warm April day, Sam at eight finally old enough to baste the chicken on the grill, Grace carefully wiping a winter's worth of dust from the patio table and chairs, paper plates decorated with red cherries, the smell of molasses and brown sugar from the pot of baked beans, a bowl of canned corn dotted with butter, late afternoon sunshine, the purple heads of crocuses announcing themselves in our small garden.

What came the next day is the hardest part, the details of it impossible to forget. Grace spiked a high fever and, after thirty six hours in the intensive care unit at our city's Children's Hospital, she died from a virulent form of strep. April remained relentlessly warm and sunny, but inside our house I shivered uncontrollably. Wrapped in flannel blankets and shawls from visitors, I could not find comfort. This was the unthinkable, the thing every parent fears. And it had come to our house and taken Gracie. When I looked out the window, I wanted her to still be there, making bouquets of chives from the garden laced with purple myrtle. Or when I walked in the kitchen, I expected to find her there, standing on her small wooden chair, plucking one cucumber round after another from her pink plate into her baby teeth filled mouth.

People brought food. Chicken enchiladas in a throwaway foil roasting pan and rich veal stew simmering in a white Le Creuset pot and cold cuts and artisan breads and potato salad and fruit salad and miniature tarts and homemade chocolate chip cookies and three different kinds of meatloaf and three different kinds of lasagna and chicken soup and curried squash soup and minestrone soup. It was as if all of this abundance of food could fill our emptiness.

We sat, the three of us left behind, and stared at the dinners that arrived on our doorstep each afternoon. We lifted our forks to our mouths. We chewed and swallowed, but nothing could fill us. For months people fed us and somehow, unimaginably, time passed. Summer came and friends scattered to beaches and foreign lands.

One day, gourmet ravioli filled with lobster and a container of vodka cream sauce appeared on our doorstep with a bottle of pinot grigio. Our garden was in full bloom by now. Hot pink roses. Ironic bleeding hearts. Columbine and unpicked chives topped now with purple flowers. I carried the bag into my quiet kitchen and thought through the steps for cooking pasta. Somehow, the process that had once been automatic had turned complicated. Get a pan, I told myself. Fill it with water. I had not done even these simple things in almost three months. Yet soon the water was at an angry boil, the sauce simmered in a pan beside it. The simple act of making this food felt right.

The next day, I once again set a pot of water to boil. But instead of expensive pasta, I filled it with the medium shells that Grace had loved. When they were al dente, I tossed them with butter and parmesan cheese. That night, as the three of us sat in our still kitchen, the food did bring us comfort. It brought Grace close to us, even though she was so far away. Crying, I tasted the sharp acrid tang of the cheese. It was, I think, the first thing I had tasted in a long time.

We think of comfort food as those things our mother fed us when we were children. The roast chickens and mashed potatoes, chocolate cream pies and chewy brownies. But for me now, comfort food is cucumbers sliced into circles. It's chicken and stars soup with a side of kiwi. It's canned corn heated to just warm. In losing Grace, there is little comfort. But I take it when I can, in these most simple ways. On the days when grief grabs hold of me and threatens to overtake me again, I put water on to boil. I grate parmesan cheese and for that night, at least, I find comfort in a bowl of noonies.

Not long ago, I was in the supermarket and a small basket of bright orange kumquats caught my eye. I remembered that long ago trip to Italy when Grace developed a taste for these funny fruits. I could almost picture her in the front seat of my shopping cart, filled with delight at the sight of kumquats. I reached into the basket of fruit and lifted out one perfect kumquat, small and oblong and orange. When I bit into it, tears sprang into my eyes. The fruit's skin is sour, and it takes time before you find the sweetness hidden inside.

Peaches or Plums

Alan Michael Parker

Oh, how I hate my mind,
all those memories
that have invented their own memories.

Take my first love, for instance,
how after Mass we'd kneel
underneath the back stairs

and kiss and kiss and kiss and.
Were her lips like peaches or plums?
She was Catholic and she wanted

to be bad, and I loved her
more than baseball,
but all the other days

divided us, carry the one,
nothing left over. So strange,
only to kiss on a Sunday,

to hold my own breath again
for a week, another 10,022
minutes of wretched puberty,

until she moved to Iowa
or Ohio or the moon.
Oh, I can still remember

CHAUTAUQUA

nothing about her,
only kissing, and the impossible
geometry of the descending stairs

that rose to the church kitchen,
her breath like hot nutmeg
and a little like the ocean;

and once, oh my god, she bit me,
a first taste of my body,
blood in her smile.

My Son Asks If I've Ever Worn a Bikini

Kristin Kovacic

and then apologizes, assuring me
my swimsuit's "very fashionable for a woman
my age." He's ten and the world is blinking,
turn signals everywhere he turns, and me,
I've come around the other side, a mother, finally
accustomed to my costume, and suddenly
I'm exposed again, and think of my huge
sad friend, and understand his sadness at last,
how no part of him—knuckle like a walnut,
disappearing chin, not even his tree-trunk
wrist ever escapes the easily astonished
children of the earth. Somebody, please, turn
the lights out. When I wake up, he hugs me,
inhaling. "You have that morning smell,"
he says. "I love that smell."

Said

Ann Pancake

Said when them boys jumped out, ours was already loaded, safety off, and cocked. Said nobody thought. Said who could of lived through that close of range, what the hell we gonna do now? Said it was the other two fired first, but ours aimed best, what the hell? Said both of them got up afterwards, the least hurt dragging the most hurt away. Said it'll be all over town by evening, all over the county by morning, what? Said get our goddamned story straight, that's what they said.

They come off the mountain with their own boy in a purple-lipped panic, lips a-quivering like you took a finger, flick. Eyes frogged out and reared back both, horse at a snake, and shiny with a crazy crying, at first I thought it was just a crazy crying, only later did I hear the guilt. And him a big boy, at least fifteen, you'd thought it was him'd got hit, but although it was him they wanted, he wasn't so much as grazed. While I just went on a-peeling my potatoes, scooping out the little eyes. Lick your finger on the nick.

First I thought it was an accident, then I started hearing how on the other side it must of been planned. First thought it was only our boy pulled the our-side trigger, then started hearing I was at least half wrong. Heat off that woodstove, heat off fourteen scared men, and already five different stories fighting for what would be said. I was getting my taters going, bacon grease out a cup, when I felt the oldest one, Franklin's first son, Bunk, come up on my back. I shifted my head and I looked at him there. "Chester. Ches." Was all he said.

Aside from Bunk, they brung me only because they could stand my cooking and was always short on people to drive, I knowed that. And because, at sixty-nine, I was still my father's son, them theirs. And because they knowed I couldn't talk good when I could talk at all, and most people thinks what comes out your mouth is one and the same with what runs in your head. Which works against you most of the time, but sometimes it works for. With them it was usually for. Hunting places around here have shrunkt up smaller every year. I needed fresh meat in my freezer. Now Bunk had slumped away from it, into a back-cracked chair between the cookstove and wall, and he dropped that gray chin in one hand.

Got to slicing my onions, sharp of the odor a-stamping at theirs, boots and blaze orange and gun cases and guns, all of them still in their coveralls and coats, they was a-raising a steam with what they thought should be said. Closest to my age were Franklin's three sons—Bunk, Gordon, and Kenny Lee—and them three'd had five sons, and out of their son-in-laws, two who would hunt. And then that bunch had a whole slew of boys, Franklin's great-grands, but only four with us now. A few was too little, and others only hunted on video screens. And some of them argued nasty, and some argued reasonable, and some argued crazy, and some argued half-sweet, but only the Ryan one showed any hurt for them two shot kids, kids, I heard them say, he knowed from school. And other things. He was the youngest with us, Rusty's son, Gordon's grand, Franklin's great, I'd never paid him much mind, him a-surlying around under stringy red hair, fingering spots on his face. But now he was carrying on like a just-cut calf, snotting and bawling where he curled on a cot, until one of em said get out there in that johnny-house til you get hold yourself. Then another one said, no, just go out there sit in Uncle Kenny's truck. I poked the rings out my onions. Felt the thin curl of trigger in the middle of his finger. Before pot, before cocaine, before crack, oxycontin, and crystal methalatum. . . . My daddy wasn't a drinking man. Franklin, he wasn't neither.

Started my onions in the skillet next the taters, they said the boys was a-waiting for theirs, couldn't have known how this family hunts. Because most people these days still-hunt, that would have made the Ryan alone, but they did it the old way, drive and watch, which meant there was all kind of family nearby them boys didn't know about. Now Frankie, Bunk's boy, was a-stepping out his coveralls, and he dropspilled a whole box of cartridges on the floor, and if that didn't rattle em higher. They was big men, I tell you, they got fatter as they went the generations down. They was bearchested and bullheaded and they knowed more about guns than they did people, woods, or sense. My daddy talked good, walked tall, stood right alongside Franklin even if he never did own not one acre of land. But Chester, he told me, you watch his boys, and that was before the grands come along, and long before the greats.

Now Bunk'd got up, he was trying to talk sense to the younger ones, his brother Gordon was, too. Me with my back to em, moving onions, moving taters, I was hearing more than I could see and smelling more than either. Heat of em beading water on the winders, water a-starting to drip, and it'd already come to me I was smelling em when before I couldn't, but then it come to me that I couldn't before because before they'd smelled like me. I flopped a liver out a bread bag and onto the heat, stepped back when the bacon grease popped high.

"Oh, he won't say nothing."

There it was. Me the only one not related by blood or marriage.

"Course he won't say nothing, but he can still tell!" Hothead Rusty talking, even fireder up than usual with the Ryan being his.

"You know what I mean," that was Bunk again, we'd come up together, him just two years younger. But although Bunk had always wanted different, wanted us to be like Franklin and Daddy, me and Bunk could never be.

"Well, we got to know for sure, and he's got to keep it straight," another grandson, I couldn't tell which, but I could hear the walleye scare of his eyes.

"Hell, I don't even know if he can remember something right for that long," and one or two snickered despite everything else.

"He's ever bit as bright as any one of you!" Kenny, the third and last son. Liver colored like the boy's shivery lips and jerking in the pan. Like its nerves not yet shut down from the deer it got cut out of.

Then somebody's chair legs went a-scudding crosst the boards, and "Make eem write it down!" and then they was thrusting for paper. Slamming through kitchen drawers and outturning dirty pockets, and they ripped off part of the tater bag, but decided that was too small. Bunk fell back into the chair, I seed him. I seed his gray face spiderheld in his hands. My back still to em, water dribbling down the winder insides, and guess drug dealin and deer huntin don't mix too good, I wanted to, but never said. Then one fished a doughnut box out the garbage, and another grandson took a knife to it, and that gave them some room.

I couldn't see who it was grabbed my arm, but I heard the spatula hit the floor. "Write it down!" Turned me, and then I seed them all, but their faces had done run away. Their faces had gone away and they was stubble, they was glasses, they was orange and camouflage caps, and I could feel in his arm he was still holding back, I could hear it in the way his breath left his mouth. He slammed my hand on the box piece, and one stubble-cap turned into Gordon and turned away, and with a stub of a pencil out of somebody's pocket "I won't say nothing," I said.

"Naw! Naw! Put 'I'll tell it exactly like they want'!"

I felt me swaver a little on my feet. Them winders were a-swimming, they took no reflection, they let in no night. I steadied myself with my left hand on the table edge, and I pressed down hard to keep the mark from wiggling, and how little you all are a-knowing, I said in my head. Then it got so quiet, all of them watching my hand, you could hear the sugar crust crunch under the tip. Quiet enough you could hear Kenny or Gordon a-walking away up the stairs, I could tell it was a son by the heavy slow in the step. Then I laid the pencil down, stepped back best I could, them all up around me, when Rusty yapped out "Put 'I swear'!" How little you all are a-knowing. I pulled the pencil to the very edge. I squinched the "I swear" in. How little you are knowing, and nothing about said.

Rusty grabbed the scrap, jammed it in the thigh pocket of his canvas pants. And for about three seconds, they all of them looked at me there. For about three seconds, all of them's faces come back, each one clear, and dark, and at a great far away. And I seed Franklin, Gordon, Kenny, I seed Bunk, even in the by-marriage ones, I seed. Then they turned from me and back on themselves. A-arguing again over what would be said.

I picked my spatula up off the floor. I lifted that liver out, still bleeding a little, and laid it on a plate. Shoved the taters on a back burner, figured if they scorched, they wouldn't notice much. Then I walked out of the said. And into a dusk so silent you could hear smoke leave the roof.

My daddy'd been a few years older than Franklin, I was older than all his sons. Old enough to listen. Old enough to not have said. Franklin called that an accident, too, but only one man pulled the trigger then. And that story didn't have to get made and straight because the woman didn't get winged and run away, and she was from back in the hills anyway, her good looks didn't save her there. And no one seed it happen but Franklin hisself, and just one man, Franklin's tenant farmer, my daddy, seed it after, as he helped to clean and cover up.

My daddy told only me. Me still a wee little boy, but already understanding way ahead of where my mouth would ever get. Somehow Daddy knowed that then. He said to me just once what happened, but he said to me the other many times more. That he never knowed forever afterwards if he was a friend or a debt.

I grabbed me a broom, dropped Kenny Lee's tailgate, felt it sharp in my knees when I swung up in. I waited a second for the pain to ease. Then I walked the bed to the cab.

The Ryan laid crumpled on the bench seat there. Teary face part turned up and his hands squeezed between his legs. He looked at me out of an eye and a half, and I looked back. Then I turned, set my broom between the liner ridges, and swept the deer blood out. Nothing yet said.

Three Card Monte

Philip Terman

I walked everywhere
on that island, an island myself,
twenty, just up from the Midwest,

ready to begin that long book
called my life, aimless, swayed
by whatever was at hand, strolling

blind. On 5th Avenue—a figure,
emaciated, barely distinguishable
in the skyscraper's shadow,

on the steaming sidewalk,
inside a circle of watchers. Above
his podium cardboard box

he flashed three cards—
two clubs and one heart—
the queen—then turned

them over and the quick slide,
hands gliding like acrobats,
the cards revolving around

and over and under and through
until they lost their shapes,
spinning like blades as if

CHAUTAUQUA

by some inner force, a fast-
forward choreography.
I couldn't keep my eyes off

what I was sure to be the queen,
the one to watch, certain
if I held her attention

it would prove something
I needed, what I had to master,
this street preacher staring

straight into my eyes,
whispering, voice like gravel:
a twenty will get you a hundred—

and I was confident in the heart
I tracked, staked my savings
on what my eyes stalked.

Of course I was wrong
and I returned to the Midwest
where I had to start again

from scratch, following
in my mind the movement
of those cards and the brilliant

fingers that manipulated them
until they became a blur, like that city
I'm no longer certain was there at all.

WITH MY BROTHER AT WALDEN POND

Philip Terman

Twilight, January air unseasonably warm,
we add our stones to the pile that was

his house. Further on, at its reproduction,
we look through a window, imagine Henry

reading the Vedas, chuckling to the sparrow,
minding not the hours. Briefly we balance

the rails where he heard the train's whistle
and said it will ride the backs of the laborers.

And if he heard the power saws and backhoes
clearing and layering the private property

across the road for condominiums? Earlier,
on Poet's Ridge, I tried to be quietly desperate,

to not keep pace with my companion,
my brother the mathematician explaining

the Theory of the Steady State, about how
a system's recently observed behavior

continues into the future.
Thoreau, too, had a brother.

CHAUTAUQUA

They traveled rivers together.
When he came down, suddenly,

with lockjaw, Henry nursed him
but he died in his arms anyway and Henry

loved him so much he completely lost interest
in nature. He became, he said, "denaturalized."

He loved him so much—this rugged individualist,
this stone cold solitary, this disobedient,

this misanthrope, this independent, who wanted
only trees for company, this loner about whom

Emerson said, "when you touched him, he felt like bark,"—
that he developed lockjaw himself, sympathetically.

In the blurred light of this new dark,
either a thin pine leans across the surface

or Henry is a-fishing. Why not?
Behavior continuing into the future.

Henry bragged like Chanticleer, standing on his roost,
to wake his neighbors up. I tried to wake

my brother up once. The younger, I splashed
ice water on his face so he'd rise and toss

the football. He beat the deserved crap
out of me instead. Now we look for stones

Philip Terman

flat enough to skip, a skill at which he's
proficient, the advantage of a life of absolute

concentration. Sidearming an obscure slab
he had to scrape for in the hard soil that—why

not?—Henry sparked for his reading lamp,
we follow its hops and circles and widening

undulations, like the motions of the planets,
or our souls rippling back round to water.

message

Leslie Rubinkowski

I suppose the question began to ask itself in the woods behind the red-sided house. Back then when I was small my father and I took long walks among the trees. He would smoke a cigar and sometimes I would hold his hand and always we would talk about things that mattered to us both—books, sled riding, my cocker spaniel Taffy. Through crossed arms of maple and locust and oak waited our house: swing set and sandbox in the backyard and down a bank along the driveway a creek that rushed with the sound of a far-off crowd. As we walked I would lean in and swipe at the sleeve of his suede windbreaker, impressed by the pale tracks my fingers made.

And then one day my father stopped.

—Do you hear that? he whispered.

I stopped too. Nothing but the normal. Branches cracking their knuckles. Distant talk of water over rocks. Smells of cold suede and smoke, kaleidoscopic decay of leaves at our feet.

My hand slid from his.

—No.

Behind his glasses his green eyes wide:

—INDIANS!

Along the creek I tore upstream screaming as fast as my skinny legs could go—past the swing set, beyond the sandbox, up stone stairs into the sleeping garden, until I crashed through the back door into the kitchen where I stood panting and babbling bulletins of imminent attack as my father strolled in. My mother glanced up from what she was doing.

—What did you do to her now?

Leslie Rubinkowski

He shot her a look to inform her that he was offended she was accusing him of something and pleased that he had done whatever she was accusing him of. An indignant deadpan smirk.

—What? was all he said.

I GUESS IT SAYS something about my view of life that this is one of my fondest memories of my father. I know it means something that the man I trusted most in life—I will never trust another more—spent a great deal of our time together messing with my head. Now that he has died my father has left me with a mystery and my only means to solve it: a series of concentric recollections. On one level it makes a sort of sense—you follow a trail of information until you reach its source. But memories lack logic's clockwork; they don't proceed like a creek on the way to a verifiable source. One switchbacks off another, leaving in the clearing nothing that looks anything like home. It is not that memories are meaningless. But memories are not answers, and I am beginning to think they work best as a tool to help you accept that to some questions, no answers exist.

SOME THINGS HE told me, and some things I saw. He was left-handed. He served as an altar boy until he was eighteen. He was colorblind, though he insisted he was not, though he knew he was, and favored clothes in gray and beige and black. In his sixties surgery allowed him for the first time since childhood to see the world without glasses. On his first job he made five-cent Skyscraper ice cream cones at the Isaly's delicatessen on Butler Street in Pittsburgh, in the Polish neighborhood of Lawrenceville. He was quiet, even a little shy. He told my mother that the first time he saw her, leaning against a peanut machine in the drugstore in the small town where they met, he knew beyond all doubt that she would be his wife.

From his sixty-third year on he wore a diamond earring in his left ear, a Father's Day present from my brother and me. He paid his way through pharmacy school by working four years at a slaughterhouse, beating rats away from the meat furnace with a broom.

Every year he and my mother spent winters in Key West he bought deli turkey and roast beef to feed the bands of lawless chickens cruising the townhouse grounds. While he napped on a patio chaise the birds roosted on his chest. He owned two tuxedos and a burgundy velour bathrobe matted with so many blotches of melted chocolate that my mother begged him to surrender it long enough for her to wash. He grew up in a rowhouse with a dirt backyard. He pitched a tent there where he kept a cigar box filled with cigarette butts he'd collected off the street to smoke when his mother wasn't watching. He looked just like his mother, who died when he was sixteen. He kept a pair of polished black dance shoes in the back seat of his car.

SOMETIMES HE WOULD ASK,
—Do you still have that piece of hair?
And I would tilt my head so he could see it for himself: a curl growing out of my left temple that was an exact match of the curl growing out of his temple on the right – mirror images that always made me imagine our DNA corkscrewing straight out of our heads.

HALFWAY INTO HIS FORTIES during the age of disco my mother got them front-row tickets to see Peaches and Herb. During "Shake Your Groove Thing" Peaches boogied into the audience, leaned down, and pulled my father onstage. He stood there for a second, took in the assembly grooving. Up in the balcony my friend Henry screamed—I know that guy! I know that guy! My father regarded Peaches, long legs and beaded cornrows, and let it sink in, this exquisite instant of disco kismet. Then he raised his long arms above his head, swiveled his hips and smacked his hip with hers to execute a perfect bump. Peaches shouted—*Hey!*—and joined in. The crowd went wild. My mother watched proudly through the fingers of the hand covering her eyes.

ONE EVENING EARLY when I was five the two of us walked down a street toward our Buick. We had just seen *The Sound of Music* at the same theater where twelve years later he would dance with Peaches. I tightroped in my dress and patent Mary Janes along the curb until my father put his hands on my shoulders and steered me so that we changed places.

—The gentleman always walks on the outside, he explained. The lady always walks on the inside.

Around the same time I learned that he worked in the drugstore of a PX in Korea during the war, and that the first time he laid eyes on me I was six months old.

—I came down the stairway of the plane and I saw your mother holding you, he told me many times. At this point in the story he would grow sad, shake his head. I took one look at you and tried to get back on the plane, but they wouldn't let me.

For most of my life, he kept my fifth-grade picture in his wallet. He was fond of reminding me that I was not really his, that I was in reality the bastard child of my mother and Mr. Maxwell, the ancient caretaker of the apartment complex near Fort Bragg where they spent the first months of their marriage.

—You have Mr. Maxwell's feet, he insisted.

FLEE ENOUGH INDIANS, hear your paternity questioned from the time you recognize the concept, you become a certain kind of person. You become the kind of person who studies her feet in the shower and understands that they look exactly like the feet of the man who says you do not belong to him, the kind who knows that just because you trust someone with your life doesn't mean you have to believe him. By the time you are eight and this man tells you the story of how he met your mother while she was stealing hubcaps on the street, able to communicate only in grunts, you just roll your eyes. Or you simply shoot him a look, an indignant deadpan smirk.

CHAUTAUQUA

I ALSO LEARNED there is a reading beyond words. Because after kindergarten one day my mother and I went to the library, as usual leaving with so many books we both had to carry them into the house. When my father came home from the drugstore for lunch I pushed a slim one at him, stern with the fury of a kid who was proud that she could read.

—Look at this, I challenged. It's a *picture* book.

—Well, wait a minute, he said. Let's see if we can tell the story ourselves.

He turned the pages, we decoded the illustrations. The mother and the little girl are baking a cake. They measure the flour. They crack the eggs, drop them into the bowl. There is a spoon, there is an oven, there is a smile of pride. And in my mind, in reply to some echo deep in a helix, the switch tripped. My eyes jumped from his face to the book and back even though I was nearly blind from all the words doing a tickertape glide inside my head. We were on to something here. Side by side on the living room floor we shaped life from what we could see. We created our own plot, we made a world—nobody needed to tell us anything.

I wonder sometimes if he knew how much I was going to need this.

IN HIS SIXTIES my father ceased to believe in an afterlife. The scandals of abuse and betrayal in the Catholic Church saddened him, and he turned from God. He fought this turning: whenever I visited he was reading books that might call it all back, about the source of the Scriptures or historical reconstructions of the life of Christ. Still, he had concluded that once you died you ceased to exist. He and I debated this nearly every time we spoke.

—I don't know, Dad, I would say. How can this be *it*?

When you two would start, my mother told me after everything happened, I would just leave the room and let you talk.

During one of our debates we discovered that, without either telling the other, we had read the same books about Buddhism in an attempt to stanch the violence of our tempers.

—You're like me, aren't you, he said to me in the family room the last time we spoke.

—Yeah, I said.

HOME ONE SUMMER from school I walked into that same family room and found my father on the sofa balancing on his lap a black dog—a swirly-coat loaf of male cockapoo that belonged to the Costellos next door. The youngest Costello girls christened him Lisa, though gender issues were not at the moment his keenest predicament. A German shepherd had mauled him as he'd trotted down the next block of Vine. Punctures sunk deep in his pink-gray belly.

My father cradled Lisa so that the dog's knobby spine rested against his skinny legs. On the sofa next to them lay gauze pads and Neosporin. He swabbed and bandaged the wounds and Lisa leaned back, her brown eyes taking in his face, watching his mouth moving, murmuring words I couldn't hear—though the voice, its message, I understood. I remembered it from third grade, that weekend I had stomach flu. The two of us sat on the bathroom floor long past Saturday midnight talking to pass those infinite minutes of waiting for someone sick to throw up. He was holding a warm washcloth and I was telling him how that afternoon during square dancing in the multipurpose room Raymond Frederick had punched me in the stomach. Why would he do such a mean thing? And how come stomach flu besides? He laughed at my questions in a way that made me realize what made them funny was that they were not funny at all. That it is possible to be so serious you can make anything a joke.

Years later, grown and at my lowest point, he was more direct.

—You've got to get a grip, he said to me in that same soft voice. The world is not a very nice place.

ON A TUESDAY MORNING in the middle of July he trimmed the yews, read the mail sitting on a bench next to the door, then began sweeping the green clippings off the front porch. That is where my mother found him lying when she leaned out to ask what he wanted for lunch.

The next afternoon in neurological intensive care I watched a doctor and a nurse perform the second round of tests to determine brain death. I had to assign words to the images on the x-rays: different angles of that shroud of white inside the skull. White in real life being red. Aneurysm, the doctors reported. An insult to the brain. Their certainty was an insult to mine. I refused to believe that a mind could go away. The dancing and the doubts and the sweetness and the playful evil—how could so much just stop?

—What's your father's name? the doctor asked.

—Ron.

The doctor leaned in and put his lips a fraction from my father's right ear. He screamed:

—RON! WAKE UP! He clapped his hands. RON!

Oh, God. If anything of him is still in there he's got to be hating this. This is so undignified.

With a syringe the doctor jetted ice water into my father's left ear. If he retained any brain function, his eyes would immediately track in the direction of the chill.

His eyes stayed closed and still.

The nurse wrote something on her clipboard. The curl on my father's right temple flipped up wet from ice water and the liquid leaked from the catheter bored into the back of his head.

You've got to get a grip, I told myself. *The world is not a very nice place.*

AFTER THEY'D GONE I touched the hole in his earlobe where until the day before he'd worn a diamond. A social worker had brought it to my mother in the emergency room while she, my brother, and I assured each other that he had just fainted from the heat. The woman's cupped hands carried the diamond, a watch, a medallion he had worn around his neck. The head of Christ.

—Do me a favor, I asked him in a voice as soft as I could manage.

Remember what we talked about? If you can, let me know. Could you do that? Come back and let me know.

THAT WEEK MY MOTHER discovered he'd contributed to at least three animal protection groups. I found all of my grade-school report cards in a metal strongbox; my third-grade teacher judged me hopeless at keeping my materials in order. My mother said my father had recently repeated to her several times what he'd told me during our debates: Once you're dead, that's it. You're gone. There's nothing.

A FEW DAYS later I called my mother and I heard my father. For as long as I can remember his voice on their answering machine greeting said:

Hi. We can't come to the phone right now, but if you wait for the sound of the beep, leave a message, we'll get back to you as soon as we can. Thank you.

Now the same message played. But this time there was something else—a skip in the tape.

Hi. We can't come to the phone right now, but if you wait for the sound of the beep, leave a message, we'll get back to you as soon as we can. Thank you.

Back to you as soon as—

Beeeeeeeep.

As soon as *what*, Dad?

That question: my God.

Of all death's mysteries, this one most seriously messes with my head, a situation I am certain would please my father. The world is not a very nice place, yes, but it is also beautiful–and *holy* scrolls past my eyes as I write this and so there it is, too. This then is his legacy: Question everything, but believe as deeply as life will allow. Where doubt lives, there also dwells the possibility of belief. A death is not always an ending and an ending not the same as resolution. For the rest of my life I must seek some balance between skepticism and acceptance, but now I alone hold the book, and my only guide into the future is the insistent and serpentine past.

LONG WHITE SKY
Jan Beatty

It was something about the long white sky,
the open highway feeling of no stops
that flooded me when I was washing her hair.
She had never let me touch her, never
hugged much, so when I had my hands
in her thin brown hair, careful not to hurt,
I found myself in the inner sanctum
of the body in the way that only happens
when someone allows you to assist.

What did I know of her daily scars?
> *here, tender,*
> *where you fell on the stairs. here,*
> *where the priest patted your head*
> *at first communion. here where*
> *your brother hit you?*

This head covered by so many hats
in your 94 years, now my hands
on your scalp, rinsing water through—
knowing I can't retrieve you,
you have let me near:

I will never hurt you, never pull or
overstep—I'm in love with finding
what you need, can I help, really

Jan Beatty

in the smallest way:
here/no/ not
there/ too much/
   wait—

Standing with you in the long white,
handmaiden as you ready your body
into next sky:
   you lie back,
   inch your body deeper in the hospital bed
   arms at your sides,
   you pat the sheets smooth,
   then hands crossed over your
   blue nightgown, and yes.

another kiss

Nancy Reisman

There were never enough, really, not within the family, not beyond it. She imagined walking past the glossy windows of downtown dress shops and department stores, the elegant mannequins gazing over Main Street, untouchable and untroubled, dress after dress promising a life of afternoon teas and cocktail parties and fast, bright dances, the company of expensive suits, and on the crowded sidewalk men occupying those suits, and workmen, fashionable women and shop girls, pausing to see not the window display but Ruth herself, calling her name, *Ruth*, their faces filling with light.

These were her daydreams from childhood onward, the dream of being dreamed, her own singular radiance made real by irrefutable longing from everyone. When in adolescence the dreams first became sexual, she often imagined the love-drunk faces of young men and the girls she most admired all wishing to touch her, to be what they could not live without, though most of the time she believed herself invisible.

Always, she searched for beautiful things, hair clips and ribbons, brooches, something to smarten up the plain dresses and stockings, the right bit of color to change her. She had dark wavy hair, large dark eyes and olive skin, but her face, her body, seemed to her haphazard and graceless, and she felt herself, always, peripheral, peering in, pressing her nose to the glass as meaning unfolded without her. Red suited her, and until she was older and wore lipstick, her clothes had small flecks of it, buttons or pins or embroidered collars, which changed the way she felt in a room. Did her sisters understand about color? How you could die without it? And in Buffalo, winter became for her a colorless wilderness she had each year to cross, and from her teenaged years on she took refuge in those department stores, and along Main street, where even in snow there was light from shop windows and the interiors of restaurants. She studied the shifts in fashion – dropped waists, rising hemlines, cloche hats, earrings swinging, half-way to the shoulder – and these she would talk to her older sisters about. Sometimes they would listen, and often they would nod and wait until she was finished to pose entirely unrelated questions, as if they had not heard her. She'd offer news of the neighborhood, instead: a pregnancy, a friend's cousin visiting from New York, a local boy admitted to law school. But either her sisters had heard the news already or found it to be of no consequence. They spoke with a clever ease she didn't share, and it seemed her own language – clear, plain – was, to them, neither, and the Ruth sitting before them was dull to the core, immune to rapture. Once in a while they would disassemble her outfit, taking as she stood there the hair clip with painted forget-me-nots (Jessie's, borrowed when Jessie was not home), or the green scarf (Leah's, taken from her drawer), and continue with a conversation about ice on the walkway, or a poem Ruth had not read and had no wish to read, or a novel for the Liberal Arts club, and then it seemed as if her sisters were in their own separate room within the room.

1927. LATE JULY. Thick humidity and rising heat, even in Buffalo, the lake winds still, heat shimmering up from the streets. Too warm to window shop with the other girls from the office: on her lunch break Ruth carries her sandwich to Lafayette Square and finds a patch of shade. The benches fill early, and she's taken to bringing an old pillowcase, just big enough to sit on, the fabric cool on her legs. Though the heat falls away at night, Ruth has been restless, her sleep fragmented and thin, so the lunch hour has a drugged, irritable quality. She is sweating with the city, thirsty and strangely weepy, and there's no apparent antidote: if only she could swim at one of the lake beaches, if at least a breeze would kick up. Or better, a thunderstorm, a vast, drenching thunderstorm.

It's then that she thinks of the roses, blooming early in her sister's yard, flourishing in the heat. A passing image of red, and the climbing vines; she thinks to reapply her lipstick, and buys a soda from a street vendor and presses the cold bottle to her face.

She doesn't make a decision to take roses, then or later, the impulse doesn't work like that. The next morning she's awake before dawn, even though the night has cooled, and then she's dressed, leaving her apartment, crossing Butler Avenue to Jessie's house, Jessie's yard, where the roses have climbed a trellis beside the house, perhaps two dozen in bloom. She chooses six large ones and cuts the stems and wraps them in newspaper. The neighborhood seems gloriously empty. It's just dawn when she returns home. The roses she places in water-tumblers around her bedroom, the increasing light fragmented by oak leaves and window sheers, blurring with the fragrance and secrecy, so that the room seems exquisitely private. Maybe the feeling will be there when she returns from work, maybe not. She delays, sticky again, by the time she leaves, and she rushes through the saturated air to the streetcar and the paper-ridden clerk's office at City Hall.

"RUTH." IT'S JESSIE, at Ruth's door, her yellow summer shift still covered by an apron, round dark patches of sweat beneath her arms, hair loosely pinned. It's evening. Jessie's face is closing. "Don't touch the roses," she says. Jessie's face is not so much angry as loveless and tired, tired of Ruth: this will not be the face she shows to her husband Harry, or her infant son, or to Leah. A few orange streaks remain over the rooftops, and along the block porch lights appear, little yellow moons, echoing Jessie's dress. Ruth says nothing. It's as if the roses in her bedroom belong there, have always been there, the cutting nearly forgotten. Jessie closes her eyes and Ruth listens to her soft breathing through the screen, and when Jessie opens them again, her expression is still unyielding. "Goodnight," Jessie says.

In a neighborhood of closely built two-flats, someone is always looking out a window. What's surprising is that anyone noticed Ruth.

Had she walked through her sister's tiny yard, leaving it untouched, or even lain down on the patch of grass, who would have remarked her presence? The roses were visible, and made her visible. She hadn't thought. Idiocy, really, to think that no one would notice a bunch of roses, carried that morning by Ruth.

It was the second time that month she'd been out, alone, at an odd hour. Only two weeks earlier, she'd awoken at one in the morning, and there was a small-voiced crying, like a baby's cry, or a cat's, which could have been coming from anywhere. Windows stood open all over the neighborhood. She put on a house dress and shoes without socks, and walked out into the street. There were other sounds and then the small crying, which came from the other side of the street—Jessie's baby, perhaps? The night seemed darker than it had a moment earlier, the air less clear, and she hurried to Jessie's house, and let herself in with the hidden key. Quiet inside, quiet and dark. She heard the crying sound again, but coming from somewhere else, another house or an alley, further off. And then other sounds in the apartment, and she realized she needed a reason to be there. What to say? She'd had a dizzy spell, and it frightened her. Ruth was frightened, that part was true, though she couldn't say why, only that she needed to come here. And she moved in the direction of the hallway, her eyes adjusting to the dark now, and through the doorway she could see Harry's shoulder and the back of his head; he was kissing Jessie, and moving on top of her, and they were both softly moaning, pleasure sounds. She stood watching them through the doorway. There was a shuddering in Harry, and she could see Jessie's hands touching his face, and the two of them kissing again, and then the sounds of sheets, movement, and Ruth retreated to the living room. And when the house seemed quieter again, and she sensed the sleep breathing, she let herself out, and stood on the unlit porch for a moment before hurrying across the street to her own apartment.

For days the images would float up before her, Harry's skin, his back and shoulder in the shadowy light, Jessie's hair loose against the pillowcase, her hands tensed against Harry's back, pulling him, their sounds, which seemed half-animal, half-bird. Twice she saw Jessie in the morning, watering potted plants, as Ruth walked to work. She waved, and Jessie waved, her hair now pinned up, her body hidden beneath her apron and dress and undergarments, hands immersed in work. That Sunday, Ruth baked a coffee cake and brought it to Jessie and Harry. On the table, daisies in a milk bottle, craning toward the light, a glass bowl of plums gleaming beside them. Harry offered a plain, unrevealing hello, nothing that spoke of his skin or his night movements, a simple "Hello, Ruth," and returned to his preoccupation with a torn window screen. The baby was awake, and for several minutes Ruth held him, only a little awkwardly. He had a sweet, powdery smell, and wide dark eyes. He'd learned to grab, to see what he wanted and grab, this time her beads, which he tried to eat. She did not know how to gently take them away and distract him, though she'd seen Jessie do it a dozen times. He began to fuss, and squirm as she held him, and the fussing became crying. She made hushing sounds and rocked a little, but it seemed that his discontent was in fact a response to Ruth, as if he sensed all that was inadequate about her, and could not bear to be held by her. Jessie scooped him up and walked him around the kitchen, and then he was gumming the fabric of her dress. She sat at the table and unbuttoned her blouse to nurse him. She'd lain a cloth over part of her chest, covering herself, but her left breast was still exposed. Ruth was unable to keep her eyes off it. She pretended to watch the baby, and sometimes she did—the workings of his small mouth, the way his eyes tracked Jessie's face—but found herself wanting a glass of water, and wondering about Jessie's nipples, and the milk, and the feeling on the tongue, the taste. Then she snapped awake, and stood, poured water to drink. She washed Jessie's breakfast dishes and swept the floor, while Jessie nursed the baby to sleep. When Ruth stopped moving, the kitchen seemed impossibly still. Jessie mouthed "thank you" and Ruth retreated to the stillness of her own rooms, the warm dull afternoon never cresting, just sliding into a too-warm evening, and its routines of clothes-pressing and organizing dresses for the week, a curtain falling over the moments with Jessie and the baby, and then the curtain gradually solidifying, so that in later years what she remembered of that day were the billowing white shirts on Jessie's clothes line, and the brown-sugared ring of coffee cake and water poured into a glass.

The yellow dress, Jessie beyond the screen: this image remained.

HARRY. HE WAS handsome, slim, with thick wavy hair and hazel eyes and well-shaped lips. When Ruth was nineteen, he began to date Jessie, and though Ruth herself had regular dates, her daydreams seemed to lead her back to Jessie and Harry. She imagined herself at the lake beach not with her school friends, but with the two of them, sleeping in the sun on a languorous, drowsy afternoon, lulled by the warm scent of grass and lake and skin salt, and the sensation of a rolling embrace. Sometimes Harry was embracing her and sometimes Jessie was embracing her but at no time was she separate from them. It was all one sweep of feeling, gorgeous, like a kiss, a long kiss enumerated into several and throughout her body, and with it the sensation of hands on her skin. Sometimes she was wearing nothing, nothing at all, on this beach, and it was as easy as sleep and she was beautiful. In this dream she got to be beautiful. She would fall into this scene late in the afternoon if she could, during a nap before supper, but then she would wake, damp and tender, and to move, just to move, gave her small rippling shocks. There were household sounds beyond the bedroom door, like a small alarm, and a smell, a scent she couldn't name, except that it was that scent, damp and briny, and she had to wash quickly. And then set the table and sit for supper, all the lake dream still whirring in her head, enough so that Jessie's direct gaze, or the mention of Harry's name, would make her glance away and flush with embarrassment.

Her sisters married and took other flats on the block. Finally, Ruth moved into a smaller place. It seemed now there was even more separateness, the need to cross the street to find her sisters, and sometimes she would panic and imagine herself an ice floe cut loose. Solitude was excruciating, though in fact much of her time she was not alone, but at her city hall job, or on weekends with girlfriends, walking on Main or taking in a picture. She spent as much time in her sisters' parlors as she spent in her own, mostly Jessie's. Too quickly, Leah would lose patience, her delicate features turning sharp. Eligible young men took Ruth out, to dances and dinners or to the pictures. She wore red lipstick and red earrings and waited for something to happen. Often there was a second date, and on the second date she would flounder, listening eagerly but not knowing how to respond or what to say after she had told about the city clerk's office and her sisters' lives.

THE MAN IN the photo is Sammy Glazer, in his late twenties then, and the beach Crystal Beach, a rare picture of Ruth laughing, laughing because Sammy Glazer is carrying her in his arms, half-threatening to drop her in the water, and because Sammy has already kissed her, and because they are only wearing bathing suits and the sun and wind feel so fine on her skin. Rare because it later became Ruth's habit to rip her own image out of photos. This remained because of Sammy, and because in the photo their bodies are inseparable.

Sammy was a cousin of Ruth's school friend, Maura Glazer. Ruth had met him before, but only briefly, and in a crowd, her awkwardness keeping her on the periphery. That August at the beach, clumsiness seemed to fall away, her eagerness pushing forward. She'd gone to the beach with Maura and Maura's younger sister, and Sammy met them there. He had a Mediterranean handsomeness and an easy charm, and Maura liked to speculate about his romances. He easily could have married several women he'd dated, but had not. Once he had told Maura he wasn't financially secure yet, and once he had told her he hadn't met the right girl, and once he had told her he wasn't in a hurry to be a father. Maura believed all of these things. He liked nightclubs and music and he was known as a wonderful dancer. That first day on the beach, Ruth was still in the spell of her own body and what she had seen at her sister's, the heat, the impulse for roses, and with Sammy she was strangely un-shy. She asked him if he'd like to walk with her to the concession, where she shared her soda with him, all the while wanting to touch him. And then she did touch him, as they returned to the beach blanket where Maura and Ellen were dozing; she touched his cheek with her hand and let it drift back over his hair. She was standing very close to him then, and she could see a change in his face, a small light, and later that afternoon he kissed her, and they swam together. Aloud, he wondered if she liked to dance.

What was it he saw? The yearning, the desire, the implicit invitation. Yearning changed her face. Touching him had been spontaneous and tender, and not the gesture of a beggar; it was in fact the gesture she had seen Jessie make, one she herself had never made before. For a moment something lively and unafraid took hold, and that was the moment Sammy saw her. And when he took her dancing, she felt at first awkward, but then her movements became smoother, the dance floor becoming a silk-bright world she did not want to leave. He drove her home and kissed her goodbye. For two weeks, they met at the beach and in the dance hall, and Ruth became bolder, wanting to hold him, her hands hesitating on his shoulder, on his chest.

The first time they made love was in his car. They'd been kissing for what seemed an hour, and his hands were under her clothes, and she wanted nothing more than to be rid of the clothes. And she was amazed by the pleasure he took in touching her, in his hands and then his mouth, the liquid, almost biting pressure—astonishing. And he stopped and gazed at her for a minute, his eyes glossy in the dark, all of him somehow glossy. He was fussing with a small packet and then she felt intense pressure, a burning, a pause in the pleasure, but then he was touching her breast again and starting to move the way she'd seen Harry move. The pleasure returned through the burning sensation, an exquisite burn, and a frenzied feeling began to overtake her, her body traveling beyond herself. Then he was shuddering and they were quiet in the car. Quiet little kisses. There were two other nights like this, both of them in a park he drove her to, with a great green field and a small woods, a farm field with no one around, and they lay on the beach blanket and afterward watched the black, star-thick sky. At work she was dreamy, and if she found herself thinking about him at all, she'd feel aroused and would have to find a way to stop the thought.

Her sisters knew only that she'd gone on dates with Sammy Glazer. These presumably meant evenings at the pictures, which might include hand holding and mild kisses. She did not think to name the way she and Sammy were together those nights, which seemed to belong to a separate, private universe. No one warned her of anything, and it seemed there was nothing to warn her of. In those weeks she did not think of the future, the present so immediate and strong it would naturally wash into and overtake any other season. She did not think of marriage. She thought of Sammy's mouth, and Sammy's joy at the beach, and his weight above her, and his solidity below her, and the earthy, sweet-salt taste of his skin. She floated from visit to visit with Sammy, and when she was with him the present seemed inexhaustible. A luminous sleepwalking.

In September, the beach closed. One weekend, Sammy took Ruth to a matinee, then dropped her off at home. He called again late in the month. He wouldn't have time for a nightclub, he said, what about another picture? At a Hippodrome matinee, they sat three rows from the front, Sammy mesmerized by a film Ruth struggled to keep up with—imagining instead the beach blanket and the texture of Sammy's skin. Now and then he patted her arm, and she waited for him to hold her hand, but he did not. Afterward, he took her to a tea room for sweets, and there her anxiety bloomed. Why was he not holding her hand? And what to say? He'd want amusing conversation. He'd want charm. "Sarah Kaplan's cousin Mel is going to medical school in Boston," she said. "Dora Steiner's going to have another baby." But as usual, whenever she talked of the branching and crossing networks of other peoples' lives, boredom settled on his face, changing it to the polite mask of a stranger. Nor did he care about shifts in fashion, despite all that touching and physical joy. Why wouldn't he care, at least, about the textures, the ways clothes touched your body, if not the ways they might transform you? Or the colors that you would never otherwise have? She sipped her tea quietly, and asked him about his family, and said that she'd seen Maura.

"Yes, Maura." He paused and took a long drink, his gaze tracking something beyond her, beyond the walls of the tea room. "Ruth, do you like to travel?"

An unexpected question; she hadn't been prepared. Maybe she should have known that on dates people talk about travel. It seemed no more part of her life than horseback riding.

"I like Crystal Beach," she said.

"We all do." Sammy spoke almost gravely. Why did it seem like his agreement was a correction? He wanted to see the great cities. Paris, he said, London. He wanted to see the British Museum. He wished he could visit Italy. Greece.

Ruth nodded and smiled and listened to him describe antiquities he'd read about, Greek statues with broken arms, urns, Egyptian artifacts found in tombs. She thought about English bone china, the flowered cups she'd seen at Maura's, and elegant blouses from France. Maybe he'd be willing to talk about gardens. Or paintings—she liked to look at paintings—but now he was speaking of the Acropolis, and with a politician's fervor. It was still afternoon when he dropped her off at home, the maples and oaks splashing yellow and red against the slate sky. Ruth pulled her coat tight around her. Sammy walked her to her door, and kissed her on the cheek. "You're a great gal, Ruth," he told her.

A Tuesday lunch hour. The lake wind had kicked up. "Evie Rosenthal," Maura said. She and Ruth were standing outside of Florsheim Shoes, Maura's hair tucked into a red cloche hat, brown overcoat buttoned to her chin. Ruth pictured Evie as she'd last seen her—a quick-witted brunette, petite, with gray-green eyes and long lashes. "A sparkling girl," people called her. She was two years younger than Ruth.

"I know how fond you are of Sammy," Maura said. "He just doesn't stick to one girl very long, you know."

The curb wavered, a tiny horizon line breaking up near her shoes. "Oh."

Maura scrutinized Ruth's face.

"Thank you for telling me." Ruth made a show of checking her watch, and pretended her lunch break had ended. "I'll see you soon," she said, and strode off, her dull body rushing her away.

Dates, just dates. The sex she had told no one about. It was part of the long dream she wanted to keep dreaming. But now it fell into a different light, and her body, which had seemed those nights beautiful, was not beautiful, never beautiful, only Sammy was beautiful. She'd thought—hadn't she?—that the wild, unstoppable feeling alone would forever extend her time with Sammy, that Sammy's wanting was, like hers, infinite. Those nights had felt infinite. But his wanting ended. Somehow, she'd become "a great gal."

Ruth secluded herself, leaving her apartment only for work and groceries, sleeping heavily, doggedly washing her clothes. In quick fading bursts, she embroidered a doily the size of a handprint, bright tiny x's giving way to a white cotton field. After ten days, Jessie appeared with the drowsy baby, and sat him in Ruth's lap while she brushed Ruth's hair and picked out coral earrings for Ruth to wear. "Come for a walk," Jessie said. "Come over for supper."

Jessie smelled of milk and vanilla. Ruth focused on Jessie's face now, and blinked, as if adjusting to daylight. She bundled up and followed Jessie out the front door, pushed the baby carriage around the neighborhood, and returned not to her own place but to Jessie's kitchen, where Jessie brought her soup and sliced chicken, bread and coffee. Now her seclusion extended to Jessie's apartment, as if the two places were in fact one, despite the doors and intervening street. Throughout the week, Ruth used the hidden key to Jessie's door. Sometimes Harry was returning from his office, but often he was not there, or leaving for evening insurance collections. When Ruth arrived at the kitchen, Jessie would smile. "Good, you're here," she'd say, and ask about Ruth's day, the same way she asked about Harry's day, and listen attentively, and pour cups of tea or glasses of cider. How strange that Ruth had finally stumbled upon a route to the interior, the center of things, where her dullness would leave her. Her contentment there seemed almost worth the loss of Sammy, though she often thought of Sammy not as Sammy, but as "that one" or sometimes just "that time."

In November, Jessie's invitations came less frequently. On Sunday, Jessie would say, "Why don't you join us on Wednesday?" and on Wednesday, Shabbos, and on Shabbos, perhaps Monday, perhaps Tuesday. At first, Ruth would show up anyway, but soon she could not find the hidden key, and when she mentioned this to Jessie, Jessie would say that Harry must have taken it, or Leah had borrowed it, or she herself had forgotten to put it back. By the end of the year, Ruth was invited to dinner once a week, as she had been in August.

One minute at the center of things, and the next, outside again. What missteps had Ruth made? She hadn't borrowed anything of Jessie's, not even the beads to match the coral earrings. She'd rocked the baby, diapered the baby, washed Jessie's dishes. And now the door was closing again. "I don't get to see you enough," Ruth complained. "It helps me to see you."

"I know," Jessie said, but she didn't invite Ruth to dinner more often, even when Ruth offered to cook. Instead, Jessie invited her to her book club meeting, at which of course there would be other women, none of them particularly interested in the rhythms of Ruth's day.

CHAUTAUQUA

JANUARY, A FROZEN evening. The meeting was at a house; at least Ruth and Jessie didn't have far to walk. A small foyer opened onto a living room with a fat green sofa, heavy rose-colored chairs, and smaller wooden chairs pulled in from the kitchen. Leah arrived, and a few women Ruth knew from the neighborhood, and a few she did not, all of them bundled in heavy coats and thick scarves, cocoons from which they emerged as ordinary-sized women in dresses and stockings and cardigans. "Hello Ruth, Hello Ruth. Hello Ruth." No one could say they weren't friendly. Fresh tea, a plate of sweets: all of this seemed promising. But after the tea had been poured and the women had shared the sweets, they began to talk about Chekhov. Jessie had said Ruth might like his plays, but when she'd tried to read them, it wasn't dislike that she felt as much as a kind of petulant disturbance. Among the book club women, the air in the room seemed to shift to stifling seriousness. They began talking of absurdity, and of longing—how useless, how persistent. Ruth could have faded from the room, washed away by all the talk. The auburn-haired woman on the green sofa said, "He doesn't like empty-headed people." Another woman lit a cigarette. "It's worse for the ones who think too well of themselves, but he pities them, doesn't he?" Ruth couldn't follow the conversation, and no one seemed to notice. Did they know how to laugh, these women? Yet they did laugh, even Leah laughed, and several of them smoked, and she wanted to laugh with them. She smiled while they laughed but she could not fathom them, except her sisters, partly, and she found herself watching Jessie and Leah and wanting them to say the things that would make everyone else nod. "There is no such thing as simple love," Jessie said. "This woman cannot hide behind her class," Leah said. "It's fallen apart." And as the others nodded, Ruth too would nod, and try to look thoughtful, and thoughtfully sip her tea.

Ruth did not return to the club, and she could not keep herself from Jessie's apartment. That winter, she showed up whenever the loneliness began to overtake her, sometimes knocking on the door, or shouting up from the front porch. Once inside, she'd stay for hours. In March, she began pocketing small things of Jessie's, and the next day or the day after that, silently contrite, she'd bring baked goods and secure another dinner invitation. In May, Sammy Glazer married Evie Rosenthal. In June, on Jessie's Liberal Arts Club night, Ruth, agitated, found Harry alone at home. He invited her into the parlor, offered her a glass of lemonade. She was standing a few feet away from him, and her body seemed to follow its own will, drawing her close enough to brush up against him and reach for his face. He stepped back abruptly. "Ruth," he said. "Please go home."

About Ruth's hair: coincidence. Coincidence that she had such a need to see color, coincidence that she dated no one seriously after Sammy and for decades everyone but Sammy thought she was a virgin. But it's true that her hair never grayed, that while the texture changed, the color remained the same deep brown, and her sisters' hair dulled and shifted to salt-and-pepper. The changes in her face did not come until later, and to others it appeared that time had stopped for her. A gift. But she also felt stranded in time. The sociability of her twenties gave way, and by her early thirties she had only two unmarried friends. Evenings she spent listening to the radio. There was war brewing in Europe again, and what seemed to be massive pogroms, and she stayed close to Jessie and to Leah. And when the US entered the war, younger men and even some men her age disappeared from the streets. Women did not. Women without men were everywhere, all of them, it seemed, worried and lonely. Her own unmentionable loneliness became a badge of a new sorority she immediately embraced.

Although Ruth would not admit it, not to anyone but Jessie, and then obliquely, she found comfort in the national crisis. At kitchen tables throughout the neighborhood, women offered her a chair. Always she found a companion for the pictures, or for walks through Delaware Park. She felt part of a legitimate common purpose then, as she did during small local crises, all of which she handled beautifully:

snowstorms, street floods, power outages. She did not mind shoveling walks and pushing cars out of snowbanks, and there was nothing suspect about bringing tea to the brigades of shoveling men, or delivering candles to the next-door neighbors. These moments offered instant permission to enter the other people's lives, at least for the day. During her loneliest times, an almost frenzied quest for usefulness would overtake her, and she'd make large pots of soup for her sisters' families, and cakes, and one after another noodle casserole. Maybe it was this sort of helpfulness that swayed Harry in the end—the snow shoveling, the pots of soup. Maybe her unchanging hair color, the perennial youthfulness of it, in combination with the pans of beef brisket. There's more to it than that, of course.

THESE CRISES—the war, the snowstorms—left her unscathed. Who, then, would have predicted her tornadic hysteria? Ruth herself did not see it coming, though she'd always suspected that the world could fly apart. In the spring of 1951, Jessie was struck by a swooning fatigue, and at first Ruth swept in with soup, ran errands, and sat at Jessie's bedside relaying neighborhood gossip, her worry laced with contentment. But after a few weeks, Jessie showed no sign of improvement, and slept instead of listening to Ruth. An annoyance, and then, with the diagnosis of leukemia, a terror. For months, Harry and his sons and Leah all moved quietly about the apartment, escorting Jessie out on good days, ferrying her to the doctor and later to the hospital, a small determined collective, while Ruth floundered. At moments, she glimpsed a tenderness between Harry and Jessie she had not witnessed in years, but she was simply an audience to this intimacy, excluded and uncomprehending.

As Jessie declined, Ruth became volatile. During the first hospital trip, Ruth raged at the nursing staff, sobbed, shouted even as Jessie tried to sleep. The nurses barred her from the room, and escorted her to a chair in Hospital Reception, where she eventually fell into a quieter and more static panic. After an hour, she glanced up to find her sister Leah's pale, oval face, hazel eyes flat with fatigue. "Go home, Ruth," Leah said. "You need to go home." After Ruth resumed weeping and accused Leah of coldness, Leah dug into her pocketbook for bus fare, and led Ruth to the bus stop. "We're okay here, Ruth." Leah said. "Get some sleep."

Most weeks, Leah set Ruth to small errands, marketing and trips to the pharmacist, housekeeping at Jessie's and Harry's place. Perhaps this was why, later, she said nothing about the widowed Harry dining regularly with Ruth.

HARRY'S KISS WAS nothing like Sammy Glazer's kiss. Not the kiss she had dreamed of, not the kiss she had seen him give Jessie when they were still young. It was a tentative, consoling kiss, without passion, the sort of kiss you might get from, well, a relative. When she kissed him back, Jessie's presence seemed almost palpable, and she kissed him more insistently, as if kissing Jessie through Harry and also kissing her away.

They honeymooned in Florida. The first time he touched her, she felt at once a welling desire and a wash of grief, the impulses inseparable, inchoate. The turquoise and white hotel room became a box for Harry's slow, quiet movements, and for the brief feeling of elsewhere, of the world dropping away, and an even briefer instant of she and he blurring together before the distance between them—a space that was and was not Jessie—broke open again.

IN LATER YEARS, Ruth's hysteria recurred, often in hospitals. She was the last survivor, and only at the very end did her hair color change. When she comes to me in dreams, her hair is dark, but her face is gaunt, white, frightening, the way it was in her final days. Still, her expression is of surprise and pleasure, and her eyes shine. She is happy to see me. I am stunned to see her, but it seems rude to tell her I thought she was dead. She finds a seat in an auditorium, and someone helps her from her wheelchair, but as I approach, she remains standing. She wants me to kiss her, to kiss that white drawn face, and I know that any hesitation will wound her; yet if I kiss her, I might tumble into her, into her deathliness, where I will dissolve. Her gaze does not waver. She is my grandmother. I lean forward and kiss her cheek, and fall into a quietness. I am in my bedroom; early light plays against the wall, and the air seems a soft blue-green. Beside me, my husband sleeps, breathes in the blue air, and I find myself kissing his face.

Are You Out There?

Mark DeFoe

Burgess Hale Shriver 1914-2005

Outside his window, in my father-in-law's
Last days at the nursing home, was a red
Dirt field scattered with wind-blasted wheat stubble.
The field gave no message—blank, wordless nature.
Beyond a ragged hedgerow stood a new oil rig,
A mock Eiffel Tower, gaudy with lights,
Shrill, clanking, loud as a carnival ride.

His hands, heavy even now, lay torpid
On the sheets supplied by the kind hospice folk.
Why did he cling so, wife and home long gone?

His last month he mumbled maybe fifty words,
Wandering down that tunnel of loss, seeking
Rest from a body that would not relent.

Before he shrank to a boney rack, he
Sold insurance, dabbled in real estate
And played the land lord, yet was a kind of
Odd-ball populist who had seen bankers
Devour a thousand farms and hated it.
Who longed to be a lawyer, and was by God,
Contentious enough. Who could have been a
Big band leader or sultan or pasha,
Charming wheeler-dealer in fine carpets.

CHAUTAUQUA

Craver of meat, of all that gave him bulk.
Big graceful tennis player. Big dancer.
I saw him rise from the lake on the planks
Of his homemade water skis, spilling
Water like a great white walrus, skimming
Behind the boat, an elegant elephant.

Sometimes a cruel man, sometimes tender,
Trapped in his big stubborn German bones by
His demons, plundering his thesaurus
For a word that could describe his anguish,
Believing in some cabala, some secret, some code
Of life dancing just beyond his reach, buried
In the language and waiting just for him.

But if you were drowning, he'd likely drag
You out, then toss you back and shout, Swim! Swim!

Yet, Burgess, you left me this: Some of us on
Your creaking green lawn swing, some of us
Reclining on the old quilt. And around me
All who matter—Jeanne, Who you gave me for wife,
And my daughters, laughing, and talking low
In the cooling prairie night that thrummed
With locust and cricket. And you, always
The Potentate, commanding Marie to forthwith
Bring forth the creamy homemade ice cream, the sweet tea,
The dark, thick and mysterious coffee.

Why should I not forgive you, my second
Father, like I have forgiven my own.

Mark DeFoe

Are you there, in God's workshop, whacking
Away at some zany homespun project?

Give me a sign, Burgess. Give me a sign.

I was flying and you were driving

Mark DeFoe

Moment of tilting space. Lights wheeling up.
I was descending through the clouds to you.
Alone, you came to fetch me that spring night.
You drove the serpentine roads to reach me.

I was descending through the clouds to you,
the plane sliding down on final approach.
You drove the serpentine roads to reach me,
past dark hills and farms with blue TV's.

The plane sliding down on final approach
and knowing better, I sought your headlights
past dark hills and farms with blue TV's.
Your light was down among ten thousands lights.

And knowing better, I sought your headlights
among the crosshatch of diamonds flashing.
Your light was down among then thousand lights,
your car a small blink on the interstate.

Among the crosshatch of diamonds flashing,
the pilot's voice murmured while we glided.
Your car a small blink on the interstate,
You had drawn your half of the path before.

Mark DeFoe

The pilot's voice murmured while we glided,
the engines softly whining in his hands.
You had drawn your half of the path before—
All departures and returns are plotted.

The engines softly whining in his hands.
Two lines must bend and intersect in time.
All departures and returns are plotted.
Wheels shriek—earth, oh earth—jets reverse and roar.

Two lines must end and intersect in time.
I spiral down through cold geometry.
Wheels shriek—earth, oh earth—jets reverse and roar.
I grab what's mine and join the jostling line.

I spiral down through cold geometry,
crowd gone mad for luggage, ears to cell phones.
I grab what's mine and join the jostling line.
I find your smile and touch it with my own.

Crowd gone mad for luggage, ears to cell phones.
Moment of tilting space. Lights wheeling up.
I find your smile and touch it with my own.
Alone, you came to fetch me that spring night.

Milk Toast

Maura Stanton

Do you float your toast in a bowl of cold milk, or pour the milk over the dry toast? Perhaps the milk is warm, straight from the cow? The translucent light from winter snow has summoned this old-fashioned word into my brain, and now I'm driven to thumb through old cookbooks. Milk shake, milk punch, milk toast. Turns out you butter the bread first, then serve it in hot milk. Use sugar, or if you prefer, salt and pepper. So of course I get out the toaster, stick in two slices, butter them, cut them into chunks to fit in my bowl, heat up milk in the microwave. I hesitate over the flavoring, finally pouring on a teaspoon of sugar. Now I'm ready. Is it dreadful? Is it good? The toast grows soggy, at once, the sweet milk is speckled with crumbs. But it tastes wonderful, and I stand in front of my kitchen window, loving each bite. Why, I've invented cereal! And I'm as proud as a poet inventing another sonnet, never mind Kellogg or Quaker Oats, never mind Keats or Shakespeare.

Welcome the Demon

Jane McCafferty

I was never a consistently great sleeper, but ever since I gave birth to my children, I've been a terrible one. Like the miser of hours I'm always counting. Did I get at least six? I ask myself each morning, calculating on my fingers. My husband used to hate this counting. You're obsessed! You make yourself crazy! His frustration was understandable. One night in bed he checked his watch around three in the morning. I'd been sleeping beside him, but that tiny circle of watch-light woke me up. Upon this rude awakening I said, with exasperation that might have been warranted had he struck a large gong several times next to my ear, "Can you please not check your watch?" He couldn't believe it. *Are you telling me I can't check my watch?* he kept repeating. *You're actually telling me you can't sleep through me checking my watch?* He loved telling this story to our friends as an example of what a ridiculously bad sleeper I was, and it was good for a laugh.

I agreed with his theory that I might have made the insomnia worse by being obsessed with the idea of sleep. The first step is admitting you have a problem. That I could do. But I didn't know what the second step was because I'd tried everything and nothing consistently worked. I knew about hot baths, warm milk, melatonin (worked sometimes), chamomile tea, kava kava, valerian root, no television before bed, avoiding alcohol, a solid routine (yeah right), creative visualization, meditation, desperate prayer, exercise during the day but not in the evening, waking at the same time each morning, lavender, eye-masks and eye-pillows, not having a digital clock biting orange letters into the darkness of the room, no computer on, closing the blinds or curtains, leaving the room when you can't sleep and finding a boring book in another room. I'd been briefly addicted to a seriously wonderful drug called

Klonopin that made me feel absolutely, exquisitely normal. (Tylenol PM was like taking a hit of speed for me.) I'd also been on Trazodone, which sometimes worked but was not reliable and also could leave me hung-over in the morning. I'd sent away for "Sleep In A Bottle" and tried "Rescue Remedy." I'd gone on-line for advice. "Have you ever considered your body might be *rejecting horizontal sleep*?" Dr. Dave from London inquired. "Did you know most animals sleep on inclines?" At three in the morning I once actually dragged a mattress onto the steps and tried sleeping there. This is sad.

I'D BEEN TRAINED by babies not to sleep well. I nursed them—two of them born two years apart. I could not do "the Ferber method" when they were infants. I didn't have the guts to leave them in their cribs crying their hearts out. I did try once. When the baby sobbed behind bars I couldn't help assigning language to the wrenching sounds, perhaps a variation of personification. To me the crying said, *How can you be such a monster, I am a helpless infant who is afraid of being alone in this prison of a crib, and you have all the power; you can come pick me up and stop this agony, recognizing that I am the most vulnerable of creatures, or you can lay there denying the reality of my ferocious need, pretending you are deaf or made of stone. It's your choice!*

I endured this infant diatribe for twenty minutes, then ran to the crib and rescued her, tearful with relief that by accepting my limitations I wouldn't have to experience this torture again. My husband had the same tenderheartedness (some would say stupidity), so we were doomed. By fervently flunking Ferber, we had signed on for many years of kids waking in the middle of the night, and until they were two and four, kids in our bed, between us. They both liked to sleep horizontally. My husband would often say, "I'm getting tired of waking up with a foot in my mouth." Finally we somehow got them in their own beds, but they'd visit us. Usually once a night. *I had a bad dweam. Can we weed a book? I'm thusty.* Irresistible, they'd more often than not climb back in.

Jane McCafferty

They can say their *r*'s now—they're almost ten and twelve. My husband, turned ex-husband, doesn't live here anymore. I can hear women of my mother's generation thinking, well no wonder, honey! Children in the bed! Hello!

But it's not that simple, of course; we had years without them in the bed, too. Had we passed Ferber with flying colors there's an excellent chance we might still have divorced. Had we *all* been great sleepers, we might still have this unwieldy contraption called joint custody now. Who knows. But sleep, in my estimation, is the biological equivalent of the balm of Gilead. Sleep is vacation. For Shakespeare it was the "chief nourisher in life's feast." In sleep you sail. And heal. I go through some fairly long stretches (like an entire summer, just last year) where I sleep beautifully and deeply, night after night, so I know of what bliss I speak.

And I know that when sleep eludes me for two or three days, I become intimate with a dangerous edge. I read the newspaper with the eyes of exhaustion and it buries me: the world's evil we're supposed to live with—with a good night's sleep this all is somehow strangely palatable, a backdrop. But without sleep? I get tearful; what energy I have goes to fighting despair. The absurdity of this life becomes acute, and it's harder to breathe. All the ordinary tasks of life seem overwhelming.

Like a trip to the grocery store where I recently read that *20,000 new items* are introduced yearly. When I am tired in *The Giant Eagle*, Pittsburgh's chain of grocery stores that my friend calls *The Giant Vulcher*, I feel overwhelmed like a newly arrived Mongolian immigrant, blinking, paralyzed, bombarded by the blast of choice. When I'm exhausted, the items scream; I feel myself dodging invisible force fields. I confess that even on my best days, I'm usually capable of buying, at most, four or five things at a time. I was made for the old world, where tired women went to the small market on the corner each morning and bought fresh veggies from a portly Italian man.

Once I was so tired I waited for a bus for a half hour. The bus came, and I forgot to get on. I stood there in a daze while the *others* got on. I only woke up when it pulled away. "Hey!" I called out, "What about me?" So it's not very consoling when people say, "Don't worry about sleep. You'll sleep when you need to." Because not sleeping really changes everything. You want to get on the bus with everyone else, but you can't.

My boyfriend (do I still call him that if he's fifty-two?) says this lovely thing to me most every night, something his grandmother said to him. "Sleep with the angels." I always say, "You too." He is a sleep pro, and comes from a whole family of sleep pros. They nap in chairs whenever they please. The TV can be on, sunshine or lights blaring, other people scattered around the room, but when it's time to sleep, off they go. Something bovine about it all. I watch them with a mixture of mystified reverence and jealousy. My boyfriend himself is perhaps the greatest sleeper among all these pros. He sleeps so deeply, so unselfconsciously, that he can snore like a great splayed beast on occasion, shaking the entire house, and not wake himself up. It takes him between two and five seconds to fall asleep. You can be talking intensely about something; one moment he's fully engaged, the next, when the delicious lure of sleep arrives, he vanishes like a fish lured back to his real home. There will be no warning that he's about to go down. Please, I say (and it's always too late), can't you please take me with you? But he's gone, he's in dreamland, and already deeply happy, it seems to me. It's hard not to poke him.

At least he's not a sleep snob. (Suffering insomniacs really can't bear sleep snobs.) These are the people who think sleeping fewer hours than other people means they are morally superior. (I've sometimes secretly suspected this is true.) They make great use of the wee hours and have no concept of insomnia. "I don't worry about sleep, since I never really needed much. A few good hours, and I'm fine. People who sleep seven and eight hours are just wasting time. I'm so productive I work until about three in the morning, catch a cat-nap, then I'm totally refreshed."

I much prefer the opposite of the sleep snob: the unapologetic sleep lover like my old friend Jackie who once said, "I've noticed that if I get my thirteen hours, all seems to go pretty well."

If a given sleep snob delivers the news of how little they sleep with a particular brand of arrogance, I always like to remind them that they're in the company of Margaret Thatcher, who once said, "Sleep is for wimps."

In contrast, Mr. Rogers *loved* his eight hours.

SOMEONE IN A coffee shop today said, "You have to befriend insomnia." This is not a new idea, and I've tried it before, but for whatever reason, when this particular person in her red and gold cape said these words, it seemed a new and powerful idea. She added, "Insomnia is a demon that takes its fuel from your fear." I heartily agreed. "So tonight," she instructed, her dark eyes brightening, "what you need to do, is welcome the demon. Set a little table for him. Tell him to sit and eat and stay as long as he wants.

Kick up your feet, Insomnia, but first take your shoes off.

What kind of shoes would Insomnia wear? I believe they might be ancient wing-tips pilfered from a garbage can. Or is he in clown shoes? Envision his ravenous eyes, his wrinkled grey suit, the long, greedy fingers. What a sad creature. He can't help himself. Nobody likes him. He has been everywhere in the world, haunting people like Van Gogh, Edna St. Vincent Millay, Proust, Carey Grant, Edison, and W.C. Fields, and all have wrestled him. Kafka despised him. Imagine being hated by all these souls? Napoleon, Horace, Dickens, Madonna, the guy next door who cuts his lawn in what can only be called plaid trousers, the insomniac list goes on.

So let your heart open to this derelict demon, this rejected rogue of a sleep thief. If you do this night after night, despite his lack of charm and terrible greed, you will help him dissolve into light. And you'll sleep. Eventually you'll become someone who hits the hay like it's no big deal,

CHAUTAUQUA

like it's your God given right. You'll glow like a farm girl. One day you'll stop the miserly counting of hours in the morning. Whoever wants to check his watch in the middle of the night can go right ahead. You'll be sleeping with the angels.

WHITE GIRL

Diana Hume George

An excerpt from the memoir-in-progress, White Girl: Living With the Senecas

*Our memories are imperfect; thus I changed all names,
except for that of my friend Nancy, to respect privacy.*
–DHG

THE FREEDOM WHEEL

I was a white girl. When I was growing up this fact seemed the least important thing about my ordinary and predictable life: regular, spiceless meals, pet turtles and fish, thank-you notes to aunts whose faces I couldn't remember for presents I didn't like, interminable Sunday school and church every week, carefully monitored television programs, planned family recreation (a museum; a concert; a play), kickball in the back yard, tuna fish sandwiches on which I was not allowed to put enough Miracle Whip. I collected stamps and marbles, and sometimes I pasted old postcards into a black album. For a few years I had a dog, but it died. On the occasions that I was allowed to go to the movies in the small town where I grew up and lived for my entire childhood, I had to be home ten minutes after the movie ended. I hated my life. I was a middle class white girl with a bad case of wanna-be.

One night when I was fifteen, I snuck out to the carnival that came to town for a few days every summer. I met my best friend Nancy behind the Rexall store and together we wandered through the back lot of the Main Street stores where the rides were set up. I was smitten. At the cotton candy stand I bought a big pink cloud from a woman who looked like a gypsy. Then we turned toward the Ferris wheel because it was the biggest ride on the lot. I followed the elegant circle with my eye, around and around a ring of white light. I wanted something that big in my life. I wanted something to happen. The music from the speaker above the wheel—it seemed to be the music of the wheel itself—made me feel free.

We got out the string of tickets while we strolled to the wheel. The closer we got, the higher the wheel looked. I felt a grab of fear and pleasure in my thighs. A few feet away from the wheel, I stopped in my tracks, and put out a hand to stop Nancy. She glanced at me and told me I had cotton candy on my mouth. I licked the sugar without turning away from where my eyes had settled. Look at him, I said, pointing to the dark-skinned man in sunglasses who leaned against the wheel, not three inches from its turning spikes, hands folded across his chest. I walked in a kind of trance to where the carnie unloaded the last riders, and got in line for the next ride, Nancy right there next to me, as she always was.

The man worked entirely without words. Closer up, I saw that he was Indian—from the bone structure of his face I figured he was probably a Seneca from the reservation bordering our town. But because he was a carnie, he could have been from a faraway tribe. That might be even better. He unloaded a car by tipping it forward and extending a hand if there were women or children inside. When a car was empty, he turned his head and gestured slightly to the next group. Sometimes, I noticed, he only indicated with a small nod of his head, not using his hands at all. All of his movements were smooth, seamless.

Summoning me and Nancy with the merest angling of his wrist, he made my knees weak. I gazed straight ahead while I mounted the platform to the car, afraid that if I looked at him I'd melt or float away. Once I got seated, I peeked at him while he leaned over us, placing the bar in the safety latch. Up close he smelled like summer, his skin was a deep brown, his shoulders were wide. His mouth was open slightly and I could already feel that open mouth on me.

After latching the car, which seemed to take him a good while, he took our tickets, turned on the wheel, and we jerked up a few feet. Then he stopped it and loaded the next one. I leaned over and looked down at him each time. With the wheel loaded, the man turned it on and leaned against the motor casing. Every time our car came down past him, I hoped to catch his eye, but he just leaned back impassively and smoked. When the ride was over and the unloading began, our car was stopped at the very top of the wheel. The car swayed in the summer night breeze. I looked down on the people and the lights and the rides, and that small parking lot in back of the Main Street stores turned magic. Then I closed my eyes and let myself sway.

    He reached over us to unclasp the safety bar, and I held my breath. I must say something now. But he didn't look friendly, didn't invite conversation. He seemed remote, detached, and that was why I wanted him. As soon as we were off the car, I walked straight to the back of the line again. Nancy followed, interested to see how I was going to play this. We rode the wheel again, and then again. And then again. Still I had said nothing and done nothing. In line for the fifth time in a row, Nancy asked if we were going to ride this thing all night.

    Once more, please just once more, I promise I'll do something this time. But I didn't have to. This time, when he had placed the safety bar and we extended our hands with the tickets, he didn't take them. Without looking at us, he simply turned the motor and up we went. I stared at the ticket still in my hand. It was working. On the next turn of the wheel, when our car swooped by him he reached out a hand and barely touched it, making it rock back and forth all the way to the sky. After he unloaded everyone else, he kept us on through another batch of riders, and then another. And when he let us off at last, he smiled at me. But still he said nothing, his eyes invisible behind sunglasses. I managed a lame thanks when I rose to my feet, stumbling slightly from all that airtime. I was pushing my luck, being gone from home so long. Mom could be checking my bedroom any time now.

    At home I slipped in the back door, walking hurriedly through the living room and hall to the stairs. Knowing that Mom might have heard something, I was in my room with the door closed within sixty seconds, slipping out of my clothes in the dark and sliding into bed. I lay there practicing the even breathing of fake sleep. When my mother opened my door a crack and looked in, I was turned toward the wall, breathing heavily. Exhale. One. Two. Three. Inhale. After a moment, I could hear her walking on the front of her shoes and I knew what she was doing. A zipper sounded. She was checking my purse for evidence of forbidden acts. I could hear the click of lipstick tubes and makeup against each other. My mother left the room and shut the door.

Now I was free to think. I reached a hand out to my radio and turned it on low. *Well, she was just seven-tee-een, you know what I mee-een, and the way she looked was way beyond compa-are.* I wanted out of my dull life, and I knew how I was going to do it. It would have something to do with the dark man in sunglasses leaning against a giant lighted wheel, hands folded across his chest.

The next night I was back at the carnival. I had to be—it was only in town for two nights, and I had no idea who he was. I wanted him, of that I was more certain than I'd ever been of anything. That night I ended up under the Aldridge Street bridge with him after tear-down. For the next two years we met in secret, under that bridge, in fields, in woods, in the back seats of cars, in cemeteries. By the time I was seventeen, I was purposely pregnant by Lennie. Rather than risk the public disgrace of an illegitimate grandchild, my mother consented to sign papers for my marriage, and well into my sixth month, I stood at the front of an empty church exchanging vows in maternity clothes. Lennie and I left our belongings in an apartment just off the reservation, using it mostly as headquarters while we drove to nearby towns for the last few weeks of the carnival season. In the back lots of the small towns, from my place near the cotton candy stand beside the woman I'd thought looked like a gypsy, I could see the white girls who lined up for rides on the wheel, again and again and again.

Diana Hume George

Lena Who Knew

LENA AND HER HUSBAND Dusty were Mohawks from Canada living on the borders of the Seneca Reservation. They spoke in slightly different speech patterns and moved more quickly than Senecas, it seemed to me. Mohawks and Senecas are both tribes of the Iroquois Nation, but it was the Mohawk men who grew famous as expert ironworkers. Dusty was often gone for long stretches in Buffalo or Niagara Falls, working on the bridges. Lena raised her kids, cleaned white people's houses, and ran their world largely without his help.

I always intended to get back in touch with Lena to thank her for what she gave me for almost three years in the late sixties. But when I left that world, I left for good, and the decades somehow passed without my returning to see her. A few years ago, talking to my ex-mother-in-law on the reservation, I asked if she ever sees Lena. Don't you know Lena died, she said, over a year ago now. I staggered forward slightly, thinking for a moment I might fall down or pass out. Ruth gasped, realizing that I hadn't heard, and remembering that I'd been close to Lena all those years ago. I thought you would have heard, she said, some kind of cancer, it took her quick.

But in my remembrance she's still there where I left her, so I keep reforgetting that she's gone. I know what she looks like, because women like Lena stay the same from the time they let go of girlhood until they die. Lena is cooking dinner for a huddle of big men in work shoes and flannel plaid shirts gathered in her tiny kitchen. The men are shifting their weight from foot to foot, trying to warm up. Maybe they're drunk, maybe they're sober. She's always sober but always laughing, treating the men like overgrown boys, telling them to get out of her way so she can get food on the table. Her glasses are falling down to the tip of her nose and she is reaching up an impatient finger to jam them up while she stirs stew in a cast iron pot. She's wearing baggy wool pants and a sweatshirt, and her hair, curly for an Indian's, is graying only a little.

CHAUTAUQUA

Or she is on hands and knees in some white man's house, cleaning a floor. She is not using a mop, because mops are for lazy people. She left early this morning from her small rented house just off the reservation and drove down to the main road. What she is thinking about as she drives I don't know. I never knew what Lena thought about when she was alone, because she never offered to tell me and I would never have asked. It's Tuesday today, so if the school principal in the white town is still alive—he would be long retired by now—she is cleaning his house, then picking up his family's dry cleaning.

Or she is making coffee for a dazed girl in a shabby apartment with low ceilings, and finishing the breakfast dishes that were on the counter when she came in. The girl is dressed in clothes Lena got from her employers. Lena has altered them and installed elastic in the waist so the band won't hurt the girl's still-distended belly. In a room off the kitchen, a baby begins to cry. The girl starts to get to her feet, moving slowly and painfully because of the extra stitches from the hemorrhaging, but Lena sits her back down with a gesture and hurries to pick up the baby. So the girl sits at the kitchen table, which is rusty-legged but very sturdy because Lena chose it. The girl blinks vaguely while she runs her hand in circles on the porcelain surface of the table.

Lena's easy laugh—she was always amused at something—poured into my bones because we were always together. Since Lena always thought of my husband as family, I became family the moment I married him, and my baby became what she called her first grandchild. Her own children were grown, but neither was married and it didn't look like they were in a hurry. Her son drank too much beer with my husband. Her daughter was in trade school.

When I came home from the hospital, Lena was at my apartment, the first of the ones we rented on or barely off-reservation. The apartments got smaller and darker over time, and all were sparsely warmed by gas space heaters with no automatic shut-off valves, but I still loved this one because it was my first. Weak from blood loss, I was supposed to stay in bed. For the first two months of my son's life, Lena was my mother and his. She left to clean other people's houses and her own, made meals for her family and guys cutting wood or working iron, but she spent the rest of her time at my place, cleaning and cooking for me and giving me "the sane feeling," as I called it. I didn't feel it with anyone but Lena.

She had to teach me to change diapers because I'd never changed one, never even picked up a baby before my own. I wasn't one of those teenagers who'd had babysitting jobs, or any job at all except selling pumpkins I grew one fall. Lena found this entirely unbelievable. My lord, she'd say, how'd you *get* so ignorant. But she never said it meanly, and she played with BJ endlessly. Though he does not remember her, I think he owes his easy laughter to Lena.

When Lennie came home from the winter logging camps, she made supper for him and the crew. There were often five of them, big men in big boots, most Indian, maybe one white guy, all gathered around our table. I'd walk slowly to the kitchen in my bathrobe and sit at my own table like a guest, while Lena brought in bowls of mashed potatoes, heaps of sausage and onions and peppers, piles of homemade rolls. She was making my home like hers, which was just what I wanted. She paid for a lot of that food herself, and I knew it. Lennie made about fifty dollars a week under the table, and sometimes on payday he came home with some of it already spent on beer. She made huge pots of spaghetti sauce, the best I ever ate, and chili, and all kinds of soup. One night it was meatloaf, but this was not like any meatloaf I'd ever tasted. My own was Presbyterian. This was messy and greasy and gorgeous, and somehow a little bit sweet.

I knew how to cook basic meals when I got married—some kind of meat, boiled potatoes, a veggie. But Lena used spices, and then I realized I didn't know anything. We'd stand by the spice rack in the supermarket, with BJ in Lena's arms as often as he was in his carry-all, and Lena would point and explain. This is oregano. You know what oregano is, don't you?

I didn't. My family was Presbyterian.

You don't know oregano. Geez. She'd shake her head as if I'd been culturally deprived beyond imagining.

When I was completely recovered, I started going with Lena to clean white people's houses, nice residences in nearby towns, the homes of lawyers and bankers and insurance men. She knew each house as if it were her own, knew exactly what was to be cleaned each week and how, what items were monthly or bi-weekly, when the special jobs, like windows, came due. She kept it all in her head. The people treated her as people treat their valued help, with friendly regard, easy authority, and a superiority that almost didn't show. They gave her bags of clothes that would otherwise go to the Good Will, and sometimes they offered an old couch or a refrigerator when they were redecorating. She knew there was a gulf between their circumstances and hers, but she didn't care. These worlds weren't hers, and she didn't envy them. I never actually met the owners—she brought me along to teach me to work—but she told me little secrets about each family, stuff she knew about their foibles and quirks from cleaning their houses for years. One man kept porn in an old suitcase in his study, another was allergic to the perfume his wife wore on purpose, and one of her most prominent male employers dressed up in garter belts and stockings. She never said how she knew about that one.

It got so I spent most of my time with Lena. After the carnival season, I saw less and less of Lennie, who disappeared for long periods of time drinking with his buddies. Lena was at my place, or I was at Lena's, both worlds seemingly manless except at mealtime. When her son stumbled hungover through the kitchen, she shooed him off and he'd leave for the whole night and she'd have no idea where he was or when he'd come back. I don't know what I'm going to do with him, she'd say, shaking her head and looking earnest. But then she'd notice that I was putting on BJ's sleeper backwards, and she'd turn around in circles laughing. Later I'd wonder how we avoided talking about how empty our lives were. But women can be good at that, and if it hadn't been for the meatloaf night, I might never have known that Lena thought about such things at all.

Although I'd heard stories of how Lena would scream at Dusty when he came home after he'd been gone a few days too many, I never felt the aftermath. People figured Dusty must have a woman somewhere else. Everyone knew that on occasion, Lena would throw things at him. Sometimes he retaliated. It had been going on for over twenty years this way. But if Dusty waited out the storm and sat at the table, Lena would finally say, What do you want to eat? and he'd answer, and she'd put it in front of him as if nothing had happened.

Once when Lennie and I went there unexpectedly to eat dinner because there wasn't any food at home, her daughter said there'd been a big fight just before we came in. But here were Lena and Dusty and their two grown kids at the table, Dusty silent and shoving food in his mouth, and Lena telling everyone how BJ had walked to her from fifty feet away. His puppy-walk, she called it. Even though I tried, I couldn't find anger in her voice. It was burned away, maybe screamed out.

How could she be like this? I was almost sick with my own dull ache. Lennie was cheating on me and I knew it. My marriage was a sham and it was only a year old. In his world, cheating on your wife wasn't just tolerated, it was almost expected. As close as we were, I didn't feel free to ask Lena what to do. I could ask her about anything else, but not this, not the one matter that was most vital. Instead I was watching her, trying to figure her out. What kept her from flying apart? Where did the laughter come from, her vast amusement about life that had no trace of the cynical or the bitter? I didn't know if I could learn this from her and I didn't know if I wanted to.

At least I'd been able to hide from the facts. I had to surmise everything about Lennie's activities. He lied consistently and well, and it was tempting to believe him in order to make life simpler. I couldn't be Lena, Lena who knew.

❦

making Lena's meatloaf

I'M GOING TO go find him, I said one night after we'd put BJ to bed. I think I know where he is.

It was the first time I had said anything like this.

Never mind, she said. He's just out drinking with the boys. (To Lena, all men were boys.)

No, he's not, he's with a woman and I think I know who.

Lena sighed in a way that made me think she'd known this would come sooner or later. I should have known she knew.

So what? she said, shrugging her shoulders. He'll be home.

So what? Did you say *so what?*

It was my turn to be incredulous toward her, as she so often was toward me.

Okay, she said, you go ahead and get him. And tomorrow night and the next night and the next night, you can go get him again. You want to spend your whole life hauling your man out of bars and beds?

No, I want it to stop, I said, and it was probably then that I started to cry. I was eighteen and terribly in love. I'd thrown away every last shred of security from that sheltered life of mine, and this new one had instantly turned to dust in my hands. There was no going back home, truly no home to go back to any more. And I was responsible for a baby, an actual human being I'd created, and I had to figure out how to care for him—Lennie clearly wasn't going to. Although this conversation with Lena took place decades ago, long before I took notes—back then I was *living* instead of writing about it—I know what else got said that night because I committed it to memory then and there, and worked over it in my mind for the next year or more, trying to comprehend my situation. It wasn't until many years later that I again heard anything remotely like what Lena told me then. It was wasted on me that night, or I took in the wrong parts of it, or some damn thing, but it was strange enough stuff that I always remembered it in later years.

She told me that what Lennie was doing wasn't ever going to stop. Don't you know that? Don't you know anything? She patted me.

No, I don't know anything, you know I don't.

But it doesn't matter, she was saying, you've got better things to do than track down a drunk husband.

No, I don't, I wailed, he's my husband!

That's right, she said, and then: he's only your husband.

Only? Who was it, I wondered, who didn't know anything?

You've got to live with him when he's around, but you've got to live with you all the time. When you made promises to him, you made those promises to yourself. How could you promise him you'd make a home if you didn't promise yourself the same thing? It's not even a promise if you don't promise yourself.

But if the man breaks *his* promises, I started to say.

That's his own problem, that's got nothing to do with you, honey.

Then she'd apparently had enough of this nonsense, because she said, Let's make meatloaf. How could she talk about meatloaf? I didn't want to make any damn meatloaf. I followed her out to the kitchen, telling her so.

Then you're a fool and I can't do a thing with you. When he comes home, he'll eat the meatloaf. In the meantime, we'll eat it.

She was clanging dishes and opening cupboard doors. Where's your wooden spoons? Do you live here, lady?

So we made Lena's meatloaf, with dill and lots of carrots—that was the secret, the grated carrots made it orangy and sweet. That's still how I make meatloaf. We sat together at the table and ate it with mashed potatoes. I'm sure it felt sudden to her when I asked if she still loved Dusty, but I knew this would be the only night she'd ever talk to me about such things.

Sure I do, what a silly question, he's my husband, he's the father of my kids.

Don't you want to—leave him sometimes?

Well, sure I do. But I can't or I won't, and there you have it.

She was laughing, but for once there was an edge to it, even a tinge of contempt. I thought: she loves him but she doesn't respect him. How can that be, I wondered. I was very young.

He knows you'll never leave him, doesn't he?

I suppose so, she said. If that bothered her, I couldn't tell.

DURING THE NEXT YEAR, I tried to learn what kept Lena going. She knew exactly who she was, and Dusty wasn't as central to that as I'd thought. Lennie was gone more and more, and we moved twice, each time to dingier places with lower ceilings. Sometimes I sat up half the night near the window, waiting, watching snow fall into streetlight beams, until we ended up in an uninsulated log cabin on a road without streetlights and then I waited in the pitch-dark, counting occasional headlights. When Lennie came home drunk and broke, I protested. Her name was always Kenny and Richard and Ray. I felt helpless. Lena's laughter was contagious, so I laughed, too, but mine was raw. We never talked about it again. She'd said all she had to say.

Then came Johnnie's wedding. Johnnie was in the group of friends who gathered around Lena's kitchen table, one of her many honorary sons. She helped Johnnie's sister plan the wedding. I was there, too, standing against walls, listening. The reception was to start at two o'clock on Saturday in the legion hall of an off-reservation town. Dusty was supposed to be back from Niagara Falls the morning of the wedding. He didn't show up. Lena gave no sign of looking for him. I turned around in my seat every few minutes in the church, checking the door.

The reception was large and drunken. By four o'clock everyone was dancing, even the men who had to be trashed in order to get on the floor. Lena danced with Lennie and Kenny and Richard. I watched the door for Dusty, Lennie got drunker by the minute, I watched Lena bringing food from the kitchen and dancing with the little kids. Hours later, when everyone except the hardcore drunks had gone, and only a few couples stood on the floor, Dusty strolled in. Lena was in the kitchen cleaning up. I walked straight over to Dusty, with whom I never really spoke. His detachment had always scared me.

You son of a bitch, I said, you knew this was important to her.

He was too drunk to answer. He just leaned against the wall, then reached for my arm. Les dance, he said. Before I could say more, Lena was there, pulling him silently into the kitchen. I followed. I had to see this. In the kitchen, the women went on working at the sinks while Lena pounded on Dusty, calling him useless, a snake, and finally descending to vulgarity. I'd never heard her use such language. I was delighted. Dusty raised his hands to cover his face and head.

Get him, Lena, I said under my breath. Johnnie's sister, a severe woman named Rene, raised her head from the sink.

You stay out of this, she hissed. She slapped a towel at me and told me to dry some dishes. Lena was still shouting at Dusty.

I don't know how she takes it, I said, and banged a plate down on the counter. I didn't care what Rene thought. Usually I was afraid of her, too.

It's none of your business. You keep out.

Other Indian women looked up from the dishes line, interested to see Rene angry with me.

I turned to face Rene, but there was sudden silence in the room. Lena was done yelling. She was standing over Dusty where he was crumpled in a chair.

I'm sorry, Dusty said, looking up at her. Then, after a moment, he said, Les go dance. He stood up and held out his hand unsteadily. Lena stood for a moment, breathing hard, then took his hand. They walked out of the kitchen. I threw down the dish towel and slammed my body against the counter. The women all looked at me, their faces blank. She's going to dance with him? Rene didn't bother to disguise her contempt for me. I always knew she didn't like me.

Of course she's going to dance with him, you imbecile, she said, he's her husband.

If she had any self-respect, she wouldn't even *talk* to him, I said.

For a moment, I thought Rene was going to hit me. Instead she said, Lena's got more self-respect in her little finger than you got in your whole white body. If you had any self-respect, you'd be out there with your own husband.

I suppose I'd be dancing with him?

That's right. And then she turned back to the sink.

Because he's my husband, the father of my child?

I had never talked this way to Indian women, never even thought of doing so. They were silent. It was clear that they had no more to say to me. I was too young and too stupid to bother with. I stood by the counter, swallowing convulsively. The only other thing I remember is the sound of dishes clanking. Then I walked back into the main hall. From the wall, I watched Lena and Dusty dancing in a circle on the floor. Lena was half holding him up, but she seemed to be enjoying herself. On the other side of the hall, Lennie was dancing with a woman I didn't know. His hand was on her lower back. They swayed to the music. I watched his other hand moving along her arm, next to her breast. I walked over to them.

May I cut in? The woman opened her closed eyes, looked embarrassed. She floated off in a breeze of polyester. Lennie held out his arms to me and we swayed in the dim light. I could feel him leaning against me, and I wound my arms around his neck. This man had been my route to a kind of freedom, even if I was now his prisoner. He smelled familiar to me, like home now. I buried myself in his neck for a while, then put my head down on his shoulder. Out of the corner of my eye I could see Lena and Dusty. They were standing in one spot on the floor, empty now except for the four of us. Lena caught my eye and smiled. I smiled back. I turned my face back into Lennie's neck. It took me two more years to leave.

My Son Makes a Gesture My Mother Used to Make

Laura Kasischke

My son makes a gesture my mother used to make, the sun in their eyes, fluttering their fingers over their foreheads as if to disperse it. The sun, like so many feverish bees.

I keep driving. One eye on the road and one on the child in the rearview mirror. A man on the radio praying. That awful kid down the block where I was a child who buried a toad in a jar in the sandbox, dug it up a month later, and it was still alive.

He does it again. The sun, like the drifting ashes of a distant past, the petals of some exploded yellow roses.

The miracle of it.
The double helix of it.
The water running uphill of it.
Such pharmacy, in a world which failed her! She died before he was even alive, and here she is, shining in his eyes.

Light nodding to light.
Time waving hello to time.
The ninety-nine names of Allah. The sun extravagantly bright and full of radiant, preposterous spiritual advice—like a bible rescued from a fire that killed a family of five. I squint into it and see both a glorious parade of extinct and mythological beasts, and an illustration in a textbook of a protective sheath of protein wrapped around a strand of DNA—all cartoon spirals and billiard balls, and the sole hope of our biology teacher, Mr. Barcheski, who, finally enraged by the blank expressions on our faces, slammed it shut and walked away.

Naked Ladies
Sara Rath

Nudity has always made me uncomfortable, especially my own. Will's been dead for almost two years and I still undress in the closet. Stepping from the tub in my bathroom I'm grateful for the steamy mirror. Even with the fog from my shower I always avert my eyes.

But extra pounds have a way of sneaking up at menopause, and my daughter Emmy, physically fit and fanatic, determined that I ought to swim. The Y offers a class for Seniors, but it will (thankfully) be a few more years before I'm ready to become a Water-*Spryte*.

When I wanted to start jogging years ago, I bought a pair of expensive running shoes. Guilt kept me running until my knees gave out before the shoes did. I got an exercise bike and watched television while I pedaled. Never a fan of daytime TV, I found the task doubly boring.

Swimming would be easy on my joints, I was assured, and it wouldn't be hard to learn.

I *knew* how to swim, I told Emmy with a huff; I had once earned my Junior Lifesaving Badge.

And I knew she was right; I had to exercise. For additional persuasion, I went shopping for a flattering bathing suit.

Back home the high school football coach gave lessons every summer at the millpond. We didn't have a Y and there wasn't anything like an indoor pool. Our bath houses were tar paper shacks where we changed under our beach towels. Boys peeked through the knotholes, and we hung our clothes on rusty nails.

The Y was definitely different. Finding myself in a sleek and slippery locker room with damp tiles and echoed splashes, I was in a chlorinated haze. Frankly, I was frightened. This was foreign territory for me.

I managed the transitional maneuver from street clothes to bathing suit while facing an open locker, shielded by its open door. But my polka-dot bodyshaper with tummy control, guaranteed to make me instantly look ten pounds slimmer and to flatter "rectangular figures," bore no resemblance to the sleek Speedos and racer-backs around me. Apparently I'd need a duffel bag and swimming cap, too. I was ill prepared.

Back home we learned to swim mostly because we aspired to reach the raft, a wooden platform that floated on empty oil barrels. There we could lie in the sun and bake all afternoon, idle and tanned.

Here, through swinging doors I found a ceramic pool of Olympic proportions. Divided into six long lanes, men and women thrashed to and fro with intense deliberation. The closest lane had three older women who dallied a bit, and I watched them for a while. They spluttered down to the other end on the right side of the lane, then turned and swam back on the left; that way they cleverly avoided collisions in the narrow corridor between the yellow ropes.

Already conspicuous and barely able to breathe (shoving ten extra pounds inside taut Spandex takes a toll) I struggled to sit down on the side of the pool and casually dangle my legs.

One of the women glided up to my knees and pushed a pair of plastic goggles above her eyebrows.

"I'll wait if you want to go ahead."

"It's my first time," I admitted. "I'm not sure where I should be."

She eyed my polka-dots and pinched a drip from the tip of her nose. "You swim much?"

"No," I sighed. "I gained some weight. My daughter sent me here."

"This is the lane for you then," she patted her ample belly. "C'mon in. The water's fine."

It really was: the heated water was soothing. I vaguely recalled the sidestroke and reached the other end after swallowing only few mouthfuls of water. Then I clung to the curb with white fingers to catch my breath before starting back. I tried it again.

When I headed to the locker room my eyes burned from chemicals and a fuzzy white aura surrounded everything. It was just as well: the scene in the showers was dreamlike and surreal.

I had never seen so many naked women in my life.

Thin women, all sharp angles. Other women who were Rubenesque. Wrinkled women and firm women, skin shining and slippery on all. Soapy women with sinuous muscles. Large women puffed and swollen in rosy mounds. Graying women glazed with suds. A hairy woman with stretch marks; a totally exfoliated woman who'd had an appendectomy a long time ago. Black women, white women, tall, short, old, young....

All bare naked. Stark raving naked. Naked as jaybirds, exposed with abandon beneath shimmering clouds of shampoo and hot spray. I frantically searched wet faces of strangers to see if I recognized anyone. Then, just as abruptly, I stared at their bare toes instead ... just in case there *were* women in there with me that I knew, God forbid!

Oblivious to their preposterous state, the assembly conversed as if meeting for a relaxed cup of coffee downtown.

I found a vacant nozzle, intending to rinse off quickly, then rush home still squeezed inside my damp and strangulating suit.

"How'd you do?"

Was someone introducing herself?

"Hello," I replied cautiously, "How do you do."

"How'd you do? How many laps?"

It was my friend from The Fat Lane, under the nozzle next to mine. She was peeling her straps over her shoulders and down. And down. And down.

"Terrible. Only four."

"Don't give up," she said, "You'll be surprised how fast you improve."

I concentrated hard on her face while she spoke and not the cruel scar on her chest where her left breast must have once matched her right. Except for that, she was all curves, generous curves, extravagant flesh lathered in soapsuds that bubbled and sparkled and danced.

I felt dizzy. It may have been the scalding water or the woozy effect of chlorine fumes. On the street, constricted by clothing, I'd find this woman unattractive and overweight. But here, liberated and stripped, this bountiful woman had a brave and undeniable appeal.

"Amber," she said, extending her hand toward my navel.

I backed away without thinking.

"What's your name?" she chuckled, ignoring my *faux pas*.

I reached. I shook.

"Elizabeth, Liz...Lizzie, to my friends."

Amber closed her eyes to soap her face and I rushed to my locker still suited up as planned, and pulled on my slacks. I hated feeling out of place. I was not a competent swimmer, all of this took too much time, it was not natural to shower with a crowd and I seemed to have discovered a latent perversion or something really weird that I could not explain.

But there was the matter of the $304 Emmy had shelled out for the YMCA, and the fact that she said if I didn't go back I'd never hear the end of it from her. I was more than willing to give her the money, but my daughter's sharp tongue pushed me over the edge.

The next day I packed a new duffel bag with my towel, a bathing cap I found in the attic, plus new goggles with yellow lenses, non-fog, $18.50. I did not include shampoo and soap. I would shower when I got home; one day, one step at a time.

I even wore my daughter's old Speedo swimsuit under my dress. She had not worn it since middle school when she went through the usual plump adolescence. The suit was washed-out pink, formerly shocking pink, as a matter of fact, which, I reflected later, could not have been more prophetic. The white latex cap had become suspiciously sticky and ripped when I tried to get it unstuck.

Amber joined me again as I slid into the pool.

"Giving it another try, Lizzie?"

I replied with a wry grimace, adjusted my new goggles and tried to repress the memory of my unfortunate fascination with her in the buff.

"Go ahead," she said, and I did. It wasn't so bad.

I began to contemplate the rhythm of my breathing, the sensual flow of the bubbles and the sensory deprivation in the serene and tranquilizing womb of the pool. I did seven laps without stopping (well, I paused once at the end to catch my breath).

Amber swam over as I bobbed up to my chin.

"And…?"

"Seven."

"Seven?"

"Down and back, down and back. Seven times," I said.

"But that's fourteen!" She laughed. "If you do eighteen, that's a quarter-mile!"

"No kidding? Wow!"

She slipped away with a graceful backstroke that I desired to emulate.

"Fourteen laps!" I said aloud, bending my knees and gliding on my back after Amber. "I swam fourteen laps! Unbelievable!"

When I reached the shallow end of the pool again I turned and did another two circuits. Amber was waiting for me when they were completed.

"Four more," I coughed, "That's a quarter mile!"

I ripped the goggles over my wet head and raised my fists high in the air with a leap, in what was, for me, a rare exhibition of unbridled joy.

But Amber reached out at the same time I jumped and roughly shoved me back into the water.

"What. . . ?" I sputtered, angry and confused at her rude assault.

"Your suit!"

"What about it?" I inquired, looking down where I found more of myself than my daughter's Speedo. The fabric had entirely disintegrated. There was almost nothing left.

I had swum the backstroke in a transparent web of rotten pink nylon, with conspicuous (promiscuous!) disregard!

In shame, I sunk to my nostrils, my entire body and especially my sizzling cheeks more "shocking pink" than that bathing suit could ever have hoped to be.

"I'll grab a towel," Amber said, and she heaved herself up over the side. I could hear her wet feet slap to the locker room, and waited impatiently for her assistance in liberation.

THE SHOWER WAS again filled with rounded, mounded, folded flesh in a symphony of steamy hues. But this time I found them less fascinating than I had before. Instead, trembling and forlorn, I busied myself by picking the remaining shreds of suit from my own chubby body with fingers like prunes. Fragments of dead elastic, like pale worms washed up after a rain, stuck to my skin despite sharp rivulets from the needle spray.

It was disgusting. *I* was disgusting. I would never be able to show my face (if only it were just my face!) at the Y again, membership deposit be damned, and Emmy could go soak her head.

Those victorious eighteen laps, that quarter-mile, would remain my personal best and my humiliating *last*.

"I watched your backstroke," a voice spoke next to me, "And I knew you had no idea your suit had dissolved. . . ."

To my right a tall woman brushed aside a strand of wet hair that shielded her eyes and smiled brightly.

"That happened to me once," she laughed, "But it was mostly the bra."

An older woman on my other side chuckled. "I remember that, Wendy!"

"Well, *I* didn't know it until I climbed out and stood there with my boobs bobbing east and west," Wendy continued. She squeezed some shampoo into her palm and offered the bottle to me. "So I know how you feel."

"Chlorine is hard on bathing suits," the older woman said.

I sudsed my hair and rinsed.

"Right," I mumbled.

"Amber, tell her about the guy in the yellow trunks, the one who was so cocky until he lost his jock in the deep end."

"Tell her about the time your strap broke and your prosthesis floated away...."

"What about Mary Beth, when her elastic stretched and her suit ended up around her knees...."

Suddenly the showers were filled with stories of all kinds of indecent exposures. In spite of myself, I had to giggle. Then I even heard myself laugh.

I forgot I was standing in the shower with a bunch of naked ladies, every bit as shameless and as much of a spectacle as the rest. We were sudsing and rinsing and gossiping, talking up a splattering storm.

You could say I finally "got in the swim," that morning of my baptism at the Y. It wasn't long before I mastered my Australian crawl and now I swim a mile at the pool, three days every week.

When I'm doing laps I adore the sensual sweep of the water, the way the rhythm of my strokes opens a passage in my mind.

Emmy says she's proud of me, but she can't be as proud as I am of myself.

Sara Rath

Occasionally I catch sight of a glistening knee and note the graceful arc, or the luminous drops of water from the rise and fall of my elbow. I'm always surprised to realize it's my own leg, my own arm. I'm amazed to see my own bountiful body, so magnificent; so much *of me*.

Loss Has Left the Moon Charred

George Looney

for David Citino

The sky cannot hold itself
down. What we want
to see as romantic, hues so full

of themselves that, in another
context, we'd call
them arrogant, we can't

show lovers today & ask them
to let their hearts take up
some old sixties ballad about love.

It always comes down to loss.
That's what the crane,
who must have taken the wrong current

to end up here, the only crane
for thousands of miles, is
trying to tell anyone who will listen.

Maybe it's better if those hearts,
trapped & separate in
the lovers looking to the sky

George Looney

for solace, get drunk on cheap wine
& sing some hymn
that smacks of cathedrals & organs.

Maybe only what Dickinson called
"Heavenly Hurt"
can help any heart today. Loss

has left the moon charred, his
entrails still glowing
in the cold of the local

mortuary, the radiation he was
exposed to in his
last days, meant to cure,

seeping slowly out his bones.
Let's allow that
mournful crane to cry for us,

& our loss. Knowing David,
a lone bird's cry is
all the elegy he'd have asked for.

The Wave

Richard Hoffman

Grant me an old man's frenzy,
Myself must I remake
—Yeats

How does a swell become a wave?
What pushes up from under water?
Tell me; this tired body is all I have

become of all I tried to be; I move
more slowly now and have to wonder:
how does a swell become a wave?

There isn't much I wouldn't give
to feel time's promise rise and gather
again in this tired body, but if all I have

is this one heavy life then let me heave
it, somehow, all of it, into the future,
the way a swell becomes a wave

that rolls for miles to a beach or cove
or thunders on rock and shatters.
I am tired of this tired body. All I have

to live for—my children, others I love—
some days I'm so fatigued they hardly matter.
How does a swell become a wave?
Tell me! This tired body is all I have.

A Reflection

Richard Hoffman

Some days I wake feeling drugged,
incoherent, the sunrise itself
an intrusion, others I'm raw and sad

and each new thing, each person,
even every new thought, feels too late:
How could I not have noticed this? Why

did I never think of that before? Why
have I met this striking person only now?
And only the familiar has no sorrow.

These are the days, I know by now,
my dead surround me; I sense them
when the beam of my sad attention

is reflected back at me the way
the eyes of animals shine back at night:
the only evidence they're there.

mama GODOT

Jane Ciabattari

"I don't know how much longer I'll last," she says.

Nearing ninety she is between worlds, and there is not much I can do for her from a distance. Just listen. I don't really know her. Our relationship is rusty. I learned at a young age to swallow pain and keep going. It is not a bad lesson.

"How are you doing?" I ask each week when I call from my house in Sag Harbor, a former whaling village thousands of miles from Kansas.

"I'm just waiting for what happens next."

"Anything new?" I ask.

What she knows is she walks wrong. Bowlegged. Her father takes her outside after dinner and trains her to keep her toes pointed forward. Her mother buys her special shoes. Brown. She hates to wear them.

"Not much goes on," she says. "It's just as well. I have a lot to be thankful for. They take good care of us here. I sure miss my flower garden. When you plant them, you don't think about leaving them."

The house is gone now, sold to pay for her care.

"It's nice of you to remember to call me," she adds. "I'm glad I have memories still there. We can't always count on that, right?"

Her parents have taken her to a new town. A tornado blows a sewing machine across the horizon. She is astonished. She wonders who gets it when it lands. She wants it.

"I'm sorry Francis didn't live longer," I say, using my father's first name in hope that she will remember him. "You're bound to miss him. You were married sixty years."

"I'd forgotten how long."

"You met when you were only thirteen. He said he'd had his eye on you for a long time. Still does, I'll bet."

"Do you think so?" She laughs coyly.

She curls around the pit of adolescence, fragrant with lust. She wants Paris gowns, hats with little veils, a wasp waist. She wants to be a fashion designer in New York. She swerves, tempted to linger, and is caught. He sits behind her in Latin class. He wants her to drink sloe gin. She refuses.

"He didn't live to be eighty. You're eighty-six."

"I don't know how much longer I'll last."

I want to say, 'don't be afraid.' But I stick to practicalities.

"What time is lunch?" I ask.

"Noon."

"Dinner?"

"Five o'clock."

She cooks every day for decades: meat loaf, chicken-fried steak, pot roast, veal birds, scalloped potatoes, Floating Island, Anadama bread. Peaches and berries on a Pyrex plate, fifteen minutes at 325 degrees. Done in a jiffy. She is so busy in the kitchen she has no chance to try her hand at anything else.

"Breakfast?"

"I don't know."

"Where are you now?"

"In this house where I live."

"But where in the house?"

"I'm where the telephone is."

THE NEXT WEEK when I call, the nurse tells me that she has trouble breathing at night. They are giving her morphine four times a day. It helps her breathe easier, the nurse says. "But she is...." The nurse searches for the word. "Disorganized."

"I'm getting my money together," she says when the nurse puts her on the phone. "Out of my dresser drawer, to get some patterns."

"Patterns?"

"Sewing patterns, a couple of patterns for the things we make. Let's see ... I have ... I'm a little ... I've got a cold. I'm supposed to see the doctor. It's a little hard for me to keep track. I'll get some new patterns, we'll go from there."

After several years of trying, at last she has a daughter. She sews her a ruffled organdy frock. There is a long interlude of diapers and bottles and Madame Alexander dolls, with tiny dresses she makes herself, then piano lessons and golf clubs. Everything costs so much.

"Are they giving you oxygen?"

"Someone was smoking. That was trouble."

At first she won't let Francis kiss her. He is a smoker, and she can't stand the smell. He is smitten. The two of them, too young for their parents to agree for them to marry, elope.

"I've had a bad cold for a couple of days. Hope it will soon be over. Then I can get on with the rest of my life."

"Your daylilies bloomed this summer," I tell her. She had sent me a couple dozen before she moved out of the old house. She wrapped each one in newspaper with a tag giving its name in delicate tracings of pencil. Stella d'Oro. Mary Todd. Wine Cup. I planted them. In the spring, all the nametags were blank, erased by rain and snow.

"I've been reading the paper," she says. "It's the *Kansas City Star*. I've had it all my life. I'm used to the headlines. That carries me along. I read the newspaper. Then I think a bit about breakfast."

"I'm just waiting for what will happen next," she says again.

"While you're waiting, what do you think about?" I've always wondered. She has never revealed herself, only glimpses.

"I don't know quite. They keep me in charge. They keep me notified. This is a real good set-up. I have no complaints."

"I FIGURED IT WAS you when the nurse brought me the phone," she says after a long interval in which I can hear her labored breathing.

"Happy birthday. Did you have a celebration at lunch?" I had asked the nurses to give her my gift at lunchtime, when she was most alert.

"Lunch? I just had . . . Nothing special. It was all right. I was glad to get this phone call."

"You made it to eighty-seven."

"I don't know how much longer I'll last," she says. "I'm not feeling so hot."

She is in a wheelchair now, too heavy to walk. She is five feet tall and weighs 235 pounds. Her lower legs are swollen with edema. I think of the Willendorf Venus. They put her in a whirlpool and use ointment, but still there are blisters. She has fatigue, shortness of breath, lung congestion. The diuretics give her kidney failure; without them, she swells up.

For much of her life she has "sick headaches." Coca-Cola is the closest thing she has to a cure.

"How are you managing?"

"Just fine. I just keep going. The same things. The plant arrived." So now she remembers my gift.

"I thought you might like to have an amaryllis. If you water it, it may bloom in a few weeks."

"We had fun deciding where to put it."

"You have lived into the twenty-first century."

"How about that."

THE FOLLOWING SUNDAY she is sitting right by the phone. She has already had breakfast. She has a bad cough.

"When was Francis's birthday, November fifth or sixth?" I ask.

"I don't know."

"You were married sixty years."

"I can't recall when I didn't know him."

"You met him in Latin class, when you were thirteen."

"It just clicked."

THE NEXT TIME I call it's a day of falling leaves, not a cloud in the sky. In the backyard in Sag Harbor I hear a steady sound as if there is a creature in the trees. It's the leaves detaching and falling. It's the time for that. Something or someone drifts past, making the lower branches in the oaks by the side of the house sway in rhythm. That sound again: leaves, like the shadows of birds.

"I'm just out of my shower," she says. "My hair is all curly."

She always said she hated her curly hair, now she seems to enjoy it.

"That's on the program this morning. That's all I know."

"Your lungs sound better. You were coughing last week."

"It's just something in my throat. Don't worry about that. It's not an ailment."

"Did you have a flu shot?"

"They may have given me one and I've forgotten it. It looks like a nice day."

I look up: jet trails, falling leaves, a blue sky.

"Last night I watched the Leonid meteor showers," I say. "It was better than fireworks."

"I'm glad you have access to the outside world. It means a lot. I miss my garden."

"How is the amaryllis?"

"I don't know what happened to that."

She is quiet on the other end.

"I love you." I throw it out, taking a risk.

"I love you, too."

It is a first. I want to ask her to repeat it, but I'm afraid she might not remember she has said it. I don't understand this love, how much it hurts. It makes no sense. We have nothing in common. Just blood.

"I was thinking today about the story you told of being in a tornado as a little girl and seeing a sewing machine flying down the street," I say.

"I don't know what happened to that sewing machine." She is silent so long I fear she has fallen asleep.

"What did you have for breakfast?"

"I don't quite recall."

"What are you doing now?"

"Just waiting. To see what happens next."

"Me. Too."

I AM IN the New Orleans airport, having visited a friend expecting her first child, when my cellphone rings. Kidney failure. She is not expected to last the night. Last. I imagine a long corridor lit with candles, her exit.

She rarely left home. She never went anywhere without telling me where she was going. It is unprecedented, inexcusable even, for her not to be the weighty anchor back there in the center of the country. She was short on tenderness during the years I was growing up, but she was always there.

I think of the last time we spoke. The sound in the trees. The heavy leaves, brown with age, heavy as leather, letting go.

On Father's Day

David Valdes Greenwood

Today, with one subtle shift of an apostrophe, my family will change Father's Day to *Fathers'* Day. The meaning of the new term is perfectly clear, but the punctuation nonetheless looks slightly off at first. There, in a nutshell, is the core truth about our first year as gay dads. As incontestable as it is that we're a real family, we still throw some people off.

To be sure, most of the people in our lives see us for the Cheerio-wearing, diaper-toting, perfectly average parents that we are. When I sit at a picnic table with my parents' group, all of us trying to keep our children from indiscriminately swapping binkies and colds, it's easy to forget that there's anything extraordinary about my family. The moms and dads of Lily's playmates have welcomed us wholeheartedly into a community bonded by struggles with midnight feedings and post-teething stress disorder. When we held our daughter in our arms on our first Fathers' Day one year ago, this was precisely the life we envisioned.

But a year is a long time. As Lily has transformed from a wet bundle into a girl eagerly taking her first steps, recent events have forced us to grow up as well. We've had to admit that it was an illusion to think that our family, even in the quasi-liberal bubble of Massachusetts, was just another family. We already knew our governor decried gay parenting as being "not right on paper" and "not right in fact." But it was still shocking when, in the very week that we finalized Lily's adoption, the longtime agency Catholic Charities of Boston abruptly decided it would end all of its adoptions rather than place kids with same-sex parents. Soon after, parents in a nearby town sued school officials for civil rights violations when a teacher read a fairy tale that involved two princes but no princesses.

How should we react? We could argue till we're blue in the face that we're good and moral dads, telling how we took turns sleeping with Lily in her hospital room when she had pneumonia. Or point out that Lily's birth mother picked us because she believed we were the family God chose. But when all is said and done, the facts don't alter the first visual impression: "Look, Ma—no *ma*."

One Sunday, we went to a diner with another pair of gay dads, a child between each set of men. Still, the first thing out of the waitress's mouth was "Wives' day off, huh?" Even in the land of gay marriage, she reverted to the most traditional story line for the families before her. And why wouldn't she? While single gay people are now everywhere in pop-culture fare, families like ours never grace the silver screen nor merit a rhyme in song lyrics; we barely show up in greeting cards or on TV. And look what happens when we get mentioned at school.

Even as we try to raise Lily with love and a sense of safety, she's always going to see that her family isn't the established norm. Is it any wonder, then, that we get dreamy-eyed over ads for Rosie O'Donnell's *R Family* cruises, designed for gay-parented families? Or that we plan to make an annual tradition out of Family Week in Provincetown in hopes that, for at least a few days a year, Lily will see her family as the yardstick, not the exception to the rule?

But we don't plan to live the rest of our lives on a cruise ship or in a beach town. We plan to raise Lily at home in her own community, where, if she looks closely enough, she'll see as many configurations of families as there are constellations in the sky. Two moms packing their girls off to school. Two dads and their son welcoming a new baby. A mom and a dad redoing their backyard so their toddler has a place to play. A mixed-race couple singing lullabies in two languages. A single mom raising the daughter she went to Africa to adopt.

CHAUTAUQUA

We want Lily to see all of this and to keep it in her heart for those times when the world stubbornly insists there is only one family picture. We cannot shield her from people who would erase us, whether from storybooks or society, but we can teach her to celebrate Fathers' Day, and every day, with unfettered joy and fierce pride.

Mantle's Knees: A Kind of American Prayer

Mark DeFoe

May 22, 1963–Yogi cried, "This is it!" But the ball struck the right field façade just inches from the top. Eyewitnesses swore the ball was still rising. A computer projection calculated the distance at 734 feet.

An all too American Drama, played out
In played-out hard-scrabble Oklahoma—
Cherokee red earth, Hanging Judge Parker
Badlands, bootlegger territory, Knife-
Fight Saturday nights towns, Belle Starr country,
Jesse and Frank's neck of the woods.

Where Mutt, his dad, with his big splayed hands, pumped
it at him right, and Granddad winged it left,
taught him to crush the ball from either side.
The lead mines sucked lean life from such lean men,
Throwbacks tossed up from endless rust and dust.
Towns of folks hanging on for the dear
Life of those who had legs enough to run
For glory and sign on the dotted line.

All waiting for those scouts from The East—
Wily as Indians, cagey considerers,
Seen-it-beforers. Squint-eyed, toothpick-suckers,
Yarn-tellers in quality boots and real Stetsons,
Scratchin' in their rumpled notebooks (Too slow.
No arm. Can't hit curve.) Code that said you'll be

CHAUTAUQUA

A bent-back miner, boy, sooner than soon,
With wife and three kids to bow you down, down.

There he was just tow-headed Mickey, with
Nice teeth, and girls buzzin' round and all that
Happy talent in the coil and sinew of him.
And his joking ways they say he got from his mom,
Thought what she had to laugh about, God knows.

And then he was legend. He was Mantle.
Baggy pinstripes couldn't hide that swing, those
Bull shoulders. Then he was Whitey, Yogi,
And Bobby. And Elston Howard, Hank Bauer,
Joe Pepitone, Clete Boyer, Rizzuto,
And tormented, fated Roger Maris.

He was Mantle, hobbling the base paths
With crumbling knees. And even later when
He broke our hearts with booze and regrets and
His cheesy restaurants, he was still The Mick.

Yet he was Mickey. You knew it when you saw
That easy country lope, tender on his pins
When he rounded the pads, not like Ruth's
Mincing, baby-stepping, stiff-legged prance.

Knew it when you looked up and saw the ball
Rising toward you, over the Bronx, over
Broadway and the City That Never Sleeps.

And it was like you had grown up with him,
Had always called him Mick. And you

Mark DeFoe

Had been there too, one gritty, baked-out, red-sun
August evening when one of his homers rose up
Out of god-forsaken Commerce, Oklahoma.

And all you could do was sit with your hot dog
Halfway to your mouth and whisper, "Jesus,
Jesus, that ball ain't ever coming down."

The Last Days of Amelia Earhart

Mark DeFoe

"Mother said she wanted me to fly, but
I have flown the coop. I'm off the charts,
this sun-racked spit not Howland, but some
island too unknown to be forgotten.
No Prospero. No Caliban. No luck.

Leaning back on a scraggly palm, facing
the mindless sea, I indulge in what I
was never good at—keeping my diary
in my head, logging my earth-bound days.
Poor Fred is down the beach where I dragged him,
where I covered him with great sobs and sand.

The leg is stinking and water is so dear.
Why, when out of the green and copper sea
the Jap destroyer emerged like a swift
gray spectral fish did I hide? Why not
one shout and a wave, one smoky signal fire?

If they had put ashore they would have seen
the ghost of the Electra inverted in the reef.
Surely my smile, my famous tousled hair,
would have charmed them out of rice
and a ride to Yokohama? Oh, Georgie,
did I fear their strangeness in this place so strange?
But my choice was my choice.

Mark DeFoe

The leg must go; I know such things. You can
call me Stumpy, the one-legged wife of
a confessed legman. But one eye never
stopped that pirate, Wiley Post, now did it?

Sorry I will miss the signing at Macy's.

Sometimes I try to talk with the babies
we never had—boy like me, girl like you
—but I never know what to say.

Kansas sunsets, your champagne and berries and cream
and coffee and books near Columbia U.
But remembering creates such drag
I can't get my wheels up. And I'm airborne
most of the day, Georgie, making tracks,
the wind always on my tail, chasing clouds
in the Kinner Canary again.
What a sweet little ship she was!

I told you I knew from that day skating
on Hinson's Pond when I was five how speed
made your Meelie want to leap from this earth.

I swing in the arcs with auks and albatross and
frigate birds and never plot a course.
The wind is heavy and the birds never cease their cries,
but I know the wind and the birds speak my words.

I rise up, and they call out to me, courage.
Follow us, Oh, beautiful human girl.
This way home. This way home.
And my heart knows a pure clean emptiness."

There never was a time when, in my opinion, some way could not be found to prevent the drawing of the sword.

—Ulysses S. Grant

Our National Life

Reincarnation of the Peace Sign

Jim Daniels

In 1972, my father-in-law, painting the flashing
on his roof, asked his daughter arriving home from school
what he should paint on the chimney.

He escaped Yugoslavia in 1960 without the language
to tell his war stories. He had an inexplicable love
for Mohammed Ali, and nostalgia for simple bread.

You could drive by that house and never notice
the red peace sign, but once it's pointed out
you'll never miss it again.

He was always on a high ladder, trying to color
the miracle of his own home. So quiet up there,
he once told his daughter it was safe to cross

the street, then a bike ran her down, broke her leg.
The world always exacting its slice
of cruelty. How could he have forgotten?

In 2004, he gives me permission to repaint peace.
My legs tremble on the thirty-foot ladder. I try to trace
his old lines, but make a mess of it. Beneath me,

my children shout my name. I can barely hear them
in the rarified air. If you drive by now—*peace*,
a little brighter, a little harder to make out.

Jim Daniels

If you drive by now, honk your horn and wave.
The old man's getting a little deaf. His English
as good as it's going to get. He's inarticulate

with rage at the war's daily news.
But if you raise two fingers into a V
he will nod, and nearly smile.

THE PLASTIC HORSE OF TROY
David Bouchier

Last time I visited the ruins of the fabled city of Troy, some forty years ago, a man in a faded Arab robe intercepted me at the entrance and offered a genuine piece of the original wooden horse. Now I am a sucker for relics of all kinds—I treasure my lock of Patrick Stewart's hair for example—but I was doubtful about this one. Not only did the wood look suspiciously like fragments of a modern packing case, but also I had my doubts about the very existence of the original wooden horse.

Consider the story line. It comes from Homer who is the ultimate unreliable witness and would never survive questioning by a Congressional committee. As Homer sketches the tale in *The Iliad* and *The Odyssey* the Greek warrior Achilles came to Troy to rescue the incomparably beautiful Helen, whom the wicked Trojans had kidnapped. After a siege of ten years, and the death of Achilles, the Greeks hit upon the clever wheeze of pretending to retreat, leaving behind a keepsake for the Trojans in the form of a large wooden horse. The Trojans were dubious about this Greek gift but wheeled it into the city anyway. That night, soldiers hidden inside the horse crept out and opened the gates, and Troy was doomed.

Homer wrote this tale in about 900 BC, which was already hundreds of years after the events it purported to describe, which is roughly equivalent to a historian of today writing a history of the Wars of the Roses based on hearsay and without the benefit of The History Channel.

But it is a splendid story nevertheless and has survived three thousand years of skepticism from cynics like me. When I returned to Troy with my wife a few weeks ago I was looking forward to both of us meeting the man selling genuine relics of the wooden horse. Relics never run out, that's why they are miraculous. This time I was determined to buy one for my collection. But, alas, the imaginative salesman was gone, replaced by a tacky gift shop. And there, outside the gate of Troy, was a huge brand new shiny reproduction of the famous wooden horse. I don't know how dumb the Trojans were, but this horse wouldn't have deceived a five year old. There were windows all along the sides through which the Greek invaders would have been clearly visible.

But we hadn't yet plumbed the depths of this particular fantasy. In the nearby Turkish town of Cannakale we found another Trojan horse on the harbor, a splendidly dramatic sculpture made (we were told) of fiberglass reinforced with steel. This horse was a replica of one used in the 2004 blockbuster movie "Troy" starring Brad Pitt as Achilles. I haven't seen the movie, and hope not to, but the critics said that, in terms of historical accuracy, it made Homer's epic poems look like scientific reports.

Right beside Hollywood's steel and fiberglass wooden horse was a stall selling miniature plastic wooden horses. So here was a plastic representation of a replica of a movie representation of a highly unreliable three thousand year old story describing events that probably never happened—a copy of a replica of an imitation of a symbol of a myth. I almost bought one of these miniature plastic Trojan horses, to assuage my disappointment at not getting a piece of the real thing. Then I remembered that there was no real thing: only the myth is real, except of course that it's not.

It's hard to escape the conclusion that all of us—Homer, the archaeologists, the tourists, the cinema audiences, Mr. Brad Pitt, and possibly even bold Achilles himself—have been conned.

QUIPU OF THE SCORCHED LORD
Gregory Donovan

Horse-men came with their rum and dust,
their beer and flags, squealing armor, stink of wine,
the beatings they gave themselves under the sun
and inside the drizzle and gritty rain
with the *nine-tailed cat* and the black tarred
rope and the cane for the boy who must *kiss
the big gun's daughter*. Cruelty alights in power
without knowledge, and so it was without wonder
the black mouth would kill wherever it was
pointed. The long-faced conquerors sailed out
from the hiss and surge of their wooden belly's dark
laced with what was written in secret and sea foam
to fall upon the back of the promised world,
wolves in the eyes of the thousands of thousands
waiting to welcome the fevered dreams of men
who night and day talk to their books and their charts.
Buzzards rule where eagles have fallen from the sky.

The Inca was already at war, no time
for the runners and their tales, the warriors of steel
with impossible appetites, the fiery gods
kept close as lovers sleeping,
the sudden blood. The Lord sent them
such presents, the well-worked masks and useless
trinkets the white-faced hair-faced men wanted
to eat, ignorant of the rite of touching gold dust

Gregory Donovan

to tongue. Wild men, lost, distracted and sick
with lust—the Lord sent young wives to calm
them, the angry ones, and sweet wives, too, for their
angry horses, which ate real corn, like real men.

When Atahualpa at last understood
they meant to burn him, he submitted instead
to be strangled so that his dried body might
live on as lightning among the Incas of the Incas.
They burned him anyway. And his ancestors.

Daily now the black-gowned priests drag
the ancestral mummies into the fire,
by night the people steal them back again,
lightning to parade the streets.

Broken by knives of flame, crushed
to dust at the hands of the wind,
the dry ancestors thirst for time and the strength
the Jesus-priests have taken away for their distant
god who hangs in the sky beyond the sea, their one god
the white men have killed and raised from the dead
so they might kill him again. The white men nail his endless
agony to a cross and make us kneel to kiss it.

Come back through the flames, we pray. Give us water
for our thirst, o Lord. In the dark of every eye you burn.

Sarah Henry, Phantom Wife: 1775

Gregory Donovan

It is the cool light in the white room
in the white voice of the lizard.
It is black flies banging at the pane.
It is the grey and silver tensed in the spider's web
and the hoarfrost sparkling in the brittle grasses.
It is the shuttered moon in the reptile eye.

It is a woman buried to her breasts
in the damp of the earth rolling away
from her place in a window in the ground
where she waits in the hard white dress
for the cloak, the dark buttoned trousers to mount
three stone steps into nothing with its red carriage wheels.

It is the rustling in the petticoats of a daughter,
it is the silence in the skirts of a slave.
It is a woman spreading her hair to dry
over the bent-backed chair before the fire.
The woman believes at times she can see its shadow
thrown against the wall, whirling and beating,
the squealing engine of the madness of the times.
The lizard says no mirrors here.
Mistress Henry has developed *a strange antipathy*.
It is a woman jumping up like a spark fading out.

Gregory Donovan

In the wood above her head, demons busy
with their work, knocking and laughing,
sometimes dancing to the lizard's fiddle tunes
and eating the good food she gets cold.
Mistress of demons, fed on air and candles.
Soon, soon, they moan, and promise to leave her
to slip into the unmarked grave of her long dream.
It is waking in the scratch of her name across a deed.

It is the leg crushed in the accident at the mill.
After it was cut off, the hired man said he felt it
again at night, a phantom lying beside him in bed.

What makes a man think he can own anything?

The lizard steps from his trapdoor in the smoke,
scales of smoke-grey tipped with smoke-black, candle
in hand, leaving the pewter tankard to warm
on the andiron shelf, checking her bonds, taking off
his powdered hair, his one blue horn jutting . . .
if broken off, she has been told, it simply grows back.

The lizard eyes dart their many directions.
The swift lizard says sometimes the wrong herb
will make its way into the soup's shining face,
sometimes the lovely arched fireplace will smoke.
The lizard says he will set her free. A lizard's head
bobs up and down. Shoulders, too. Up and down.

It is a husband at night burying a wife in shame
like a dog in the open field, snakebit
yet given, he may assure himself, *every loving care.*

CHAUTAUQUA

The master, Patrick, swears never to speak her name again.
It is a man burning wax myrtle candles, the strait-dress
smoldering on the fire in an empty basement room.
Sarah, name of his mother, name of the dead.
It is a name whispered, broken off. It grows back.

GOOD PEOPLE

Joan Connor

I *am the fairy who stole Bridget Cleary.*

AMONG THE YELLOW gorse and the sudden rocks, around the scraggly thorn bush, the good people sat in the circle of the rath. A white horse or perhaps the glamour of ground fog pawed the earth and huffed. One of the folk muttered, shoulders hunched, webbed feet splayed as he brewed tea in a broken eggshell, bruising with his stumpy thumbs the John the Baptist's herb. He resumed his seat on the grass tuft, peered through his squint eyes.

One of the wee folk, a nose with legs, asked in his half-voice, "Does you believe in them then, people?"

But the web-foot just sipped his tea.

The one with cowtail hair snickered, said, "I never seen one, but I heard tell that they walk beyond the ringfort. More and more of them all the time."

The nose's hands covered his nose as he squeaked.

Then the web-foot said, "Aye. They're there. They live always adjacent and highly visible lives. A bad lot. They take changelings, some of them, switching one of their symmetrical kind, a babe or a maid, for one of our lopsided own. One long leg keeps you safely walking in circles. Their kind walk straight."

"No," the nose said.

And cowtail nodded, her eyes as solemn as moonlight, quiet as moss. "They make bad butter, clabber the milk. They pen their cows. I heard a story once of a farmer who kept his cow all the while indoors."

"Pishogue. Pishroguery," the nose said. He shook his nose sadly. "Poor cow."

Web-foot said, "I heard tell of a Kerryman roasted his bairn on a shovel."

"Great Jenny Greenteeth. But why?"

"Pixilated. Peoplated."

Light dappled and spangled the rath. The shadows piped, and gibbered, and snuffled.

"The baby made small fire, small meat. Wrap red thread thrice 'round your thumb, bear your four-leafed clover. When you walk beyond the rath, keep one eye over your shoulder." Web-foot cupped his shell in his snaggled fingers and smiled into it. The smile of a secret kept.

Over the grass blades, the midnight wind played harp. The will-o'-the-wisp flitted from stone to stone, jigging to the wild music.

The cowtailed one crossed her arms over her long dugs and whispered, "They have rounded ears."

"No," Nose shouted covering his pointed own.

The light filtered and flittered. Web-foot drained his eggshell and set it beside him on the tuft. "At the Puck Fair, their people wind up into the hills to wrestle a mountain goat and bring him down to crown him king."

"Poor goat," Nose said, pulling his long legs up beneath him. "Poor goat of the unruly rule. Eerie." He shuddered.

"True. Truly," the web-foot said, "and it's all in the name of their god, Lug."

"The big Lug," Nose piped.

"Let him speak," the cowtailed one said.

"Lug. Lug the long-handed with a shining face and a roaring spear. His druid brought him inscribed on birch paper in Ogham the warning of abduction."

"Who? The abduction of whom?" Nose asked, hugging his legs and settling in; he knew the story well.

"The fairy were to steal his wife, seven times."

A goat-hoofed one on the periphery bleated. "That ugly crone. What good people would steal a one with rounded breasts, and rounded ears, slotted nose, and yellow hair?"

The shadows chuckled and hooted.

"Nevertheless, so runs their tale. So Lug appointed birch her protectorate."

"Aye, birch is good wood," the goat-footed one said, "to hold evil at bay and madness off. That's why we plant it round our rath to keep the visible people out."

"It's good for inception, too, they say," the cowtailed one said. "Sure and none was ever planted round Bridget Cleary's cottage. Not one stick."

"Birch is vigilant," the web-foot said, "though still we get the pretenders, those who like to pretend that they can cross both sides of the veil, the seanchaí, like that one Jack Dunne."

"We have done with Dunne, that nosy one," Nose whistled. "Back to Lug."

"As you would have it, only an ensorceled good folk would take foul wife. But they are our mirror selves. Lug. Sun god. Son. Sun. Light. Blinded himself, small doubt, to his wife's deformity. She did not even have a snout."

The hircine one stamped his cleft feet. "I can't believe that. You go too far, tale-spinner."

"Oh, it's certain," the cowtailed one said. "Aye, the web-foot would know. They say he ran with the people; he knows their ways. He came back with a sign, he has even legs and an even temper."

They nodded and murmured. True. True. Even legs, he could walk straight or round. And, besides, they were in want of a good story.

"Who killed the corn king?" Nose shouted. But the rocks groaned. They had all heard it before, so many times before. These were ancient stories, as old as the tale-spinner, web-foot. As old as the rocks and the trestled Dolmens, perhaps older. The good people lived outside time but inside the cycle of day and night, the interchange of dark and light. Time transitive was their habitation.

The foxfire landed on Bean-Nighe's shoulder, and she keened, hunched over her bloody linen in the stream suddenly sprung from the rock. "It's Bridget's linen, I'm washing," she said. And she scrubbed and pounded the sheets with rocks. She smelled like foxed ale, oranges bearded with mold. The goat-one liked her perfume and nuzzled close as she wailed, "Tell the one about Bridget. Tell, tell."

And the goat agreed. "Tell. Tell."

The grass music strummed and hummed. The light flickered spangles like snow sifting.

"No," Web-foot said, "I cannot. It makes no sense. Flame like Lug has long hands. In people-land, death's hands too extend like Lug's. Her dog mourned her, Badger; and Dotey, her cat. But she left no child to cry for her. And no one birch-like watched out for her, no one stood by her graveside. When Death extended his bony hand, he said, 'Charmed, I'm sure.'"

The fay ones sniggered.

Cowtail said, "They say she was after meeting an egg man on the low road."

"Who killed the corn king?" Nose asked.

Web-foot said, "On their side, Death goes by many names and many roads, high and low."

The fog horse bucked, cords whipping from his bridle. The washing woman keened. "Bridget's gone up the chimney. Up in smoke."

The goat-one snorted. "It's just a people tale, an old husband's tale. It has no matter."

The web-foot flinched. "Grave matter. Grave matter."

"Who killed the corn king?" Nose wheedled.

The ground orchestrated weird chords. Whispers. Rustles. Patches of light. Old ground spins stories until dawn when shadow selves dissipate back to ground. Wound round. Wound down. A goat bleat. Dawn.

Joan Connor

I AM THE fairy who stole Bridget Cleary.

Johanna Burke, Ballyvadlea, Co. Tipperary, 1895

THEY SAY SHE had pansies in her blue eyes when she looked on William Simpson, the Emergency man, but, pish, that's just talk. But it could be so. Saying so won't make it so. And him being a Protestant and married; it would not have been seemly. But this, I know, is true.

She was proud, Bridget Cleary, and bold with her tongue was my cousin. High spirit and high color. A fine dressmaker and milliner, she was, and she cocked and pinned a black straw hat to her brown hair, with a dark blue ribbon, and two brown feathers. Feathers, you say. A shawl would not do for her, thank you. She trimmed herself out neat with the plumage from her own hens, getting her egg money twice. She was brilliant.

Too brilliant, you ask. Did her needle make borrowed magic? Pish. She had a machine do her sewing for her, and no fairy foot pressed the treadle. But some say otherwise. But saying so won't make it so. She had a fair hand with the needle.

With her eggs and dressmaking money, she had £ 20 in a tin canister in the trunk below her handsome iron bedstead. The tin was full, but the cradle empty eight years in her marriage to Michael Cleary. It wasn't natural and them living right in the shadow of Slievenamon, the mountain of women. What daisy chains did she weave, what bells ring to ward off the babies? Her with her fine petticoats, her nice ways. The pansy bloom in her eye and no buds in the garden bed. Oh, she was brilliant.

And the new cottage they lived in in Ballyvadlea, her poor Da sleeping on a straw tick in the storeroom. No straw for the Bridgie hen. And her rooster must be leery.

Michael Cleary was a handsome man, and Himself a fine cooper, too, fashioning the butter firkins for the creamery. Saying so won't make it so, but they said she met an egg man on the road to Clonmel and that she fancied William. Pish, that's just talk. But she was full of herself, that one. You have to break a horse, they say. She carried herself apart like she carried a basket of eggs. Till she took sick.

Raving, she was, with the fever, and her husband, too, beside himself. Some say that there was matter to the illness, fairy fever. Bridget's uncle, old John Dunne put out that she was enchanted; one leg had shrunk shorter than the other, the sign that she'd walked over. But saying so won't make it so. Old Dunne limps himself, so his tale gives the lame dog a hand over the stile.

But fairy or fever, Bridget needed physic, so Michael, he fetched the Father Con Ryan for last rites. And Bridgie's father, Patrick Boland, set out to fetch Doctor Crean. But he would na come and he would na come, the doctor being always in his cups. Finally the doctor came on the fourth day, whiffy with whiskey, sozzled he was, but bringing medicine for Bridget, but Michael had already dosed her with herbs from a Fethard woman, forcing the spoon down her throat till she gagged on it. He dosed her but not with the doctor's medicine. And then he brought her some Claret to quiet her.

Old toothless, hobbled Jack Dunne says it's a changeling in Bridget's bed and not Bridget there at all. So they set about starving the fairy out and Michael got herbs from Ganey, the fairy doctor, and brewed them in beastlings, the new milk that I brought by in the morning, the dun cow having just calved.

Bridgie still took to bed, so her uncle pinned her down by her ears while my brothers, Patrick and James held her arms and William her feet, and three times her husband forced the mixture down Bridgie's gullet, she all the while raving and choking—It's bitter. Bitter it is.

And the men raised her in her nightdress and dowsed her with urine, and shook her and spun her, three times asking: In the name of God, are you the wife of Michael Cleary, the daughter of Patrick

Boland? In the name of the Father, and the Son, and the Holy Ghost.

And three times she answered: I am, Da, in the name of God. In the name of God. I am.

They were rough with her, but what could I do? Shaking her and winding her round. What could a woman do? Bridget with all her spirit and fire could not stop it. What could I do? I watched her shame.

Brought down she was then, mad with the sickness and hunger, and stinking of urine, smutched with char, and a poker brand on her forehead where they'd tried to brand her and scare the fairy out. Not so brilliant then, Bridget Cleary.

But even through all this, Bridget was full of sprite and made as if the Peelers were come to the window. But Michael only threw the chamberpot of slops at the police Bridgie would have fancied summoning there.

My mother, Mary, was after trying to coax a fire in the grate with some stumps of whitethorn to heat the kettle. The whitethorn gave off green smoke, pale fire. And the men carried Bridgie in and hung her over the grate for ten minutes by the clock on the cupboard, charring her nightdress. If she was not sickly before, sure and she would be now. And I thought to myself that they might be smoking in a fairy rather than smoking one out. But I did na speak. What can a woman do?

The men were quieter then, pleased with their remedy. The remedy was this: Bridget huddled, meek and speaking on things that were na there. Fairy-haunted she was then, conversing with the air. My mother helped Bridget into a clean nightdress and pressed a palm to her brow by way of small comfort.

And maybe after all Bridget walked with the fairy. Who's to say? Maybe she ate primroses and found herself walking a yellow lane and saw the good people and maybe she heard the bluebells knell her death —for didn't she sit up as if a fairy had pressed second-sight into her, a third eye? Didn't she sit up and ask, "Why is the house all filled with smoke? Why are the sergeant and constable here?" Her eyes wild with light.

But the house was not yet filled with smoke, the constabulary not yet arrived—though Michael did not tell her so. He let her think that the smoke roiled and that the men were there. But his saying so didn't make it so.

In the morning the father returned to say mass for Bridget, and didn't she poke out the host with her tongue and rub it into the bedclothes. I swear I saw it though no other witnessed it. And then she paid the father for his pains out of the tin canister and she gave me a shilling for my new milk. But first didn't she rub it under her nightdress, a pishogue on me? Why shouldn't I tell Michael then? Wasn't she a pretty one? Wasn't she still full of herself though?

The plowman came from his plow to calm her, and Bridgie was herself again. And her husband made her drink holy water, all the while watching her, and he made her drink milk too, and he told her to get dressed. A plain calico chemise, she wore, and green stays, a red petticoat, and a striped petticoat, black stockings and black boots, a blue flannel dress, and a cashmere jacket, a white shawl. Oh, she was brilliant.

And out she comes to the kitchen, the room well sprinkled with holy water, the doors and shutters thrown wide to chase the fairies out —though I think to myself, what's to keep them from sauntering in. But I keep my tongue as Bridget enters, her brown hair coiled neat again. And Michael, he eyes her askance, asking again after the pishogue she rubbed on my coin.

And Bridget's eyes flare. "Would you be making a fairy of me when your own mother walked two days with the fairies?"

My mother clucks and sets out bread and jam on the board. "Come on now," she says.

The kettle steams on the hob.

Michael's eyes narrow as if he is praying, his father but dead yesterday and Himself not gone to the wake. He mutters about the pishogues.

And I wonder: Why should Bridget have all the luck, she just a few years younger than I? The fine clothes, and her egg man, her tin canister.

And I with the babies, crammed in my dark cottage. Why should she wish bad luck on my shilling, on me, her cousin? And Bridget tells Michael that she casts no curses, knows nothing of pishogues.

Then Michael hisses like the kettle, his face red as the embers. He takes the first bit of bread and he jams it into her mouth, yells, "Eat it." Then a second bit of bread. And Bridgie's choking on the bread, the first bit and the second, and reaches for the milk. But Michael pulls the pitcher aside and yells, "Eat it." Then a third bit he jams into her mouth. Bridget's eyes tear. She will not eat the third piece. Or she cannot.

Michael knocks her to the floor. His hand is on her throat. His knee is on her chest as if in half-prayer. "Swallow. Swallow." And he grabs a burning stick from the grate and threatens to cram it down her throat if she will na swallow. He would feed her fire, he would.

And he strips off her white shawl, her cashmere jacket, and her blue skirt, her striped petticoat, and her red, her green stays, and neat black boots till Bridget lies there in her plain calico chemise and her black stockings, spellbound. And an ember from the stick drops and catches fire to the chemise. Just a small hole at first there burning.

"Give me a chance," Bridget pleads. But saying so won't make it so.

And Michael grabs the can of lamp oil and douses her with paraffin. Once. Twice. Thrice. All the while my brothers and my daughter own, my mother bearing witness—

She made large fire. She was brilliant.

What could I do? What can a woman do?

Bridget Cleary at twenty-six was gone. I do not know what became of the tin beneath the bed.

I AM THE fairy who stole Bridget Cleary. The husband said she walked out at night, wearing only her nightdress, between two tall men. She would ride, he said, on a white horse, corded to its back on the Kilnagranagh Hill. Three nights he waited with black-handled knives to cut her from the fairy traces. And I was perplexed. I had peeped in the kitchen window, smelling new milk and

CHAUTAUQUA

Claret, smoke and fear. I saw that one kick her charred foot as one would a cat in the creamery, or a stone in the road, and roll her in a sheet and bag her head. Great fire leaped in the kitchen as he knocked the old woman down and drew a knife on the lot of them and they cowered in the room beyond. And he made the soft one, the one with the scared eyes, carry the package out to the bog with him where he'd dug a small hole to plant his changeling in. He threw the rest, her ashes, on the dunghill and scattered chicken dirt on her new grave. I was surprised at his ferocity. I knew his mother; she ran two days with me. A woman who stepped lightly.

Midnight, and I waited till the two even-legged ones walked away, then pulled back the branches, and scrabbled at the loose earth. I pulled the winding sheet and the bag from her head. Her body was spilling out of itself through the holes burned in her flesh. She wore black stockings, a flocked chemise, one gold earring. A smudge of char decorated her brow. Her face set in a grimace of surprise. The changeling. She was sore changed. I left the earring—I had no use for hexed gold—and bundled her back into the dirt.

I watched the one who brandished knives and fire search the outbuildings and fields for his wife. I watched him wait on the hill for a white horse. I watched the cooper weep over the one gold earring he found in the manure, her half-grave for that part of her gone ashen, all the while wondering why. Why. If he grieved for his wife gone, did he not go to her in the bog corner there where he planted her?

Then the men in caps came and took her before she could root, could grow. She left a small hole, puddled with dew. They put her back in the ground in Cloneen, a larger hole, cornered with four small stones, no name. No ring of stones. Not a monumental passing. No one came. So I sat with Bridget's stones. When she lived in the cottage, she passed me eggshells out the window to brew my tea.

I sat for seven days like the seven cure for the seventh daughter of a seventh daughter they'd mixed in her new milk. And on the seventh day I knew that they meant to leave her there, in the ground, lost and found, (they knew where) so I stole her then. I exorcised their charms from her.

Joan Connor

She left her name behind—it flew up the chimney—and she walked with me, foxgloves on her charred hands, her body poulticed with Hazel leaves. I carried her in my eggshell cup. And the first words she ever said to me were: Can we bring Badger? So I whistled as I walked for the wee dog to please my eggshell enchantress. Saying so will make it so.

She became our changeling child, one leg shortened to walk always into the fairy ring.

At dusk or dawn on solstices we scamper to the Emergency man's and spit in his cream to curdle the butter or skim the fat so it won't churn. We tie red threads on thorn and thistle against him. He leads tours of the fairy cottage where Bridget flew up the chimney. He'll see small profit in it. We eavesdrop on their tales of her. She comes from bad stock, but I will not tell her so. But nor will I be the fire-starter's urges, demi-urges. I have known their men to take spirits and strike their wives and mothers. I have known them to steal cattle and beat their horses. The soul-less recognize no souls. Bad stock. And bad stock makes poor soup.

I do not tell the good people my eggshell princess's provenance, that she is one who rent the veil. She walks between the rings, her wee dog tagging after. The Mountain of Women is her domain now.

The fairy did not take her, mind. At least not until later, not until I saw that they planned to leave her, sodded. Nor did fairy take her husband either. But who knows what lives in the ring beside the good people and whom they visit? Who knows what lives between people-land and fairy-land? Perhaps some dark imago called upon Michael Cleary. But, when importuned for a chance, what imp fevers a man to offer lamp oil for a chance? Say the devil made him do it. But never say, fay. Never say, I.

Or say that their fairies live within them, dark caprices. Goatish caprices with long hands who do not know themselves or their own darkness. They will have no feathered hats, no cleverness, no barren women with quicksilver tongues and wits, no wizard stitchery, no dalliances with egg men, and every whim must be bent to their benighted wills until beside them a woman shuffles, the emblem of their deformity, stunted and hunched like a weathered stump. That was the fairy who stole Michael Cleary.

CHAUTAUQUA

The good people want no authority, just a good story, the anarchy of beauty, the ambiguous blurry moment of struggle between light and dark. We live on thresholds and leave the cottages to the others. We swing on the hinge of time. I will not tell Bridget's story, just the hinge of it. I leave them to their accounts.

Strange love that dreads a coin rubbed on a woman's parts. Strange love that yells, Swallow. Swallow. Choke on your bread or I will feed you fire. Choke on this hot stick. Strange love that strips a woman clean and burns her brightness off like peat till nothing shifts but ashes in the hearth. Strange love that steals a tin for small coin. Small coin. Lesser than a sole gold earring.

When we give food, we feast. We bury our gold in sacred ground. Weave flowers and fairy knots and bright feathers in our hair and let it down. We love all her parts in sum. When we steal, it's for large coin.

I am the fairy who stole Bridget Cleary. She is not witch. She is not fairy. She is not the wife of Michael Cleary.

My wife now. We walk the hills in bridal weeds. I had much need of her, of speed. It's a hard road waddling with webbed feet, and we ride no wild white steed. We ride ragwort in its stead. We drink cowslip for our mead. We make moor our marriage bed. Our way is wide and well-lit by wildfire and wilder greed to range wide and to range free. We sing half-songs and hold hands. Squint at dusk; you'll see us pass, hear our music in the grass. But the roses at the ringfort spike with thorn. Keep your side; we'll keep our own.

IN BALLYVADLEA, the new tenant scrubs and scrubs that stain, that stubborn smoke, from the lime wall. But it will not yield to soap and scouring. Vexed, she kicks the bucket and the water sloshes to the floor. They say that Bridget Cleary walks. She's never seen her. They say that Bridget Cleary haunts. Spanning over a century. Wouldn't you think that, if that troubled ghost had time on her hands, that she'd have better things to do than loiter here. A fireside tale. She turns back to her scrubbing. Keep your side; we'll keep our own.

SCOTTISH ROOTS

Mary Gilliland

I had wondered
    why on earth
the British count it
    among the trees.
Now, as it helps me
    climb rockface
to the left
    and keeps me from
nettle on the right,
    I know.

I know, too, its growth
    of six years
keeps concealed, keeps
    me from finding
the cave—really
    more a broad
opening—we reached,
    feet upon another's
shoulders, heads slid in
    to look up.

Legs dangling
    out of sandstone,
noses stuffy with
    dust, we could see

CHAUTAUQUA

the S spiral, the circle
    within circles,
the series of triangles
    and figures that
might or might not
    stand for humans.

The Pictish carvings I'm
    looking for—signs
of my ancestors'
    ancestors—hidden now
—have found their way
    to another place.
Rooks nest overhead.
    The river below
lofts over the rocks
    and under.

Perhaps my descendants
    are hexing my eyes,
haunting the ravine
    already, small
in the cranesbill popping
    through forget-me-not
while my vigorous feet
    hide in ropes
hands cliff climb,
    leaves of vine.

THE SONG OF MRS. HUE

Alan Michael Parker

Not because I live above my laundry
where all the shirts fly by
singing on a metal rod

ghosts on their hangers in their plastic suits
(even though I'm a Lutheran).
Or because the chemicals that burn my throat

the napalm I have chosen
mean that every dollar saved
bears in my mind

the picture of my daughter.
Or because Basic English II
in night school at the middle school

feels like talking through a shoe.
Or because the nice white man
wants his money back

and the nice white woman
wants her money back
and the nice black man

wants his money back.
Or because I dream I am on my belly
fingers first rushing sliding

CHAUTAUQUA

in a warm rocky river.
Or because I wear
my mother's smile to remember.

But because the lovely lovely lovely
people who moved next door
above their carpet store

invited me to dinner after church
and they have faces wooden faces
carved and dug out and impossible

and their home it was so nice
it smelled like a field of
flowers that have never grown

so red and gold.
What have I done?
Why have they come to me now?

Slate Headstones, Charleston, S.C.

Michael McFee

The shallowly-chiseled
winged death's-heads
and dashed biographies
of prosperous colonists,

their infants and relicts,
have been sheared off
by centuries of hurricanes
and earthquakes and wars

till they're nothing more
than rough gray fins
of anonymous strata
surfacing from the dark,

all the eloquent verses
and painstaking tributes
molted like dead skin,
leaving these rock-rows

in the walled cemetery
a museum-like display
of prehistoric weapons,
uplifted arrowheads

whose weathered edges
can still hurt God's foot
when he comes walking
in this morning garden.

Good Morning America (Courtesy ABC, 9/25/05)

Peter Fortunato

Deadly flu inevitable, only Swiss company Roche makes cure, no nation owns enough when, not if, pandemic strikes, don't ask why US never stockpiled, start now, 60 people dead world-wide, bird danger wakeup call.

Also, President's approval rating never lower as House Hammer DeLay indicted claims innocence of money laundering. "No daylight" between the two says source, while news pundits declare scandal spin must top speed handle many woes, even Senator Frist big heart-doc contender for oval office getting stock deals scrutinized, and don't forget gasoline is short, expensive, don't forget hurricanes mismanaged, Iraqi war news daily worsening, and Cheney's staff chief Libby finally admits he leaked secret agent's name, remember?

Now monster mold threatens New Orleans. Ugly stench in doctor's home, he wears surgical mask and latex gloves live amid fuzzy grime that circles parlor walls, coats picture frames, water line like river wharf splotchy black yuck. Fascinating. "This is still a good place to live!" hopeful guy declares. And from New York City studio Diane Sawyer reminds viewers round the planet—me in Qatar watching wide-eyed—these homes will all be demolished.

Being blond helps in on-line dating, results study 30,000 on-line daters, valuable as college degree in these circles polltakers conclude.

CHAUTAUQUA

Then there's the giant squid, white, long as a building is tall, photographed 20,000 leagues under the sea by Japanese, head guy smiling like a kid displays long tentacle accidentally nabbed can still suck with suction cups his fingers—so strange feeling! Used squid as bait.

Pray these stories don't escape their box, please pray peace on Earth, salaam, shalom is not just super-marketeering what you need to buy or else things only get worse—truth to say the TV never answers me when I pray.

Still, here's superstar George Clooney recovering torn dura mater membrane of spinal cord, exercising wit in Italian villa personal tour for Ms. Sawyer who gah-gah gushes, "A guy from Kentucky has a pizza room!" New movie he directed about Edward R. Murrow nemesis Senator McCarthy inquisitions title *Good Night, and Good Luck,* was signature of newsman's newsman, used years ago in a poem of mine, I'd just like to mention—Clooney, very classy, won't take bait about girlfriend preference blond or brunette, looks happy being himself, average Joe who's who.

WHEN THE SURGEON
Geraldine Connolly

When the surgeon cuts the blackened nail
from your left big toe and wraps a bandage
around the remains, you stumble clumsily
out of the office, the pain deadened
until late that night when it sears through
your foot like a hot needle. It was something
you never noticed much, your toenail,
a small windowpane of hardened horn-like
bone. When you unwrap the bloody bandage
and stare at the toe, it's a face with no features.
Nothing looks back at you but
a lump of torn flesh, a seabed of red
shifting mudflats. Skinned of its covering
the toe lies fragile, unprotected.

Walking on it causes pain so you favor
your other foot, the right one. You drag
the left one behind you like a loose rope
then adopt a stiff rocking tilt of straightened
legs to avoid the pain. A ribbon of cotton
you wad up to cover the wound, an ointment
spread across it to soothe. Walking is
a given you have to relearn but the whole
smooth glide of it depends on that tiny
missing square you never thought about.
Without it you're a peg leg. The right

CHAUTAUQUA

foot leads. The left falters. You can feel
its absence like a lack of money. Your legs
are out of kilter. Like the body and the soul,
one drags behind, the other leaps forward.

Evening Marina

Geraldine Connolly

Each afternoon, twilight, deliberate,
comes like a suitor to the marina and opens
the shades on sunset's final sizzling blast of light.

The fisherman in his boat watches, intent,
gaff hook in hand, waits for the coppery strokes
of the blaze, its last fierce plummet of light.

As it unravels, a teenage boy dives from the bridge
across the wide vermilion gaze of stunned girl.
A widow makes her last voyage up to the corner store.

Foxes leap from dens. Ash trees tug at their leashes of fire.
Along the torn cove, a leaf swirls down and finds its way,
touching the wind above the stones, before it disappears.

The migrant worker picks cherries, tastes one, drops
the others into a tin pail. Etched trees like beautiful martyrs,
burn. Two geese lift and float across the island barrier.

a HUNGER FOR THE WORLD: THE PERSONAL STEPS OUT WITH THE POLITICAL

Faith Adiele

A lecture given at the Chautauqua Writers' Center, June 18, 2005

Good afternoon. The title of my talk today is *A Hunger for the World: The Personal Steps Out with the Political in Literary Nonfiction*. I want to build on Diana Hume George's talk this morning about the backlash against creative nonfiction—the accusations that it is self-indulgent, confessional, naval gazing—to talk about some of my favorite authors to teach, all of whom argue for the political, social and spiritual relevance of literary nonfiction, memoir in particular.

In his introduction to *The Granta Book of Reportage*, British editor Ian Jack supports the claim that reportage (definition: dedicated journalistic investigations, narrative journalism) has "replaced religion as the permanent backdrop" to our existence. In the best-known essay in her brilliant collection, *I Could Tell You Stories: Sojourns in the Land of Memory* (which are the strongest—and most gorgeous—arguments I've read for the importance of memoir), Patricia Hampl claims that the project of memoir is both necessary and "surprisingly political." "True memoir is written," she explains, "like all literature, in an attempt to find not only a self but a world...a hunger for the world." In his introduction to *The Business of Memory*, an anthology on the nature of memory in the technology age, poet, fiction writer and essayist Charles Baxter talks about the transformation of private memory into public event and the betrayal sometimes required. All three make a connection between the writer's hunger to engage with the world, either current or historic.

I recently taught a class based on these ideas called, *A Hunger for the World: Memoir & Reportage of Social Engagement*. The course considered the role of the writer, as a political, historical and spiritual being, in the larger world, and assessed that role through two different literary strategies—the memoir and reportage—asking if memoir, inward looking and subjective, and reportage, outward looking and fact-based, are in fact responses to the same concerns. Why does the engaged writer choose one strategy over the other to confront the world? What is the political potential of memoir? The spiritual potential of reportage? What is the relationship between the personal and political? The implications—and danger—of forgetting, as both individuals and nations?

Each week we studied narrative (memoir, reportage, documentary film) on such themes as the politics of naming, or recovery and forgetting in families and nations. The world we hungered for included Romania, where the state had co-opted and constructed history, complete with televised performances of trials, Hollywood's nostalgic construction and marketing of the Vietnam War, the Zapatistas' post-modern marketing of their Revolution in women's magazines and cyberspace, and the mythos and misinformation surrounding Africa, perpetuated by contemporary travel writers who just can't stop themselves from reading and referencing *Heart of Darkness* even when faced with the reality of Africa before them.

Hampl's essays are performative—they both create and then analyze the work of memoir. The most famous piece in the collection, *Memory & Imagination*, is the one I use to define and demonstrate true memoir. In it, Hampl recreates a lovely little moment from childhood, a piano lesson that the reader can see and hear, and then deconstructs what she has written, discovering that many of her memories are in fact inaccurate. Beginning students are usually enraged, despite the obvious inadvertency of Hampl's mistakes. (Theresa Jordan creates a similar moment with an account of her first memory, that of her father being attacked by a bull on their farm, a vivid scene full of churning dust and flailing limbs and panicked cowboys and she the little girl screaming on the sidelines—only to discover later, much to her surprise, that she wasn't yet born. The drama of the family myth somehow wormed its way into her psyche.) Hampl explains that "we store in memory only images of value," and that investigating the connection between these memories and their true meaning to us is the job of memoir. *Why* we remember something is often more important than what.

She then reveals the link between this remembering, flawed as our memories are, to the larger world. It is because "Each of us must possess a created version of the past." The stories we tell others and ourselves that explain who we are. And if we don't do this work, Hampl says, "someone else will do it for us. That is the scary political fact." My favorite book of literary journalism demonstrates her claim. Philip Gourevitch's award-winning and meticulously researched book, *We Regret to Inform You That Tomorrow We Will Be Killed With Our Families*, contextualizes the Rwandan genocide as essentially a failure of imagination, first colonial and then national, a public narrative (perpetuated on talk radio) that created false identities between identical groups—I can only be human if he is not. The most powerful confirmation of the power of narrative is in the incident he recounts of the Hutu invading a boarding school and telling the children to separate themselves into Hutus and Tutsis, so that the Hutu children can go free and the Tutsis be killed. And the children in their brilliance and compassion say there are no Hutus or Tutsis here; we are all Rwandan. And so what can the Hutu militants do when faced with a narrative that refuses theirs? They kill them all, even their own. And thus Hampl is proven correct: "The function of memory, while experienced as intensely personal, is surprisingly political."

I encourage you to read her other essays: *Reading Whitman During the Vietnam War* moves beautifully between obtaining for the first time birth control/female reproductive freedom/triumph of technology, being disillusioned with American identity in the face of the Vietnam War, and reading Walt Whitman and Emily Dickenson as poets who ostensibly staked out different territories, the public and the private. In *Milosz & Memory* she argues for more politically engaged and responsible

American memoir, explaining that in totalitarian regimes, "the work of memory becomes politically dynamic and personal testimony approaches danger, for its purpose becomes not only elegy but survival...at stake is the survival of memory itself." We Americans tend to privilege the individual, with "history just landscape" to the essential Horatio-Alger-like drama of the triumph of self, whereas anyone who comes from a group that has been historically oppressed will tell you that we are shaped by (and perhaps therefore responsible to) larger historical moments. The beauty of memoir is that it democratizes the process of national narrative. The official history, that which appears on TV and in books, belongs to the powerbrokers, the victors, whereas the true story was often lived on the ground, by ordinary folks. Memoir upends the hierarchy, saying that voices previously unheard can write the collective history. You don't need to be a politician or a PhD or an aristocrat. If you marched in Selma; if you marched to Bataan; if you survived the camps; if you survived the death of the family farm; if you survived your *family*, you can be that voice.

In the author's statement to my paperback (which I'm seeing for the first time) I admit that it took years for me to decide to write *Meeting Faith*. Sure, I fancied myself a writer and I had the data—a journal stuffed in a drawer for years—and sure, folks leaned in whenever I let slip at cocktail parties that I'd spent time as Thailand's first black Buddhist nun. So why not tell the story? When it comes to the messy, oft-misunderstood world of memoir, however, I believe that the question has to be far more passionate—more than *why not*, more like *why*? Why tell this story? What is your goal? What can be gained (and lost) from taking a personal, intimate experience and exposing it to the world?

I was already writing one memoir, about the impact of public, political events on families and individuals, using family narratives to find connections between the legacies of the African post-colonial experience, the American Civil Rights movement, and the Great Immigration from Europe, so I knew the work involved. I knew the years of laboring before a blank computer screen, convinced that no one would want to hear from some biracial farm girl who flunked out of school and made a wild gamble to reclaim her identity. I knew that in order to sound authentic, memoirists are often forced to share things we'd rather not, to offer up our warts and weakness. I knew that I risked being thought narcissistic and eager to confess things that still filled me with discomfort. *Why tell?*

In order to move your story out of the realm of catharsis and therapy and into the territory of art, I believe that you must be able to identify the larger, universal themes that will allow others to join you on the journey. I tell my students, "Ask yourself what this story is *really* about." Is it Russian student murders elderly neighbor, Loner murders Arab on the beach, Irish family grows up poor? Is it a wacky account of life with bugs in the Thai forest or a meditation on how to live life? If we do our jobs correctly, will our readers be somehow more human than when they first picked up the book? I encourage my students to move in two directions—down into the self to call up the specific details that make your story unique and distinct, and out into the world to root your personal tale in the larger world.

A similar thing happened with that first memoir-in-progress, part of which has been made into a PBS documentary, which grew out of another transformative journey, this one to Nigeria to meet my father and siblings for the first time. When I was twenty-six, my mother gave me my father's love letters. I became interested in how they demonstrated that the personal is political, in how the three of us were all intimately shaped by external events, how world history is family history. And so I set out to retrace his steps and find out what had become of the infant nation to which he had dedicated himself. I arrived to a bittersweet homecoming, delighted to be for once in an all-black country, and yet devastated to witness one of the worst military dictatorships ever. How could I write honestly about a place as misunderstood and maligned as "deepest, darkest Africa"? How could I show love and anger, blame both Western imperialism and native misrule?

Faith Adiele

I needed a new model. I turned to my former teacher, James Alan McPherson, whose essay, *El Camino Real*, appears in the aforementioned Baxter anthology. If you are interested in the intersection between personal writing, politics and spirituality, you must read it. It follows the narrator's complicated brilliance as he, a black man staying in a gated community, encounters a white homeless person in post-Rodney King L.A. and begins thinking about memoir, making connections between St. Augustine (the first memoirist who advised that "memory is the belly of the soul") and his mentor, Ralph Ellison (who takes inspiration from Odysseus when "[struggling] with form and with America"); Plato (who established the division between inner and outer) and OJ Simpson; his former student, Kathryn Harrison, whose *The Kiss* tells of an affair with her minister father and spiritual longing; Gandhi and Martin Luther King (whose activist principles show writers how to use a "period of inward-turning, of re-identification with our own ethical systems, as preparation for moving *out* of ourselves ... to see what in the outside world can be reclaimed"). The individual encounters the world and through personal understanding makes public meaning and purpose. Steps outside the gated community and onto El Camino Real, the royal road.

ELI MILLER'S SELTZER DELIVERY SERVICE

Emily Barton

Excerpted from the essay "Eli Miller's Seltzer Delivery Service"

The next afternoon, Eli drove up—not in the seltzer truck I'd been imagining, the open vehicle with bottles clanking that my father had bequeathed me from his memories, but in an old gray station wagon. He brought the seltzer up the front steps in the four-inch-high crate my father had recalled so fondly; that first delivery, all the bottles were clear, inscribed with the names of the various local factories where they'd been made back when my father was a child. (Our most recent delivery was two cases of cobalt blue bottles, except for one that was dark green and another a pale, soft green, like sea glass. That one, Eli told me, was a safety bottle, completely encased in rubber so I could drop it and it wouldn't break. I didn't try it to see.) Eli is in his seventies, but he's tall and strong, with a friendly smile and the kind of outgoing personality you'd predict for a deliveryman. His accent is pleasantly rough and guttural, part Brooklyn—he was born on Twenty-seventh Street in Coney Island, and grew up in Borough Park—and part Yiddish. (Recently he said to me, "I'm going to see my sister this weekend; she's coming to stay by my brother," a locution my grandparents used, but which now only seems to exist in the camped-up Yiddish world of movies like *The Hebrew Hammer*.) That first time he came, he brought a folder of articles that had been written about him for me to look through, and told me about a children's book, *The Seltzer Man*, that local writer, artist, and teacher Ken Rush had published about him in the 1990s. I ordered the book as soon as I finished hauling the seltzer upstairs—it was only ten bottles, but you have to be a big guy like Eli to carry them all at once.

The book's lovely, sun-drenched illustrations in oil are a rhapsody on the vanishing world of seltzer delivery.

Eli grew up in a Conservative Jewish family. His father, Meyer, went to synagogue for all the holidays, and Eli's grandfather owned a butcher shop, so they had a ready supply of kosher meat. Meyer was a housepainter and his wife, May, worked at Ratchik Bakery on Avenue J, but like many families of their generation, they stressed the importance of education, and their children are all highly literate. Eli's older brother became a teacher and an engineer; his younger brother is a computer graphic engineer for Dow Chemical; his sister is a professor at the University of Haifa and has twice been a Fulbright scholar. Eli himself wanted to be a schoolteacher, but when in 1952 he approached his favorite high school teacher, Mr. Hellerbogen, and asked if he should enter the profession, Mr. Hellerbogen said, "Eli, teachers don't make any money at all. You'd be better off driving a truck."

When Eli got out of the service, he went to work on Wall Street. He worked his way up from dividend clerk to cashier, and found himself making $125 a week by 1960—a living wage, but no better than he might have made as a teacher. When he told this to his friend Seymour Kooperman, who drove a soda route, Seymour bragged that he made $300 a week. Eli challenged him to show him how, and Seymour drove him around to prove it. "He was right!" Eli recalls. "There was money in this business."

Not long after, he was sitting around in his cousin Lowell Wexler's collision shop on the corner of Ralph and Remsen near Eastern Parkway, wondering what he should do about his future. "You see that soda shop?" Lowell said, pointing to the place across the street. "All the black guys in the neighborhood go in and buy a beer called Copenhagen Castle. You like to sell; you should go get a truck and sell that beer."

The shop was owned by two brothers, Harry and Jerry Hittelman. Eli went over and asked about buying maybe ten cases to start a business in Bedford-Stuyvesant, which none of the beverage delivery men served. Harry told him he was crazy to think about going into Bed-Stuy to sell; there weren't any soda men there for a reason. "Whatever you do," Eli remembers him saying, "sell for cash. Don't give credit." Eli bought thirty cases for a total of sixty dollars, which he didn't have on him, but his Uncle Irving across the street vouched for him. Then he needed a truck. He found a used van, a black 1949 Chevy, "the old-fashioned kind, with the two doors that opened in back," for $190. Eli's savings, after buying the beer, amounted to $150, so he went to his mother and asked to borrow forty dollars. "I don't have it," she said, "but if you need it to go into business, you could take my silver dollars." Eli didn't want to take them—many were from the 1870s, and he knew they were valuable—but he didn't have any other way to get the money, so he accepted. ("And I still feel bad about it," he says. "I paid her back tenfold, but those silver dollars had been special to her.") He paid for the used truck with $150 in cash and the forty silver dollars, went out with his thirty cases to Bed-Stuy, and sold all of them, half on credit.

When he went back to Harry Hittelman to report his success and buy more, Hittelman said, "You gave those blacks credit on fifteen cases? You'll never see that money." Eli disagreed. "They were honest people," he told him. "They'll be very appreciative that I came around to the neighborhood and trusted them. You'll see." To me he adds, "And wouldn't you know, when I went back the next week, I got every penny."

Eli built up a good route in Bed-Stuy, first with the Copenhagen Castle, which he describes as "similar to a Miller, but less expensive," and later with soda water and the flavored syrups to make Italian sodas. By 1963 he had to sell the van and buy a big clanking seltzer truck like the one my father remembers. But soon after John F. Kennedy was shot, some black kids broke into his truck. When he asked them why, they told him, "We don't want whiteys in our neighborhood," and that they thought the assassination was a white conspiracy. This was an isolated incident; "My customers were good people," he says. "People weren't like that." But soon after Martin Luther King's assassination, a group of young men broke into his truck when it was parked at the corner of Park Place and Bedford, and these kids wanted to fight with him. Eli ran to a nearby drugstore, told the druggist what was going on, and the man came out to the street to defend him. "The drugstore man had been in the neighborhood a long time, and he knew the kids. When he told them he'd turn them in, they ran away." The truck was mostly empty, but Eli felt lucky that no one had been injured. After this, he decided he had to stop working in the neighborhood. When he went around to tell his old customers that he wouldn't be coming anymore, he felt awful. Some offered to come meet him at the curb, so he wouldn't have to come up to their apartments and leave his truck unattended, but it made more sense to move into more middle-class neighborhoods like Bensonhurt and Bay Ridge. Later he also started coming up to Brooklyn Heights and Cobble Hill. Over time, even as business has dwindled, he's also had many customers in Brighton Beach, where there are lots of Russians and older Jews—people who consider seltzer important. He gets his bottles sterilized and refilled by Kenny Gomberg at G & K Beverages in Canarsie, the last seltzer bottler in New York City.

Eli's seltzer is more expensive than the kind we got in the store, so we don't drink it with the same abandon, and the taste is different: saltier, more metallic, sharper. Learning to control the pressure was trickier than we'd expected; we had a few days of wet countertop before we mastered it. Even with soy milk, it makes phenomenal egg creams. But more important, we like having the crates and bottles in our kitchen, a tie to this city's past. I like the connection to my father's childhood, my aunts' and uncle's childhoods, and a world that was based around neighborhoods, where you knew the people who lived next door and ran the shop around the corner. I don't kid myself that Eli is my friend, but I really like him. Not since I was a child and my parents took me to Al at National Shoe Rebuilders so they could have my shoes resoled and I could pet Al's dogs, Lucky and Jenny, and his cat, Snowy, have I so been able to look forward to seeing someone I know so little; and it's a welcome relief in this world in which we do much of our shopping on the Internet, much of our communicating with family and friends on e-mail, to sit on the stoop with Eli and talk politics. He's a lifelong Democrat—a huge supporter of Barack Obama's bid for the Democratic nomination, "though I'm not sure the country is ready for him yet"—and sharp in his critique of the Bush administration. "Eighty percent of Americans want us to get the troops home from Iraq," he says, "and he won't do it. Which makes him a murderer—boys are coming home missing arms, missing legs; more are going to die just because he's pigheaded, not to mention all the Iraqis who are getting killed. And for a trillion dollars! He could have given health care to every man, woman, and child in America for that. He could have given housing to four hundred thousand low-income families. And instead he's going to go down as the most reviled president in our history."

SMALL CITIZENS

Maggie Anderson

Today was my political nap.
I lay down to it, febrile with accumulated
rage at poverty and hunger in the world,
as if they were my own shameful secrets.
I forced my eyelids shut and behind them
could still see the red roof across the street,
shiny, and healing as valerian in the sunlight.
A stone was rolling down to the tin gutter
with the thunkety assurance of my five-year-old
cries from the playground in Fort Lee
when the ice cream truck would ring its bell
and stop beside the green park bench.
We children were citizens, even then,
and our city had a chain link fence
beyond which we could just make out
the grid of windows on the brick apartments
where our mothers or housekeepers labored
and watched us from above. I couldn't
read then and thought the Newark airport
lights were Russian bombs. How could I
have known what my own mother meant
by her anger at nobody I knew? She told me,
when I asked, *Politics means money, who
has it and who doesn't*. So, for a brief time,
in the early 1950s, this was my one clear
political vision: from sandbox and swings
our high voices shouted, *ice cream*, as
warm nickels tumbled down from the hands
of women, their faces full of charity
and blessing at the opened windows.

Man is an animal which, alone among the animals, refuses to be satisfied by the fulfillment of animal desires.

—Alexander Graham Bell

THE LIFE OF THE SPIRIT

Winter Psalm

Richard Hoffman

Boston snowbound, Logan closed, snowplows
and salt-trucks flashing yellow, drifts
tall as a man some places, visibility poor,
I sit by the window and watch the snow

blow sideways north-northeast, hot cup
in hand, robe over pajamas.
You have made me to seek refuge
and charged me to care for my brothers.

How cruel. That could only be You out there
howling, cracking the trees, burying everything.
What could I possibly want from You
that would not undo the whole world as it is?

The Saint Who Could Talk to the Damned

Liz Rosenberg

There once was a saint who could talk to the damned. That man was my uncle, we'll get to him in a moment. His family was as normal as one can expect. They knew how to have a nice time. Yes, they claimed to trace their roots all the way back to Gan Eden, but the same might be said of any number of dimestore Jews. My father, G-d rest his soul, my uncle's brother, was an ordinary man. Bright and hard-working. Likewise his mother and father. My uncle was the cheese in the rhyme, who stands alone.

The damned, you may know, are nearly all possessed by demons, who force them to commit unforgivable sins. Occasionally, you find a half-formed soul who simply likes to have a good time at everyone else's expense. That person may not possess a demon at all, but after death will certainly become one, cursed to wander the earth for a certain number of days and nights.

The New York City public school system administered an IQ test when my uncle was a little stick of a thing, and discovered that he had the highest measurable IQ they had ever known. In fact he had the highest IQ measured of anyone, at any time, except for a poet and philosopher named Goethe—author of, among other doozies, *Faust* and *The Sorrows of Young Werther*. Goethe's IQ score was a shade higher than my uncle's. They were both six years old at the time they were tested, and one might say that Goethe had an advantage, having been born into a patrician family in Frankfurt, while my uncle's father Simon drove a cab in Manhattan before founding a hoola-hoop and slippity-slide empire out on Long Island.

Uncle Ian would have gladly let Goethe win the IQ contest at any rate. My uncle was beautiful, inside and out, with golden-blond hair that fluffed around his head like a dandelion. Old ladies went bananas over him. Babysitters and nannies likewise coddled him.

My father, dark, squat, roughly the size and shape of a fire hydrant, was of course jealous of his heavenly, brilliant twin. He convinced Ian to let him cut off the golden curls because a very high forehead (like my father's) was, he said, a mark of intelligence. He trimmed his twin's long eyelashes while he was at it. However the whole kit and kaboodle grew back in, and my father was in the doghouse for the rest of his life. Families never forget and they never forgive. I have often wondered how bright my uncle could have been to let himself be shorn like a lamb by my father, but then, I am not a saint.

Uncle Ian did not speak a word until he was three and a half years old, and when he did, he said, "Give five dollars to the blind man."

A blind man was begging on a street corner in Greenwich Village, with a cup of unsharpened pencils. (It has always seemed to me for a buck you should at least get a pencil with a nice point on it.) Five dollars was a lot of money back then. You could build a house for twenty, if you were clever and borrowed most of the materials. But my grandparents worried about their mute youngest boy, the twin who hung onto my father's bare heel and followed him patiently out into the world like a man waiting in the rain for a cab while others duck in ahead of him, one after another. They were thrilled when he finally said anything, so they gave my uncle the loose change they had between them, and he dropped it all into the blind man's outstretched palm.

The blind man weighed it a moment, his whitish-blue orbs rolled toward heaven. He cocked his head toward Uncle Ian as if he could hear his saintliness ticking in his breast. "The little man has a heavy hand," he chanted, and blessed him. Chances are my uncle would have become a saint anyway, but that clinched it.

At his elementary school labored many of the damned, including a little Russian émigré, a boy who would speak to no one but my uncle

Ian. Ian already understood half a dozen languages. To him alone the boy would whisper what he wanted for lunch, the answer to the question the teacher had posed, and various obscene insults and curses for Ian to convey to the other children. Sometimes the boy would tell his dreams, in a harsh, garbled voice. Sooner or later my uncle grew suspicious. One day while the little boy was spewing in his ear a vividly lewd dream, involving several little girls from the grade below them, my uncle raised his arms and called, "Demon, Demon! Come out from the body of the boy."

What a mess! Demons don't like to travel alone, they come in pairs, in trios with their arms entwined around each other's necks, in packs, like wild dogs. My uncle's first-grade classroom was filled with screaming and high-pitched squealing and the stench of burned flesh, all of it wrapped in mottled-gray smoke. It took an hour before they could be sure all the children were still there, alive and well, which they were, thanks be to G-d, though the poor Russian boy had quite a headache.

After that, the boy moved his chair to the back of the room, away from my uncle. He grew up to be a well-known dentist in Manhattan, Dr. R—, but he later killed himself, the poor soul. Some people can't live with their demons; others cannot live without them.

After that episode, it was hard for Uncle Ian to find friends to play with on the playground. Even his own brother avoided him; and he was not a welcome guest in the faculty lunch room either. But from time to time some poor soul would creep up to him, and begin confiding, and that would be the damned, in one guise or another—for instance, the overweight art teacher who wept over the children's paintings but cut them up with scissors at night; the gym teacher who could not restrain himself from shaking the high bars when the girls were on it; any number of children who committed a number of sins, from graffiti to graft.

There was even one girl whose demon had caused her to murder her own grandmother. Yes, one day the old woman was acting in an evil manner toward her grandchildren—all the fresh ginger cookies she had just baked, she insisted on keeping for visitors the next day. Not important visitors, either. All of the grandchildren were crying over the forbidden cookies, and this particular child—a dark-haired girl with dark sunken eyes—performed a dance on the floorboards above the kitchen, right over the grandmother's head. They all wished her dead, but the dark-haired one actually chanted a song about it.

Die the grandmother did, that very night, in her sleep, as peacefully as a china doll. All the other grandchildren remembered the dancing, and the way the dark-eyed girl had sung, "I wish the old lady would die, would die."

After that, she was an outcast. Poor, shriveled little thing. She was like a burnt matchstick with no light left. Ramona, her name was. She would scribble in the mud with a stick, writing who knows what incantations, and then rub them out with the bottom of her Buster Brown shoe. The kind of girl whose laces were always untied, and whose parents neglected to wash her face in the morning because they couldn't bear to look at it.

Uncle Ian had a happy childhood, despite what you might think. He taught himself things. He read history, and tinkered with machines and engines at his father's cab company. He drew wonderful likenesses of people.

In truth he enjoyed the company of certain demons even more than the company of ordinary people. He had great sympathy for the damned, regardless of their sins. He was seldom entirely alone, even in the middle of the night, when the damned like to wander out and find someone to pour their troubles to. It's not the same as a regular childhood friend, but it was better than nothing. My uncle was a boy who could play with a rubber band for hours, happy and content.

They lived in midtown, close to the central garage where the taxi cabs were stored for the night. Manhattan is nothing if not a city of demons. Beautiful demons; old, sad, raggedy ones; small and foreign ones; native demons; wandering and temporary demons looking to be cast out into the streets, into the Hudson River or into a new body.

Like humans, demons suffer in leading a split existence. Rather than be tied to a twig of goodness all their life, they will try to break the body they inhabit. My Uncle Ian coaxed many of the damned back from ledges and bridges. But to look at Uncle Ian you'd never know he'd had an unhappy minute. His eyes sparkled like two struck flints, he had a sly sense of humor, he was always playing tricks, telling jokes. He taught me a magic spell that makes traffic lights turn from red to green, but if you think I'm going to share that with you—forget it.

Like most saints, my uncle hit a wall somewhere in his twenties. He was down and out. He had wandered so far off the beaten path no one but a demon could find him. He listened to sad blues and started playing the trumpet, which got him evicted from more than one dingy one-room flat. He was driving cabs at night for his father's company, and he visited little coffee houses and bars, crack houses and opium dens.

He was addicted to sainthood, the way other folks are addicted to gambling, drugs, sex or the Yankees. He lost girlfriends to his pals. He gave away his college tuition to a friend, then he himself dropped out, got drafted into the army, and was sent home with a 4F. His father, my Pappy Simon, set him up in an art gallery in the Village—near where they had first seen the blind man begging. Uncle Ian, a poor businessman to say the least, gave away most of the store to people who liked art and said they couldn't afford it. He gave me a beautiful gold pin of two angels joined at the breast, (I still have it) but not long after that the gallery went bankrupt and he took up driving a Checker cab where my grandpappy had left off years earlier.

Uncle Ian's cab, yellow as a rainslicker and fat, had black and white checks on its sides. Best of all, inside were two extra little seats, folded metal stools you could pull up and sit on, facing the other passengers. Of course we children fought over the little metal stools, eventually outlawed by some demon working at the DMV. There was never any question of inviting Uncle Ian into the family toy business. He would have bankrupted it in a month. Instead he drove the Checker cab from my granddaddy's old fleet and lived in a fleabag hotel near Seventh Avenue in the Village.

One night, wandering along the nether regions of the Hudson River, Uncle Ian heard a faint cry coming from the edge of a sidewalk. It appeared to be coming straight from the gutter, underneath the street itself. He went closer to have a good look. It was nearly dawn, the sky blue as a ripe plum still wet from the long night.

This was the hour when most of the damned had fled for their lives, but here came a voice from a cardboard box parked near the corner of Hudson and Fourth. From the cardboard house a hand reached out, tiny. It looked like a child's hand, wearing a ring with a blue stone in it. My uncle poked his head inside and cowering in the far corner of the box was Ramona, the dark-haired girl who had urged the death of her own grandmother. She whimpered when she first saw him. This is not uncommon for the damned in the presence of a saint. Things don't often go well for them. But then she recovered, smiled craftily, and beckoned him inside. He went, stooping over, because Uncle Ian, I have neglected to say, was tall and skinny, slump-shouldered, like a raggedy blue heron.

Going inside the box was his big mistake. You need to deal with demons out in the open, where you have plenty of room to maneuver. This demon was a clever one. She had been cast out into the howling world for a long time. But my uncle, as I say, was at the end of his own rope. He had had too many conversations with the damned. It is possible they had rubbed off on him, their despair of ever conquering our tawdry little planet. Uncle Ian climbed inside the cardboard house, which was larger than it looked from the outside, big enough for two to sit comfortably, with a rag rug on the floor, a copper tea kettle and a little fire from sticks Ramona had gathered down by the wharves.

They talked about their childhood, about old school friends nearly forgotten but remembered now, as clearly as if they'd been standing in front of them with colored chalk in their hands. Together they conjured up the lost childish faces and voices. The demon confided her loneliness. She too was down on her luck. It was exhausting to have been damned so long and still to have to drag one's body around, through childhood, into adolescence, and onward. There was a fishy and a perfumed smell from Ramona's long black hair, and before you knew it, my uncle was in a trance. For the first time in his life, he felt at home —there, in the smelly little cardboard box.

There was a glinting little red flame flickering in the demon's eyes, but was Uncle Ian paying attention? Instead he leaned forward sleepily, like a man turning over in bed, and kissed her, which was exactly what Ramona had been waiting for, all night, maybe all month—all her life, curled up inside the smoky cardboard box. The demon inside her leaped out of her mouth and headed straight for my uncle's brain, that vast, bright, complicated machine, with all its gears and pulleys and buttons and levers and nerves and fibers It was a good, big brain, and it reacted fast, batting the demon back out so that it ricocheted and was heading right back into the woman's body, that doomed tunnel without a light. My uncle took hold. He reached out with both hands and pulled the demon to his breast. He said, "I will not let thee go except thou bless me," the only thing he recalled from the family bible.

Consider what might have happened if he had said, "Blessed are the meek," or "Jesus wept." His whole life would have been different. The demon would have gone howling out into the dawn and sunk into the Hudson River without a bubble. Instead they were bound together with her demon as surely as if a rabbi had crouched in there with them, and it had been a wedding chuppa they embraced under, instead of a box.

Uncle Ian surrendered everything that remained to him—a rickety wooden chair, a desk; his paint easel; a mattress, and a small white gas cookstove, and dragged it all out to the cardboard house on the corner. It was not a perfect dwelling, but it was cool in summer, and warm in winter, heated by the demon's breath, which they shared between them, like a fever lovers pass gladly back and forth. Of course when it was her turn to nurse him, she never was around—off to the park or to stand gloomily looking out over a bridge.

"What a burden you are," she would say.

But when it was his turn to nurse her, his blue eyes took on a brilliant rain-washed shine, like a June sky. He was happy. He took up whistling. He kept the Checker cab downtown, at the curb close to the cardboard box, and because my uncle was blessed, somehow he always found a parking space.

Sometimes he collected good fares from the passengers going to Newark, and sometimes a big tip which he and Ramona squandered on ice cream and nice restaurants, while other days he drove all over the island of Manhattan, top to bottom, without collecting one plug nickel. Then they would eat the berries and twigs he gathered in Central Park. Ramona would complain bitterly while my uncle tried to distract her by balancing a feather on his nose. That was almost always worth a laugh, or at least a gurgle from her skinny mouth.

One winter, Ramona came down with the flu. No matter how hard she tried, she could not hand it off to Uncle Ian. It was the fiercest winter in memory. Ice formed like a gray skin over the curved breast of the Hudson. Icicles dripped from the opening of the cardboard box, and the chill seeped from the sidewalk into their bones. Ramona's fevered ague, whatever it was, grew worse, soured like something left out on a shelf and turned to pneumonia. Uncle Ian tried to reclaim the disease. He argued with the demon, cajoled it, begged it to hand over the illness. He would crouch in front of her, trying to breathe in the writhing viral half-life that staggers on untouched in the human body for years. But the disease, whatever it was, the plague, was caught in Aunt Ramona like a hook in the mouth of a fish. Perhaps her demon was tired of this earth and wanted to die. Death is a demon's only release, and still it must wander the earth another 364 days after death, paying off old debts.

Uncle Ian was stubborn as a mule, like any saint, and refused to give her up. He sold his art supplies to buy her medicines. He drove the cab all hours, into deadly neighborhoods, trying to collect enough fares to pay the doctors and the herbalists, the acupuncturists and quacks. No use. Nothing was any use. She tried to drive him away, with howls and imprecations, with threats. "You wear me out!" she would cry.

That next morning it snowed. It had been snowing all night, snowing like there would be no tomorrow. A cold flood entered their flimsy dwelling, driving them out at last, though Ramona clung feverishly to the cardboard flaps.

Uncle Ian carried her out. She was not much more than a hank of hair and a pair of burning black eyes. Once she had been brought out of it, the cardboard box dissolved in the snow, caved, collapsed and turned to brown mush. He carried her through a multitude of falling white dots into the cab and drove in the worst snowstorm in New York's history, up toward Mt. Sinai, then back down the middle of Fifth Avenue to St. Vincent's.

Manhattan was soundless under the onslaught of snow. There was not another car in sight, not a bus, not a loose dog. Thunder rolled and lightning zig-zagged high over Fifth Avenue; it looked like the end of the world. Four tourists staggered past St. Patrick's Cathedral, tried the vast front wooden doors, found them locked and staggered on single file, like geese against the snow. Any other day, of course, Uncle Ian would have taken them wherever they needed to go. But now he hunched over the steering wheel, and drove on, mumbling under his breath. Aunt Ramona wheezed in the back seat, whispering with her demon's last breath.

"Give it up, why don't you," she croaked into his ear. "Stop it. Stop!"

He did stop. He stopped the cab. The light at the corner of Fifth Avenue and Fifty-ninth Street had turned red, burning like a small sun in the midst of the storm, red as a bloodshot eye staring into Uncle Ian's. He did not say the spell that would have turned it green, though

I know that he could have done it in seven seconds. Instead he waited, mumbling to himself. Snow fell without pity around the cab.

It came down in long, slow strokes, like a judgment. It swirled against the windshield, clogged the squeaking wipers, weighing them until they could no longer move. Now the front window of the Checker cab filled to the top with white, and then the side windows and the rear window too, as if a brush had swirled itself all over the glass. Inside the cab it was pure white, cave-like, as bright as the inside of a cathedral. My uncle continued to mumble. What else had he ever asked for, for whom had he intervened?

The engine shuddered and shook. Slowly, jerkily, the cab began to buck above the macadam, and then to rise. It swayed in the harsh winter wind. My uncle laughed, a pure sound sharp as a bell in the air. The cab touched earth again, it buckled and bowed like a leaping horse, and then, catching an updraft, it sailed swiftly above the traffic light, drifted to the top of four-story brick apartment houses, then further, above the highest buildings. It rose over the Empire State Building, sweeping above the Chrysler Building, with my aunt and uncle inside, my aunt screaming now, clawing to get out of the locked cab. But my uncle would not let her go. His hands gripped the wheel, his blue eyes glinting like the hottest part of the candle flame, his soul ascending, and the last anyone ever saw of them, they were in the old Checker cab together, flying directly into God's waiting hands.

OSSUARY, MT. ATHOS

Robert Cording

Three years after his death, each monk
is exhumed, his bones laid out on shelves

and labeled with the name he once was called by.
Shinbones, ribs, shoulder blades, spine

and skull: the final pronouncement on a life,
the monks believe, since the bones

of a good monk will, when returned to the light,
be clean and sweet-scented, a bad monk's rank

and blackened by their time underground.
The living enter this room of disrobed bones

to remind themselves how all that is now
hidden will be known eventually in time.

But surely, surely there is a monk who, looking at
those arrangements of bones and knowing all

too well his own nature, cries out: *O Lord,
whatever I know of myself is flawed, always,*

*I fear, the creation of a too supple mind
and tongue. Lord, it is not the future I dread,*

CHAUTAUQUA

but the rankness that may lie now inside me
and that I can never fully know nor escape,

despite my best intentions, despite
even my petitions that ask again for forgiveness

and correction, for the grace of praising
without self-interest, and with due love.

THE NEW EGYPT
Robin Becker

I think of my father who believes
a Jew can outwit fate by owning land.
Slave to property now, I mow
and mow, my destiny the new Egypt.
From his father, the tailor, he learned not
to rent but to own; to borrow to buy.
To conform, I disguise myself and drag
the mower into the drive, where I ponder
the silky oil, the plastic casing, the choke.
From my father, I learned the dignity
of exile and the fire of acquisition,
not to live in places lightly, but to plant
the self like an orange tree in the desert
and irrigate, irrigate, irrigate.

HOUSEHOLD SPIRITS
Jeffrey Harrison

Halfway to heaven, high up on a pole,
and the pole planted firmly in the earth,
the martin house in my grandparents' back yard
came back to me on the earth's other side
when I saw the spirit houses in Thailand:
miniature shrines for household gods
placed on stands outside of every house
where the shadow of the house will never fall.
Astrologers determine the exact location
and the right time to perform the ceremony:
flowers are scattered and ritual waters poured
to appease the spirits thought to bring
happiness and prosperity to the household.
But if everything is not done properly
they can do evil and haunt the house itself.
"Good spirits will not live where there is dirt,"
a Shaker saying goes, and I remember
my grandfather telling me the birds
would refuse the house if it wasn't neat enough.
But they hadn't refused it, and a colony
of purple martins lived in the many compartments—
flighty utopians, the spirits of that farmhouse,
gathering overhead in buoyant swarms,
water in their voices, sky on their wings.

VISITATION

Jeffrey Harrison

for my mother

Walking past the open window, she is surprised
by the song of the white-throated sparrow
and stops to listen. She has been thinking of
the dead ones she loves—her father who lived
over a century, and her oldest son, suddenly gone
at forty-seven—and she can't help thinking
she has called them back, that they are calling her
in the voices of these birds passing through Ohio
on their spring migration...because, after years
of summers in upstate New York, the white-throat
has become something like the family bird.
Her father used to stop whatever he was doing
and point out its clear, whistling song. She hears it
again: "Poor Sam Peabody Peabody Peabody."
She tries not to think, "Poor Andy," but she
has already thought it, and now she is weeping.
But then she hears another, so clear, it's as if
the bird were in the room with her, or in her head,
telling her that everything will be all right.
She cannot see them from her second-story window—
they are hidden in the new leaves of the old maple,
or behind the white blossoms of the dogwood—
but she stands and listens, knowing they will stay
for only a few days before moving on.

WHITE PEOPLE, WHITE BIBLE

Stanley Plumly

The only one in the King James version
I could find, the bleached-out leather cover
matched with notes, concordance, summaries,
and zippered with a small gold cross tied
like a tool to the zipper. There were photographs
pale as postcards in nostalgia shops
written on in pencil. *Plain of Esdraelon,
A Dead Sea Scrolls Cave Site.* Maps and pictures
of sample flora: poppies, green wheat,
the seminal olive, and branches of figs
in spring. *It is written—where?—man shall
not live by bread alone . . . Who is my mother?
and who are my brethren?*

                    But my Aunt Ora
looking up at night, at heaven, reading
the dark, reading the scattered star-point
spellings, reading, in her mind, the word indited,
how the strict oracular letters suffer print,
suffer verses to be built, compounded
into chapters, into black indelible strategies,
margins to corners, authenticating black
in column after column, difficult in density,
capacity, totem, would worry about the whiteness
of the thing. *King David was old and stricken
in years, and they covered him with clothes,*

Stanley Plumly

but gat no heat—in black and white, we say,
meaning nothing could be clearer.

                                     As for
skin-and-bones-whiter-with-disease, these,
like Ora, stricken, broken, sitting through
chain-smoking half the night, will soon enough
think poetry and prose a wiry involucre
of type, reciting, with ribbons around their wrists,
what they remember, singing to themselves
the psalms, as if the weight of words had risen
from the page in levitation of each sentence
at a time until the page is white again and pure
for the bluest or brownest eyes: a blinding light
in greeting; a burning light, a wall,
where nothing will be written,
where the spirit calling will be spiritual.

Hedge Crickets Sing: Some Thoughts on Art and Spirituality

Robert Cording

In Thorton Wilder's *Our Town*, Emily, who has died in childbirth, is granted her request by the stage manager to relive one day. During that day, she's pained by the beauty of the ordinary and even more so by our lack of awareness of it. When Emily goes back to the graveyard to be with the company of the dead lying there, she asks the stage manager, "Do any human beings ever realize life while they live it?" *That we should realize life as we live it*—isn't that the great wake-up call of the Bible, from Moses' last warnings to the stiff-necked Israelites that they must choose life or death to Christ's constant attempts to help his disciples realize the Kingdom they desire is always here and always coming. As the minister in Marilyne Robinson's *Gilead* realizes, "Right worship is right perception." And what is right perception? Again, *Gilead*: "The tree just glistened—people talk that way when they want to call attention to a thing existing in excess of itself, so to speak, a sort of purity or lavishness, at any rate something ordinary in kind but exceptional in degree." I want to look at this familiar but always strange conjunction of the ordinary and exceptional, those moments when we realize, as Keats did in his poem "To Autumn," that "hedge crickets sing": both the unexceptional fact of the song and its exceptional lavishness. When we realize, that is, that we *know* far more than our intellect tells us, far more than we could believe with our finite minds.

Robert Frost's poem "Two Tramps in Mud Time" is, in part, about the force of one of those ordinary/extraordinary moments. In the poem, Frost's speaker looks for a reason why, when two out-of-work lumberjacks approach him as he splits wood on a beautiful April day, he doesn't give them the job. Part of him can freely acknowledge that he "ha[s] no right to play/With what [is] another man's work for gain." But another part of him has already been given over to the work itself, to the delight of swinging an ax on an early spring day in New England. Here's Frost:

> The time when most I loved my task
> These two must make me love it more
> By coming with what they came to ask.
> You'd think I never had felt before
> The weight of the ax-head poised aloft,
> The grip on earth of outspread feet,
> The life of muscles rocking soft
> And smooth and moist in vernal heat.

The day has already given "loose to [his] soul," freeing him to feel the bounty of a first New England spring day. Lost in his work, in his own body, in the good weather, the speaker is fully absorbed by the enjoyment of his activity. Consider those lush, rocking iambs as Frost lingers over the pleasure of "muscles rocking soft/and smooth and moist in vernal heat." Thus, if he gives his work to the unemployed tramps, he will lose more than a few bucks. Yet, when the speaker finally gives his reason why he will send the unemployed tramps away and continue to split his own wood, he turns to a nobler explanation:

> My object in living is to unite
> My avocation and my vocation
> As my two eyes make one in sight.
> Only where love and need are one,
> And the work is play for mortal stakes,
> Is the deed ever really done
> For Heaven and the future's sakes.

This nobler explanation is part truth, part rationalization. On the one hand, Frost wants us to see that he cannot part with his own enjoyment, even when others need the work for food. On the other hand, Frost wants us to acknowledge that the aim of living is indeed the union of our avocation and vocation. To put the matter a little differently, Frost's poem tries to create the *experience* of those moments when we step outside linear time, when the rhythms of work connect with the rhythms of nature, and we live inside one of the inmost truths of religion—that there is an integral rightness to life. In that sense, our work is indeed for "mortal stakes," because in those activities where we unite our avocation and vocation, we return once again to the lost Eden where work once expressed the creative will of creation. Work, that is, resumes its deep connection to "play," when our labor is not toil (even if it is hard) because all our energies are concentrated in the activity itself and the "I" that too often sees itself toiling, disappears.

I've often said to my students, only half-jokingly, that the secret of life is to have a task that they can devote their entire life to, something they can bring their whole self to for their whole life. For the French theologian and philosopher, Simone Weil, when the most commonplace truth "floods the whole soul," it is like a revelation. The "revelation" in Frost's poem occurs when the speaker suddenly feels the grip of his feet on the earth, the weight of the axe-head poised in the air, the fluid movement of his muscles, and the intimate connection between his work and the preciousness and precariousness of an April day in New England. He understands with his whole body the truth which is evident: that our labor can return, if only temporarily, the ease and unselfconsciousness before the Fall when "love and need" were one. He is fully awake, that is, to life as he is living it.

But most of the time, we are, as Emily realizes in *Our Town*, frightfully asleep. She says to her mother at one point, "Mama, just look at me one minute as though you really saw me." We know too well how fast life goes by without our always seeing it. The older we get, the farther away we seem from those deep responses to the world we once had as children. It is no accident that in Tolstoy's great story, "The Death of

Ivan Ilyich," Ivan, opening himself at last to the possibility that he has not truly lived, begins to think of childhood as the one authentic time of his life. For him, and for most of us, living according to "propriety," or living without truly realizing what life is, brings on the gathering weight of death. What Ivan Illyich does not want to admit, even to himself, is that all his choices were dictated not by what he loved, but rather by what society prized. His experience of life has been second hand, routine. The great irony of the story, of course, is that Ivan comes most fully alive at the moment of his death.

Many different philosophers and religious thinkers have understood that we live daily on time's cross. On the horizontal axis of that cross, we live from moment to moment, day to day, year to year until we die. As Shakespeare points out, "Like as the waves make towards the pebbled shore,/So do our moments hasten to their end." The experience of living on this horizontal axis generates bumper stickers like: *Life Sucks and Then You Die*. Or *He Who Has The Most Toys Wins*. Time, that is, should be used to accrue as much as possible before it runs out. We essentially become consumers who feel lost unless we are consuming. We live as Ivan Illyich lived. But, of course, when we live only on this horizontal axis, we also realize, whether we want to or not, that we will never have enough or that what we have is never quite satisfying. And, as Ivan realizes to his great distress, we still die.

When we think of time only as a succession of moments, we cry out, recognizing that what we love and who we love will be lost. Yet part of us always knows that the fulfilment of life cannot be in its future. The future is always where things come to their end. We know, too, but how easily we forget, that the point of life is not that we should live forever. Thus the fulfilment of life can only lie in another experience of time—on the vertical axis of the time's cross. That axis cuts across linear time and points towards eternity. The "eternity" I speak of is not some "other" realm, but rather the way moments of meaningfulness—of beauty, goodness, holiness, justice, love—intersect linear time, become actual and incarnate, and bestow meaning on time. One of my favorite poems, and the poem from which I take the title for this talk, is Keats's "Ode to Autumn." In the last section of the Ode, we're told not to think of the songs of Spring as Autumn comes into its ripening fullness and, consequently, its end. Keats addresses the personified Autumn like this:

> Where are the songs of Spring? Ay, where are they?
>   Think not of them, thou has thy music too,—
> While barred clouds bloom the soft-dying day,
>   And touch the stubble-plains with rosy hue,
> Then in a wailful choir the small gnats mourn
>   Among the river sallows, borne aloft
>   Or sinking as the light wind lives or dies;
> And full-grown lambs loud-bleat from hilly bourn;
>   Hedge-crickets sing, and now with treble soft
> The red-breast whistles from the garden-croft;
>   And gathering swallows twitter in the sky.

Keats directs us not to the future but to a series of present-tense, full-bodied moments: the "barred clouds bloom the soft-dying day" in an explosion of refracted light; the "wailful choir" of gnats rise and fall as the wind rises and falls above the river. Can you hear, the poem asks, how on the hillside, lambs bleat; how, nearby, hedge crickets sing; a red-breast whistles; above, swallows twitter. The meaningfulness of autumn, its beauty, becomes actual and incarnate to us only when we are entirely present to the presentness of the gnats; to that whistling bird; to the hedge-crickets that sing. Only when we attend, giving all our attention to the here, now.

In the beautiful rhythms of Genesis 1, God repeatedly looks at his creation and says that it is "good." We sense as well the deeply intuited truth of the connection between the creation and human beings: "So God created humankind in his image, in the image of God he created them." In this story, God places human beings in the world to cherish its goodness, to love its beauty, to know its truth—to perceive the eternal in the temporal. What distinguishes us as human beings is just this capacity. We have the freedom, as Aristotle put it, to grasp the order of the cosmos through the intellect and choose to honor it. We are not better than the rest of creation; we're given "dominion" only because we, like God, can recognize the created world as "good," as having an integral rightness. As human beings we are fully capable of seeing beyond the consecutive order of linear time to the fundamental vision of Genesis: that there is something rather than nothing. The fulfilment of time does not lie in an endless future, but rather in that perennially present eternity. In her wonderful little book on faith and art, *Walking on Water*, Madeleine L'Engle quotes Leonard Bernstein's phrase for music: "cosmos in chaos." If "right worship is right perception," what is seen is "cosmos," the vision God reveals to Job in the whirlwind of a universe which is "good" despite the existence of Leviathan and Behemoth.

When I speak of "seeing" or "right perception," I do not mean, of course, the physiological act of the eye. I mean the spiritual capacity to perceive the fullness which exists in each moment and is always waiting for us to be present to it—what I earlier, quoting Marilyne Robinson, referred to as a "thing existing in excess of itself." The fine arts have always recognized that all that exists bears, as Josef Pieper, puts it, a kind of "imprint of Paradise" and art's role is to make this truth transparent. In the Pieper book I'm referring to, *Only the Lover Sings: Art and Contemplation*, Pieper calls for the renewed practice of contemplation. He reminds us that all the great thinkers of the Western tradition have extolled contemplation and, in a strange but intriguing connection, Pieper links Anaxagoras and Teilhard de Chardin. In reply to the question, *Why are you here on earth?* Anaxagoras gave this answer: "To behold." Chardin states in the *Phenomenon of Man* that the "entire evolution of the universe has as its final aim nothing else but the bringing forth of ever more perfect eyes." And while I don't think we are evolving so much as forgetting what psychologists call our "archaic understanding," a "willingness" as Madeline L'Engle puts it, "to know things in their deepest, mythic sense," I do think that, if the eternal were erased from daily life, we'd live in an alien, meaningless, flattened world, like Job's before God comes to him in the whirlwind.

Certainly the incessant stream of information that passes over the airwaves of television and radio, or through our newspapers and computers; our endless fascination and love for new electronic devices—cell phones, iPods, PDAs; our insatiable need for spectacle and sensation; and the bland homogenization of our values and tastes that goes under the banner of political correctness—all serve to block any attempt at the contemplation Pieper calls for. This past semester, I taught a book in a freshman first year program that was very popular when it came out in 1985: Neil Postman's *Amusing Ourselves to Death*. Postman did not fear the *1984* of George Orwell, but rather what he saw as the equally chilling but different vision of Aldous Huxley's *Brave New World* where people come to adore the very technologies that take away their capacity to think. Postman was quite prophetic—twenty-five years ago he saw that visual entertainment would trivialize journalism, education, religion and public discourse. In short, he saw how we might lose the ability to see the real world, exchanging that world for the world that passes across our multiple screens.

I'm not trying to suggest that our loss of sight is merely related to television, computers, Internet, and modern media. I see the problem more in terms of Ivan Illyich and the loss of a kind of individual response, even to God. We seem, even the faithful seem, to live at a remove from inspiration, revelation, even moments of ecstasy. In the *Varieties of Religious Experience*, William James accused religious institutions of making banal through routinization those moments of vision which were originally revelatory and ecstatic. Now to many, living itself feels too much like a routine. In today's world, so many feel as if they have no roots, no sense of belonging; they are confused about what can be believed and what they believe, and they are looking for something, as my friend Chris Merrill has put it, to "revitalize the language of the spirit." As in Hamlet's Denmark, there is a kind of melancholy that pervades modern life, a feeling of helplessness and hopelessness in the face of both the world's seeming meaninglessness and its perpetual evils. When the Psalmist cried out against his enemies, against the whimsy of life and the injustice all around him, he did so in a world that was self-evidently meaningful. The Psalmist may have lamented what felt like God's withdrawal, but God was God and bound to come back and set things straight. We live in a different world, where our fear and distress are not simply linked to our alienation from God, but to our living in a world where there is, possibly, no assurance of any meaning beyond the individual self.

As I have implied already no doubt, I think an important role of the arts is to bring us back to what I'll call primal moments. Jung said about humankind that we "woke up in a world [we] did not understand and this is why [we try] to interpret it." He believed that the unconscious, that place where the dreams and myths of primitive man are still with us, was being ignored and distanced by the modern scientific and technical world. More importantly he felt that we could not be whole without access to those ancient expressions, those moments when we are either confronted by the indifferent forces of reality or feel as if we've returned to paradise, to the very site of the creation of the world. I would agree. I don't mean to imply that we should look to the arts as our means of salvation. I mean only that they can help us see the world freshly again. In Wallace Stevens's poem "The Latest Freed Man" such a moment comes when the man can "be" again without a "description of to be," when he experiences the "freshness of the oak-leaves, not so much / That they were oak-leaves, as the way they looked." Stevens's word is perfect: the *freshness* of oak-leaves. I think the experience that Stevens refers to here is transcendent, but not in the sense of lifting the person into some otherworldly place. Rather the experience, like Job's, is one that restores us to ourselves. We see once again what is always there but which we have lost sight of. There's a similar moment in *Gilead* when the narrator remembers a moment when he *saw* a line of oak trees: "I stood there...and I thought, It is all still new to me. I have lived my life on the prairie and a line of oak trees can still astonish me."

Each one of us intimately knows this very experience or one just like it: the startling greenness of grass after a long winter; the lush red of a cardinal in the snow; the strange rightness of day and night (as opposed to the clock time we live by) we experience on a camping trip; or the endless discovery of something new in the face and body of a loved one. I believe that novels and poems, paintings and music, allow us *to be* more vividly, if only for moments. As the Polish poet and Nobel Laureate, Czeslaw Milosz writes, "When a thing is truly seen, seen intensely, it remains with us forever and astonishes us, even though it would appear there is nothing astonishing about it." For Milosz, to contemplate "tree or rock or a man" may bring us "to comprehend that it *is*, even though it might not have been."

The rub, of course, is how to praise all we can "for being and for happening," as Auden once put it, while remaining true to the horrific, both in nature and, especially, in human affairs. I want to end by talking briefly about some premises that I think underlie artistic works that remain true to being, to the blind forces of necessity and chance, and to history. What I have to say is not new, but perhaps bears repeating. First and foremost, art must never reduce the mystery of our lives and life itself in order for us to feel comfortable. The great enemy of art is always fantasy. In order to feel comfortable, we often end up loving what is imaginary—our own dreams and self-deceits; we reduce the mystery of existence to our theories and explanations. Art, to my mind, has to live with the "contradictions" the mind comes up against as Simone Weil said: why, for example, the innocent suffer so much more than anyone could ever deserve; why some people live out their lives in the unrelenting torment of a psychological disorder. Weil also says those contradictions must be experienced to the very depths of our being and art should provide those necessary moments of recognition. And art should help us see that we must love this world—not to figure it out or even understand it, but as Wendell Berry says, "to suffer it and rejoice in it as it is."

In short, art must shape a language that faithfully records the terrifying and painful contradictions of human experience, and must do so while remaining open to the intrinsic joy of being. The cost of doing so, I think, is total vulnerability. Consider the character of Lily Briscoe in Virginia Woolf's *To the Lighthouse*. Lily paints two pictures during the course of the novel. The first painting—all angles and blocks of colors—attempts to symbolize the relationship between the still living Mrs. Ramsey and her husband. Lily keeps repeating to herself "this is what I see, this is what I see" as she tries to command her painting into being. That painting—is, importantly, a failure. Lily arranges, but the painting has no life at its center. Lily's art keeps trying to rationally understand Mr. and Mrs. Ramsey, seeing each of them and their relationship in various and always limiting unities. In the novel's last section, Lily begins the painting—ten years later—once again, starting afresh. Mrs. Ramsey has died, there has been a World War, and the summer house where everyone gathers has nearly gone to ruin before being brought back to life. Lily is on the shore, painting, but mostly remembering all that has passed as she watches Mr. Ramsey, Cam, and James sail to the lighthouse—a journey which itself was planned but never undertaken those many years ago when Lily was working at her first painting. Now as Lily remembers, searching, as Woolf puts it, "among the infinite series of impressions time has laid down," she begins her painting. But once again the painting resists her. Woolf suggests that this resistance has much to do with the detached way Lily remembers; Lily, a single woman who pursues a serious career, has always resented Mrs. Ramsey's domestic arrangements and envied her domestic happiness. Now, Lily remembers the past with the sense almost of triumph as she thinks of all that has changed despite Mrs. Ramsey's attempts during her life to arrange things. But as memories make present all that is absent and, as Lily suffers the past into life, admitting to herself that she, too, cannot control a world where there is no "safety," where everything is "startling, unexpected, unknown" and yet "all was miracle," she finally cries out *Mrs. Ramsey! Mrs. Ramsey!*—it is this moment of utterly painful emotion, of simply loving the dead Mrs. Ramsey in all her contradictoriness, which becomes the true center of her painting. Lily redeems the lost years only when she loves that which is outside herself—the particularity and otherness of the Ramseys. We could say that she comes to truly know herself and her art only in attending to and ultimately loving the irreducible otherness of Mrs. Ramsey. Attention can only truly come with love, since only love, in its vulnerability, lets the world be as it is. And attending, we sometimes hear hedge crickets sing.

GILT

Philip Brady

Winter nights, dismissed from Fordham Prep,
I'd find him on the bus—Mr. McMann.
As the door hissed open and I stepped
into the vestibule and rendered a token

I'd feel his cloudy gaze. And even if
I snaked around the strap-hangers unseen
and sank between somnambulists
to conjure Mt. St. Ursulan prom queens,

by Utopia a force would push me up to
sit with the old man, my neighbor's father,
and lean and nod, attending to his gabble
until our bell got pulled. Then down the stairs,

and into the cold dark. Words can't express
the slowness of his gait. Out of time
it creeps over me now, as I cross
into the suburbs of old age. I make no bones.

What fixed my numb fingers to McMann
was what made me: Parental Bulls
mandating the 6:00 A.M. alarm,
and the daily interborough busses

CHAUTAUQUA

and the cramping desks where I cracked
Aquinas, and the waxy sandwiches,
and the jock-infested lockers, and the trek
across the desecrated corpus of the Bronx

back to Queens, where the row house door
snapped shut. *Caritas*, purred the Jesuits,
or *Agape* in advanced Greek seminar:
blossoming through others into Christ.

But all I felt was cold. Ruptured
sidewalks uncoupled our limp. We shouldered
into the wind to ford boulevards
and tottered under blind windows toward

a destination no doctrine can name.
I see them now, steering arm in arm
through the years to reach that occult haven—
gilt in traffic light as if blood-smeared.

man of war

Carol Frost

After there were no women, men, and children,

from the somber deeps horseshoe crabs crawled up on somber shores:

Man-of-Wars' blue sails drifted downwind

and blue filaments of some biblical cloak

floated below: the stinging filaments.

The cored of bone and rock-headed came near:

clouds made wandering shadows:

sea and grasses mingled::

There was no hell after all

but a lull before it began over::

flesh lying alone: then mating: a little spray of soul:

and the grace of waves, of stars, and remotest isles.

THE DEAD KNOW TOO MUCH
Kirk Nesset

At Zephyr, as elsewhere, the dead transmit from their graves. As elsewhere, the stones are fitted with video feeds, and mourners with cordless headsets, such that they who survive receive from they who have died postmortem tidings—recorded pre-mortem, of course, timed for release via the Internet at appropriate intervals. One will witness inset on a stone (in close up, the face deeply shadowed, retouched somewhat) the deceased lending comfort, if not placating, or softly making amends. There'll be verbal sweetmeats for dear ones, suggestions, instructions, life stories, jokes. There'll be final word, to the degree that the dead can and should be believed, on estate, on that ugly ongoing suit. There'll be reasons for living, and dying, if not celebration, if not promise or hope.

At Zephyr you won't find wandering criers—they who will for a fee bewail your departed loved one, no matter how long ago passed. Nor will you see synthetic willows, nor oaks a la Savannah, dripping the pale plastic moss; and there is no bridge of sighs here which actually sighs. Mourners are encouraged not to bring picnics, or (as elsewhere) to jog between stones, or do Tai Chi or yoga, or the sit-ups and leg lifts in black Lycra. At Zephyr, poised on this cliff facing sprawling Lake Simcoe, foaming and freezing in turn, mourners mourn with tact and respect, headsets or not.

Take Harriet Sibbald-Tuppage, for instance. One sees her here often, fixed on a marble bench in the fenced Sibbald plot, dating from 1780. She'll unlatch the ancient gate in the ancient fence and slowly take her seat, slip on her headset, click the code on the transceiver, and hear the latest from her late husband Harvey. He seems to have plenty to say;

one wonders where and how he found time to record so much before his aneurism whisked him away. Since she is a Sibbald, the top rung of families, and owns the best resort on this stretch of coast (boasting lake front cottages, an endless sculpted golf course, shimmering swimming pools, spas and massage, canoes and kayaks, badminton, squash and croquette), she isn't concerned about money. She was first to convert to laser mode, costly and rare. Since mid-April Harvey's appeared in 3-D, projected several feet out from his grave, a grinning hologram, large as life, as they say—if not the whole of him half anyway, whatever the camera caught, a broad bald bust with an elbow, a small section of forearm; or at times just the head itself, suspended head-high, bobbing periodically for emphasis.

On windy summer days like today she'll have her dark purple windbreaker on and gray warm-up pants, a scarf maybe, and the contempo black and gray shoes, which look like something somebody might wear to go bowling. Today she's here very early—in and gone, she'd like to hope before the gawkers and oddballs arrive, the necro-gothics and weirdos and winos, your idle leering car-bound Yank, morbidly curious, amazed to be on foreign turf without boarding a plane. It's dawn, or just past. Here, Harriet is on her bench, fenced in, headphoned. Harvey appears in the mist. Half of him, anyway.

As usual he offers the tender tidbits. He calls her his honey pot, his Pookie, asks how his peach blossom is. He's sorry he's been silent so long. It's been a week; he's transmitted every three or four days these eighteen months since he died. He offers the usual tips about business, exquisitely timed. There are annuities to consider, securities, commodities, futures. There'll be new shares to purchase, and sales and trade-ins. She'll need to ride the accountant, crack her whip; she'll need to closely oversee what he's done.

She's got her pad out and pen at this point—she takes cryptic notes. The lake smacks the shingles on the lakeshore below. She hasn't been exactly well herself these days. She was on her way out, she thought, a month or so after Harvey; she spent seven strange weeks in the hospital. But she recovered. Her lungs rose again on their own, her head cleared, and in time she felt good. Reasonably good. Today she feels odd, edgy and shaky. At least she's functioning.

Harvey pauses, as if allowing her time to jot everything down.

What about bullion? she murmurs. Gold futures?

Harvey's head looms larger. His shoulders and neck disappear.

Forget metals, he says. Market's too bullish, I think.

Once again her skin crawls a little. This isn't the first time he's anticipated her question, or questions. Yes, they always did think and speak from one mind—but lately it's all seeming too weird, and too much. The market wasn't bullish in the least when Harvey died, nor when he taped these epistles. Nobody'd foreseen the turns the economy took these last months, and there was no way Harvey could either. Nor could he have known who the present prime minister would be, which he apparently did, hinting as he did at the antics of this nitwit Paul Martin. And the pointed recent smut Harvey'd alluded to, occurring now in the province—well, it frightened her. It made her feel crazy, or set up, messed with, abused.

Pookie, he says, his head says, afloat in the mist.

She clicks her pen shut, melting, suspicious as she's feeling. And then sees a shape by the fence beyond her great grandmother's grave. She plucks the transceiver up, pauses the tape. The transmission.

What, she calls out.

The person stands unmoving, indistinct, leaden. The fog's thickened; the wind has picked up. Waves batter the beach.

Who is it? Harriet calls.

No one, the person replies, gliding cautiously nearer beside the steel fence. He materializes, at least partly.

He's short, slightly plump, clad in a respectable suit, not showy. The woeful expression and droop in his shoulders imply he's a crier. Criers aren't forbidden outright at Zephyr. They're hired, now and then, on formal occasions, aiding in easing the floodgates of grief. But solicitations are never, never permitted.

I don't need any tears, thanks, Harriet says.

The man stands slumped at the fence, clutching his black hat at his abdomen.

I know, he says.

Elm branches creak, to the left. The wind whips in hard. The crier sighs, if crier he is.

She does miss her husband, needless to say. They met when she was freshly divorced, or almost; they slogged through that mess as a team, carefully, tenderly, and things got better, and then incredibly good, and stayed good, despite Harvey's occasional arrogance, his penchant for sneaking sex in public (with her) and for unceasing talk. He'd fix her eggs and toast and tea each morning, he'd pack her lunch, and prepare thoughtful dinners, a creative if not award-winning cook. He didn't work. He didn't have to; he just managed her money and planned long lazy trips for them, intricate tours of outlandish countries: Iceland, New Zealand, Finland, Egypt, Nepal.

She shifts on her bench, forcing more air into her lungs. She tightens her scarf. The man stands there unmoving.

What then? she asks.

The dead know too much, he says.

She sits listening to the wind and the lake and elm branches, taking this in.

About what?

Everything, the man says.

Harvey appears again suddenly, or Harvey's head does, unbidden. Harriet tries to pause the transmission; she taps the remote. It doesn't respond. Harvey continues, as if impatient to finish. His head floats between her and the stranger, the crier, if crier he is. The scalp shines so brightly it glows; the blue eyes seem impossibly blue.

Honey, Harvey's projected head says. Don't forget the garbage goes out on Sunday.

We can't stop them, the man says, looking stricken.

Sweetest sweetness, Harvey says.

What do you mean? Harriet asks.

A jogger puffs past in the mist, skirting the row of stones by the cliff. He's got reflectors on his wrists, his Adidas.

I mean we've set them free, the man answers.

Harvey's head bobs. It's nice here, Pook, he says. You'll like it.

She's standing at the gravestone now, a fat granite slab flecked lightly with mica. She prods a button beside the monitor.

It's a scam, she says. The computer knows him so well it does him better than he did.

Maybe, the man says.

We pay to see the deception. It's fun. I want to believe it. But it's a scam.

Sweet Pookie, says Harvey.

Zephyr, a voice calls from the speaker.

Turn him off, Harriet says.

Who? the voice asks.

My husband. Stop him.

There's nothing here from Mr. Tuppage, says the voice, which may or may not be a robot's.

The man at the fence is weeping suddenly, quietly, covering his face with his hands.

I'm here for you, Peach, Harvey says.

Nothing new from Mr. Tuppage for a month, the voice says. *We're not transmitting.*

The man's weeping grows more distinct, more distraught.

Harvey, stop, Harriet says, addressing the bobbing head.

We're the same, Harvey says. You and me. The same dust from the same dead comets. The same light and heat.

The stranger wipes his nose with his handkerchief, saying something Harriet can't decipher. He takes a step back. And then disappears in the mist, as if he too were transmitted, and abruptly cut off.

Do you need help? the voice from the monitor calls.

The monitor flickers. Then the following message appears:

> *Zephyr denies outright any deception or falsehood, any ghostly trickery, any and all tampering with video feeds. The dead are dead, clearly. Mourners are expected individually to safeguard their wits.*

The mist thickens. The wind rattles the elms. The lake roars, blasting the rocks and the cliff. The head no longer floats over the damp grass. Harriet turns to retrieve her remote. She's not well at all, suddenly. For a moment her lungs seem to surrender, to fail to fill fully. And then there Harvey is, projected a yard off or more, in full, crown to brown loafers, sitting, beaming, leaning back slightly. On her bench. He's wearing his apron. The gray kitchen apron.

Are you there? the voice says.

Harvey's patting the bench now, saying Harriet, hey, I made dinner.

She backs up a step, totters, then rights herself. She can't seem to get air in her lungs. A truck rumbles west on the highway, en route to Port Bolster, or Painswick, or Sutton. Her husband beckons. A gull wings silently in.

Never interrupt someone doing something you said couldn't be done.

—Amelia Earhart

Life Lessons

SWIMMING WITH DOLPHINS
Sarah Willis

It's my own damn fault I'm making this trip to Florida with Kathy and her son. When I told my husband about the mess I'd gotten into with a few too easily said words, Mitchell advised me to say I couldn't go. Yeah, right.

"I can't say that," I told him.

"Why not?"

"Her husband's dead. She has a handicapped kid."

"Well, it's a tough call."

But Mitchell didn't know why I had to say yes, and I couldn't really tell him. And he didn't care I was going. He'd have the house to himself. Now that the kids are in college, sometimes just the two of us are one too many.

Jake keeps hollering "Higgins!" from the back seat. We have to keep the radio off, or he just yells louder. He's thirteen, and kind of fat, inflated looking. Once, seeing one of those Bob's Big Boy statues, I thought of him. And he certainly doesn't understand personal limits.

"Higgins! Higgins!"

Who would name a dolphin *Higgins*? The on-line picture of this motel where the dolphin is looks a little shady, but Jake's more excited about swimming with Higgins than going to Disney World. He's got black rubber flippers on his hands, steadily smacking them together, a constant thump, thump, thump.

"Nell brought snacks," Kathy says. "Would you like some juice? Cut up apples? Cheese and crackers? Nell brought snacks."

"Hey, what do dolphins eat?" Jake says. "Fish. Little fish. Right? Little fish."

"That's right," Kathy says. "That's right."

I don't think I'll be able to stand a whole week with people who say everything twice.

At the funeral two months ago for my mother, everyone kept saying the same thing. "Oh, honey, it's okay to cry." What made them think I wanted to do that in front of anyone? They weren't there with me in the hospital, where I sat for five weeks, next to my mother's bed, talking to the morphine, not really my mom, asking what I could do to help. And what would morphine have said, if asked? A trip to Mount Everest? Japan? We watched the travel station twenty-four seven, and one time my mom got stuck repeating a phone number running across the bottom of the screen, a number to call if you wanted more information about a trip to China. I'll never get that number out of my head. Sometimes when I think of my mom, I think, *oh, I'll call that number and talk with her*. It's stupid, the things we think sometimes.

My mom's cancer was everywhere. They found the tumors scan by scan, never expecting to find so many, like the moons of Jupiter. *Oh, there's another one!* Drawn on her back was this grid in black magic marker, squares to show the doctors where to radiate, like cubist drawing, as if my mother were some failed performance art. *Get up*, I wanted to tell her. *Run out of here!*

No one knew she did have one last wish, as I fed her vanilla ice cream. "Kill me now," she said.

"What?" I asked.

My mom just stared into space, opened her mouth for ice cream, then said, "Fred Miller brought me a big fish." The travel station was featuring sports fishing in the Keys. Now I'm on my way there.

I haven't gone back to work, running estate sales. God, once I loved my job. All those treasures! But people could be shits. One client accused me of stealing, and then there were customers who haggled until I almost screamed: *You're paying ten bucks for an heirloom! Will your* life be that much better if you get it for eight? When my mom died, my sister and I gave everything away that we didn't want. No estate sale. I made that very clear to my sister. I had my limits.

WE STOP FOR DINNER at Stuckey's, north of Charlotte, then Kathy drives until Jake says he's really got to pee, and we pull into this rest stop. On the acre of lawn bordered by pines that smell of exhaust, Jake runs in large circles around the perimeter for almost fifteen minutes.

"He's quite focused on this dolphin thing," Kathy told me that day I said, *sure, I'd like to come with you*. "If we make stops on the way down," she said, "he'll get frustrated and stressed. Let's just drive there in two days, then after he gets to swim with Higgins, we'll do a day at Disney World, then make a few leisurely stops on the drive home."

I was getting pretty sure I wouldn't want to make any stops on the way back.

Kathy was a physical therapist, and for the last couple of months, since we started talking about this trip, she'd gone on and on about how swimming with dolphins was this blissful experience, something about how the dolphins talked to you underwater, creating some kind of spiritual state—and she thought there was a special connection they had to children. She never said a special connection with a handicapped child, but I think that's what she was thinking. I mean it sounds fun, but I'm not sure I would have thought to drive to Florida to do it.

Just past Columbia, South Carolina—where I77 abruptly ends as if it were a long, tiresome song and someone finally shouted, *Enough!*—I pull off the highway and head us toward a motel. Kathy and Jake are asleep in the car.

Inside my room I can smell the multitude of people passing through, and pulling back the covers, I remember seeing a TV show about motels, someone waving a black light across the bedspread, displaying unknown fluids lit up like neon squids under dark water.

IN THE MORNING, I'm awakened by Jake pounding on the door. "Wake up, Nell, wake up. We're ready to go!" Through the cheap wood door I can hear the thump, thump, thump of the flippers. Suddenly I think of a seal, standing outside my motel room door, a huge seal out of water. I want to like him more than I do. Sometimes I hear what my sister said, right to me at the funeral. "What's the matter with you?"

I DRIVE AFTER LUNCH, and by three o'clock, crossing the Florida line, *Welcome to the Sunshine State*!, Kathy and Jake are asleep, Kathy's head against the window, the air conditioner blasting cold air. I should nudge her, tell her to be careful with her neck, but she looks so peaceful.

My husband, daughters and I moved onto the street three years before Kathy's husband died. Ted was strong then, with wide shoulders and muscular legs, but within a month of the diagnosis, his body began to fade, becoming slight and curved, as if holding in a punch. It was obvious he was in pain, obvious he was going to die. He had pancreatic cancer, and his skin turned yellow and itched; he was constantly scratching at himself, pulling at his clothes, rubbing his back against chairs.

He worked in a public relations firm, had been there for fifteen years with some title like vice-president that didn't really mean all that much. He was in a holding pattern and should have moved up long ago. "That won't happen now," he said, then laughed. "And they're embarrassed, you can believe that. Now they think they should have treated me better. My dying embarrasses people."

We were sitting on his front steps. We did this often in the last month before he died, meeting in the sunshine outside on his steps, Kathy at work, Jake someplace. Sometimes we talked, sometimes we just watched the neighborhood around us as if it were an independent movie, one of those slow ones.

At first it seemed a simple kindness. I'd seen him out there, so I went over, thinking that he might like some company. But the more we talked, the more he would tell me everything, anything. One afternoon he told me the whole story of how he and Kathy learned Jake was handicapped. He went into detail about the tests, the time he swore at a doctor and stormed out of the office, the night he told Kathy that if she believed the shit the doctors were saying, the limitations they were already placing on his three-month old son, she could just leave now and he'd take over. He said Kathy wanted to have another child, and he said no way, he couldn't, and got a vasectomy. He told these things simply, not with tears but with the understanding that there had been tears. He seemed to be trying to understand something new about the whole thing by talking it over with me, as if my presence might allow him a grace he hadn't found before.

One afternoon in late October he began to talk about what would happen after he died. "Jake takes so much energy," he said, almost amused. "I love his energy, but it's on his terms. If we slow him down, he only gets depressed. Kathy'll need help."

"I'll help her," I said, and Ted nodded. She wasn't my best friend—I was six years older and our kids were such different ages we never really spent that kind of time together, but we were friendly, and I would certainly try to help her out.

"I know you will, but that's not what I mean. Encourage her, will you, to take some time for herself?"

"Okay. I will. I promise."

Two strangers on bikes rode by. One waved. People were friendly.

"They probably think we're husband and wife," I said, "taking a day of vacation." Then I was embarrassed I said that.

Ted put a hand on my thigh, and that surprised me some. I was wearing shorts, and his hand felt overly warm on my skin. "It wouldn't be so terrible, would it," he said, "if they thought that?" After a few seconds of silence he removed his hand, and laughed. "You know, last week I had to get my driver's license renewed. Anyway, I started wondering what all those people would do if they knew I was dying. Would they let me move up in line? Should I play that card? It amused me not to. It made me feel superior, like dying was some privilege." He shrugged and shook his head.

Then he laughed in a hard way, and I tensed.

"Talking about that . . . I met Kathy in high school. I only slept with one girl before I started dating Kathy. I've been loyal to her. There's a comfort in loyalty." He paused, tried to shake off some thought. "But sometimes I wanted more. Doesn't everyone? Being good was supposed to pay off. It didn't. It's not just the cancer, or not moving up the ladder, or what happened to Jake . . . You know what I believe in now?"

"What?"

"Now I want something and I'm going to ask for it. It's completely wrong to do this, but I'm tired of being good." He rolled his head around to loosen something. "I'll tell Kathy she has to marry again, and that's only right. She'll will even if I don't tell her." He paused again, then added, "What I'm trying to get at is I'd like to make love with you. Just once."

I flinched, I know I did.

"It's a shitty thing to ask, 'cause of Kathy, and 'cause you're married, but it's what I want and I'm not going to deny it. I'm going to ask you and see if maybe you're feeling the same thing. Some kind of connected thing. Do you know what I mean? When we talk, it's like I never got to be this open, and you, you're tough in a way Kathy never was, is. . . . But we can do it only once, because my body's turning to shit and the second time you'd see that. The second time you'd notice. Yeah, it's a dying man's last wish and that makes me a prick. I don't think this will ruin your marriage. You don't seem happy, you know that, right?"

Before I could say yes, or no, he waved my answer away.

"Look, I'll never mention it again. I don't want to pressure you. If you will . . . do this, just take my hand someday. I'll know what that means. And, let's give it a limit, so it doesn't stand between us for the next few months. If it's yes, take my hand sometime in the next week. After that, the deals off." He laughed. "I'm an asshole."

What could I say to that? I almost nodded, *yeah, you're an asshole*, but how could I say that to a dying man? And it was interesting to be asked this, flattering maybe.

Ted smiled tightly, nodding to himself. "So, listen, your tomatoes, what do you feed them?"

I answered that question, then we sat there not talking for a while. Two squirrels chased by, normal in every way. One ran up an elm tree, the other following, spiraling up, making the leaves shiver. The elm was one of the few left after Dutch elm disease took the rest away.

I stood up. "See you tomorrow," I said, and went home.

It was all I could think about. It was huge, this thing he'd asked me to do, and wrong, and yet . . . I did feel this connection he was talking about. As soon as he said it, it was true. Kathy was my friend, sort of, yet she went to work every day and left him sitting on his porch. And he wanted me. It was stunning. It was . . . exciting.

By the time it happened, five days later—taking his hand and leading him upstairs to my bed, I'd thought about it so much I believed it had to happen.

I sat on the floral quilt and watched him undress. His skin was almost transparent under his clothes. There were bruises on his thighs. Just before he crawled under the cover his penis began to straighten out. I took my clothes off slowly, figuring much of the pleasure of this afternoon was mostly the anticipation.

We were gentle with each other. At first I thought I'd keep my eyes open the whole time, but there was a point when my eyes shut, and with them closed I was more comfortable and could concentrate on the differences. His body was shorter than Mitchell's. Things fit differently. He began to breath heavily, and I slowed down. He told me not to. "I swear I won't die of a heart attack," was about the only thing he said to me. He called my name a few times, which was nice. He came. I didn't, but I pretended to.

I wanted to say, *I love you*. I wanted him to be able to take that with him, wherever he went. But I couldn't. I didn't, really, not then.

We only made love that once. But the scary part is that what I didn't say to Ted became true. Now that he's dead, I love him more than I can imagine loving anyone.

"How are you doing?" Kathy asks quietly, waking up but not moving. We are almost to Florida City. Then it will be all Route One to Key Islamorada.

"Fine," I say.

"You're a good driver." Kathy stretches out her legs as best she can in the small space. "I wish Ted and I had done this before he died. We had the brochure for years, but something always came up. We were going to do it last fall, but he took a turn for the worse. You remember? When he ended up in Intensive Care for three days? But I'm glad you came with us. This will be great."

I slept with Ted, I want to say. I can't look at Kathy without wanting to say this. I want her forgiveness, but more, I just want her to know Ted and I had this connection, and she'd understand, right, because she loved him, too. It's insane, but I keep thinking it will make us closer, Kathy and I. If I tell her, we can be real friends. Instead I don't say anything.

The lot for the motel with the dolphin is full, and we have to park on the street. It's a little after five in the evening, and there's a skim of white across the sky. Opening the door, I feel the heat, solid, like something that will stay through the night, be there again in the morning.

Crooking her finger, Kathy beckons over Jake. "*Now listen*," Kathy says, each word a separate thing, slow and careful with the tone of authority, not at all Kathy's normal way of talking. Jake focuses on her face, standing still, not running toward the motel. It's like she's hypnotized him.

Jake listens to Kathy as she tells him that he can't jump into the lagoon until they get taught about how to swim with a dolphin. "You cannot go into the water until I say so. Do you understand?" He nods three times.

"Good. Thank you, Jake. Thank you for listening."

"You're welcome."

I have to turn away. It's like I watched something altogether private, like a kiss.

THE MOTEL IS BUILT like a large U, the office in the front, next to an archway into the interior. The stucco's dry and peeling. The indoor-outdoor carpeting is hard even through my shoes. No one's in the office.

"Hello?" Kathy calls. No one answers. There's a silver bell, the old fashioned kind, like in *Psycho*, and Kathy taps it with the palm of her hand. "Hello?"

"Hello," Jake repeats. "Hello, hello, hello!" With his arms hanging down, he swings the flippers back and forth, back and forth.

I TOLD MY MOTHER about Jake one day in the hospital, early on, while she was mostly in her senses, before the drugs took over. The coloring of death was in the room by then, not yellow like the walls, or grey like the floor. It was an invisible color, a new color, and I knew it would shade the rest of my life, hazing everything, like cataracts.

My mom wanted to know more about Jake. What kind of handicap exactly? What was his mother like? I described Kathy in good terms, all honest, and said Kathy was a widow, too, that her husband had died just months ago. I didn't say he died of cancer. I invented another death for him, a car accident. I didn't want to remind my mom what cancer could do.

"How terrible," she said. Then she asked more about Kathy, how she was dealing with the situation. Was she depressed? Could she go to work? Who watched the son? All I really wanted was for her to ask what Kathy's husband was like. Because if she had, I would have told her. I would have confessed everything I'd ever done, starting with sleeping with Ted down to the stone I'd thrown at a girl on the playground when I was in second grade. My mother could take all my mistakes away with her when she died.

IN THE SILENCE of this empty motel lobby, I begin to sweat. Something's wrong here, and I can't take wrong again. I realize I've been thinking I will do this swimming thing, too. I'm going to go underwater and let words bubble out, and Higgins will make his clicking sonar sounds, smile his dolphin smile, give me a friendly nudge and we'll swim about together, and everything will be okay again. I'll go home, love my husband, be friends with Kathy, and life will be like it's supposed to be.

We walk out of the motel office and stand in front, wondering what to do. And then we hear it. Singing. Phrases, words welling up, fading. "By and by. . . ." "There's a better place a coming. . . ." I look at Kathy, and Jake takes off running.

Behind the motel, by the water, there are dozens of people standing on a cement walkway fronting the lagoon. A dock planks the water, and people stand on that, too, holding hands, heads bowed. Layers of flowers float on the water. Jake's frozen, standing back from the crowd. "What are they doing, Mom?" he asks as we catch up. "Mom, what are they doing?" He looks scared, and I know he's feeling what I'm feeling. On the dock is an older woman, weeping as she sings. Everyone's faces are horribly sad. Kathy takes Jake's hand, and we simply watch until the singing is done.

Then people begin to move. Some turn to each other and hug, some walk away. A young couple notices us. "Higgins died Monday," the girl says.

Kathy gasps. I think I do, too.

The girl, who has on a baseball cap with *Higgins* printed on it, nods. "Old age. He just . . . well he . . . ." She shrugs. "Died."

What the hell? I'm not sure if I say it out loud or not, but I know I'm about to laugh. What's the chance of this happening? A million to one. It's absurd. Death is just playing stupid games, and we aren't made better by connecting to it—it's not a privilege to be near someone dying. I'm an idiot. So god damn stupid. I cover my mouth wanting to know why I want to laugh. What's the matter with me?

"What happened, Mom? What happened to Higgins?"

Jake's voice is loud and confused. People look at him, and yet, for once, I know no one is thinking *he's handicapped*. They're just thinking how sad he is and how sad they are.

"Higgins died, Jake. This was his memorial service. He died of old age, and they were singing him a song." She looks at the young couple. "He . . . Higgins isn't here, is he?"

"No," the boy says. "They took him out to the ocean in a boat."

"I'm sorry, Jake," Kathy says. Then she looks at me. "I'm so sorry, Nell."

Jake drops the flippers and staggers to the edge of the lagoon. He doesn't jump into the water, but falls onto his knees. Kathy follows, stands next to Jake, puts a hand on his shoulder. He's bawling, his whole body shaking with grief. I kneel next to Jake.

"Don't be dead, Higgins," Jake pleads. "I'm going to swim with you. I'm going to be your friend. Mom, don't let him be dead."

The older woman from the dock comes over. "Here, please take this." She offers him her Higgins hat. Jake squishes it to his chest.

"It's okay, sweetie," Kathy says. "He died of old age. He wasn't in any pain. He just died in his sleep."

No, I think. He was swimming with some kid who would be traumatized for the rest of his life. I'm furious. Stuffed full of death and self-pity. Such ugly things. Suddenly I'm crying, I can feel the damp down my face. Kathy doesn't notice because she's saying something to the older woman. I look over at Jake.

"*Now listen,*" I say, trying to mimic Kathy's tone. Jake's eyes widen. "I loved your dad. I miss him, too."

Jake blinks, then nods three times.

"Thank you for listening," I say.

"You're welcome," Jake says.

Kathy sits down next to us. I have no idea if she heard me, what she might think. "I don't know what to do now," she says, so much loss in her voice it hurts.

"We'll have to go swimming," I say. I reach over and pick up Jake's flippers. "We will just have to go swimming somewhere. Come on. Let's get out of here."

PROCESSION

Jan Beatty

Little wren, your body is breaking down into air.
I find you under my desk,
—how long dead?—
What do the hollowed black cones of your eyes
and your tiny claws have to tell me about home?
Your small patch of city yard,
droop of telephone wire on your daily flight,
the wind draft over the Allegheny?

I pray to the four directions
then put your body in the trash, cover you
with typewriter ribbons and calendar days and press down.
Ten minutes later I dig you out,
carry you outside in the styrofoam box
and we walk the streets of Etna
while big-haired women watch from their porches.

Across Butler Street,
the workers of the Tippins Machinery Plant
break open their lunch buckets on the stone wall.
At the churchyard I dig behind the hydrangea
with my father's tack-hammer and cast-iron awl.
Everything goes on without us.

If I could see the cities inside you,
if I could find my own ocean of light—

Jan Beatty

In the hole:
paper with a stamp of an orange sun on it
and the word: /FINISHED/
a piece of carnelian and last words:
I am sorry. I know you were alone in this room of poems.
I tried to hide your death.
RIP May 29th Calvert United Presbyterian Church.

Golden
Todd Davis

Not like bars or chains
but like goldenrod
at the end of August,
skin on the shoulder
in summer, the air
just before dark,
part of it yellowing
with age, drawn down
to the river plain
where the garden returns
year after year.
It's the soil
and what we give
back to the earth
that makes us grow,
the way flesh falls
together as we sleep.
Or perhaps it's more
like singing, each note
joining with another,
a song that merges
and shimmers
along the water's surface,
and the water itself,
from which we all drink,

Todd Davis

and in sharing this cup
cannot imagine
any other life
but this one.

The Sunflower

Todd Davis

The sunflower outside my window
has dropped its head, late August
and the heat of summer shattered
at its feet. Gray covers the tops
of the ridges, and rain falls in clear,
straight lines. A goldfinch turns up
to rest on the green wreath
that surrounds the yellow face
of this flower. The bird's face
is bent over as well, picking
at the seeds along the edge,
content to be washed
by these first cool days,
to eat from the face
of this dying sun.

THE LAST BLUE LIGHT

Rick Hilles

If this is my last flight may I still
have time to taste the darkness

melting on my tongue, dissolving
with the sound of sugar maple leaves

blowing around my childhood home;
may wind lift the leaves up to their branches

and air be restored to the last season,
winter's steamy breath leaving us autumn,

all shovels and rakes remaining in dust.
Unneeded. Let us reach our altitude,

each of us humming our assent, moving
with the sounds of wet machinery. Nothing

visible as we bear down through space
but the last blue light of day, glowing

at the black wings, the seat belt sign now off
and my dead friend, Michael, sleeping

in the empty row beside me. The fire highlights
in his poker-straight ponytail lighting up the aria

CHAUTAUQUA

on his lap, the one he dozed off memorizing,
the day his plane went down,

his thick lips still shivering and blue
from the icy waters off La Guardia.

Nothing yet has edged us out of the sky,
he says, to show he's listening. Each of us now

weighs as much as the city we grew up in.
And I can almost feel this sense

of being occupied, of the stampede
of population—

everyone I've ever loved
moving through rows of starlight,

and in me,
and what if the dead need us, too,

as much as we need them?
And who wouldn't give

everything if it meant
having them among us, alive again?

at Himmel's cottage

Richard Terrill

I get to Himmel's cottage before anyone else does, and I'm surprised that that's so, since I have the longest drive. McNally usually comes later, like me from a spot in Minnesota, but the other guys drive up together from nearby Green Bay, where Wes's and Blaine's flights land. There are six of us who come here.

Alone for now, I find the house key under the steps as always, open the door to let out the old house smell, then do some simple chores. This will surprise Himmel, who we always stick with these responsibilities, since it's his place. It's only early afternoon and already the cool air feels good when it comes rushing out of the dark house (the curtains are drawn, and my eyes haven't adjusted). I work the hand pump in the yard, which yields its rust colored water, also cool. I open the windows in the three upstairs bedrooms to air them out—heat rises—and carry the food indoors out of the sun. We no longer use the old icebox in the kitchen, instead keeping perishables in the coolers we bring, covered with ice. With no power, there's no refrigerator.

The weather forecast says hot and humid for the next four days, heat extreme for early June in northern Wisconsin. I open a beer, sit on the porch steps, and just look around. The siding on the house needs paint, and a screen is loose on the enclosed porch. I noticed the floor sagging a bit in the kitchen as I carried in the heavy cooler.

Some daylilies grow near the outhouse, and the small perimeter of grass and weeds around the house has been mowed. Himmel's dad has put up a mesh screen around a small pine tree in the yard, near where we have whiffle ball tournaments or throw a football around on these long weekends. Beyond the small yard is Wisconsin mixed forest, dense and green in heat. Himmel's dad's 160 acres are all wooded except for the small lake that's surrounded by his property. A creek leads out of the lake to a weedy lagoon, above which a johnboat is padlocked to a cedar tree. A stream trickles out of the lagoon to a branch of a larger stream. That larger stream is fairly decent trout water, though the trout are small, on a lucky day just more than the legal limit.

Above the creek and lagoon is the house. We light our visit with a Coleman lantern and flashlights. There are kerosene lamps, too, but they're only for show—too much a fire hazard to use. We cook with LP gas over a 1920s vintage range, the oven of which can't be regulated. Pizza or baked potatoes become a calculated risk. If we're here in spring or fall, we heat with wood. Sometimes even in early June. But this year, no need.

I sip my cold beer and think about how perfect this place is. There may not be another like it in the state, in all of the Midwest. Totally secluded. Privately owned, and by people of ordinary means. There's no mansion on the grounds, no timeshare on the beach. Himmel's cottage is just a place we use to get away from it all—that's cliché, I know, but as we age there's more and more to get away from. Not kids and a mortgage and a nagging wife. That's worse cliché. We're escaping from lives that show us what we believed when we were young has turned out to be wrong. And we haven't figured out something better to believe. The six of us knew each other when we believed the old truths, and we know each other now, and there's some comfort in that.

I think what we used to believe, what all people believe when they're young, was that the world somehow belonged to us, the way this property belongs to Himmel. Possibilities would always open up for us. We believed we were special and, at the same time, no different from anyone else, part of an undefined yet unbounded community. That was being young.

Now we come back each year, several times, to Himmel's cottage, where we wash dishes with water from the pump. Fill a black plastic shower bag and put it in the sun, then hang it from a tree in late afternoon for a coolish rinse that, while not wholly satisfying, at least won't kill or maim. Or we heat the rusty pump water on the stove for a sponge bath on the second or third day we're here. In summer, sometimes we drive to a swimmable lake, our own Pete Lake being mucky around the shoreline. We have dived out of the boat in the middle of Pete, but the water, which looks calm and warm and which we know doesn't run deep, is frigid more than six inches below the surface. That's metaphor for something. Appearances deceive regularly enough that it's noteworthy when they don't. I'm reminded what my Dad used to say to start a conversation with me when I was three or four years old. "Well, Rick, what do you know for sure?" I hadn't realized he was truly curious about what I thought I knew, that it could be an issue of contention.

I sip my beer. I've got the urge to down it all but I have to pace myself for the long weekend of drinking ahead. I can almost see the heat, so I watch it for a while, how it hangs in the weeping willow tree by the woodpile, in the space above the aspens and maples where the trees stop and the sky doesn't want to begin. It's even in the mown grass and the usually cool pines and spruce. The birds don't fly. Even the mosquitoes seem beat and don't annoy.

These five friends are the guys I suffered through public secondary schools with. We had the same teachers in plaid jackets or beige frocks, knew the same girls we had the hots for but never dated. We played endless poker on high school weekends down in my basement, on an eight-sided felt table that my parents gave me as a present for my sixteenth birthday. A few summers ago, my wife re-covered it for me.

The group gathered occasionally through college and even graduate school and after, playing poker or shooting pool at my parents' place during the holidays and summers. And once or twice a year we took trips to someone's cottage, mine or Himmel's, an easy drive from where we grew up. We were, in our late twenties, already the oldest of friends.

But by the time we were nearing forty, there was no longer an annual Christmas poker game. For a while, some of our wives had played in

CHAUTAUQUA

that dying game, the kind of thing a late twenties/early thirties couple would think that they might enjoy—"*this is what I like to do, dear; I want you to share it with me.*" But the wives got tired of poker and then the children came, and as our parents moved away in retirement, or died, there was no reason for some in the group to even come back home to Green Bay for the holidays.

So when I moved back to the Midwest, I suggested we mount an expedition back to Himmel's cottage. It had been more than ten years since the last. With friends on the East Coast and in Florida, friends with children still at home, I thought it wouldn't be easy. I wondered how many of us would be interested. All six of us were—about the right number for a good table of poker, for a weekend of drinking and laughing our real lives into remission. Lives in which some decisions we make seem to have consequence, and some have no consequence at all, and we can't be sure which moves are which.

But would we have agreed to meet again, and meet again every year as we do now, if our retreat were some ordinary modern cottage on a typical overbuilt lake, polluted by jet skis and the thud of boom boxes? Others in my group think we would, but I'm sure we wouldn't. Setting is everything, almost everything. The land counts, the seventh player at the table.

One member of our group says a sign of middle age is not being able to tell any one year from all the others. A few years back, Himmel brought us gray polyester golf shirts inscribed, "Eleventh Annual Pete Lake Festival of Trilliums." It's not the kind of thing that a guy wants to wear out of the house, and that was the joke behind the gift. Then someone pointed out to Himmel that it wasn't the eleventh year of our summer trips. It was the twelfth.

It doesn't get hot like this very often in Wisconsin, and when it does it's as if the land isn't used to it, wants to get dealt out a hand or two. Today, I see where Himmel and his son have nailed up a basketball backboard to a poplar tree, and the sight of it makes me sweat a little.

I'm glad I'm not wearing that polyester Trillium shirt. The backboard stands near where the logging road—two tire tracks kept from being overgrown only by regular use—sets out from the front yard of the place. This road rambles out from here for over a mile on Himmel's private land, then there's a locked gate, then a dirt road leading a few more miles, passing only about five more houses or cottages or trailers, to the highway. That's the way you have to go if you want to leave.

TABLE TALK: HIMMEL ANNOUNCES that he might be running a "medium pot bluff," or MPB as he labels it. He will also let us know when he thinks anyone is running an SPB, a "small plot bluff," and much more rarely an LPB, "a large pot bluff." That we've all heard this analysis a million times doesn't prevent him from giving it to us again with the same smirk we've put up with for over thirty-five years. *What a nerd. Typical engineer.* And when he alerts us to the possibility of a "medium pot bluff" when he himself is the potential bluffer, the pronouncement is meant to give the other players pause—a reverse-reverse kind of psychology designed either to draw people in when he's got the cards, or get them to fold when he's running on nothing. It's like those choices in our real lives: you just don't know which it is.

How familiar to me are these gestures and strategies. It's the same familiarity I have with the other players, who have changed so gradually over the years that on these summer weekends I think they could all pass for fifteen. I could tell you that Himmel is balding (as most of us are), that Weston is overweight (as most of us are, except he is worse), that Blaine grows more conservative every year like his Norwegian parents (most of us do—not politically, but in that personal way that means you finally have more to lose in life than you have left to gain).

But what is most remarkable to me is not that I know my old friends so well, but how closely I can relate the particulars of their lives to the way they play poker.

Just as Weston, for instance, folds easily if good cards appear to be on the table in front of someone else, so he once bowed to the father he could never please. "Aren't you a man?" I heard Hal Weston ask his son when Wes had too quickly withdrawn his hand from a hot engine block. We were in our mid-twenties by this time, under the hood, and Wes just laughed at his father's criticism. His dad had served under Patton in the War, while Wes, after ROTC during the Viet Nam era, was given an early discharge from the quartermaster corps for being overweight and somehow annoying a superior career officer. We never did get the straight version of that story, and we never passed judgment, didn't care, but the outcome was clearly not what Wes—or his father— had in mind. And poker? The honorably discharged son of Hal Weston can never bluff, won't run the pot up as much when he truly has the cards. He has learned he must never be wrong, even if it means he's never terribly right.

Himmel, on the other hand, is the most likely to bluff, and most likely to get out with bad cards early in a hand. His father was an engineer, as Himmel now is, and it's the logic of the world that's dearest to him. Two plus two is always four. Yet Himmel's also prone to odds-defying lucky steaks. I remember one such run on a weekend night in high school. After beating us yet again with another flush or full house, Himmel threw down his cards and got up and ran while another player and I chased him around my parents' basement with power tools. It's better just to drop out when Himmel is getting cards.

The best time to beat Himmel is during his remarkable *unlucky* streaks, when his common sense poker fails him. He thinks he should be winning with these cards, but he isn't. Or you can win if he's not paying attention, having too much fun, getting "loosened up" by the other guys with insults, drinks, and old rock and roll on the cassette player. For he is in many ways the most careful of us all, and we are a careful bunch—the "smart kids" ever since junior high, of whom much was expected (and just what was expected? And what did *we* expect, and what do we now? A lifetime to answer those queries). Because Himmel's wife seems not entirely in favor of the now twice or thrice annual trip to the cottage, Himmel may be the one who needs it the most. And for each of us, the trip grows more necessary every year.

"Gee," Himmel says one day, early in the afternoon before any of us has had a drink, "isn't it weird to be over forty and realize this is all the farther you're going to get in life?"

Himmel always wanted to be in management, and never got the call. Just as Arnie was a musician and now is a pattern maker, and Wes was a salesman and now is a house husband, and McNally quit IBM before being dumped in a downsizing and is now back in graduate school, and Blaine survived yet another merger of his New York bank with a bigger one, but wonders if he'll survive the next. And I, too, as a tenured full professor, will know not advancement in my career, but just the coming of the next semester.

So now we wonder why it's turned out that way. We're facing the downward free fall that comes from the top of the arc of career and life more than half gone. Except here at this cabin, where change is suspended. We're stationary here, docked somewhere around 1974. In the woods, here in our Wisconsin, there are no doors that will be either closed or opened to us. Just maples that redden in fall and small beech that hold their yellow leaves into winter. Hemlock, the only conifer that turns.

It's true that we're more or less forced to play our old roles in these annual reunions, roles based on the people we each were in college and high school and even junior high, seventh grade when we met. The roles wouldn't hold all that each of us has become, not for more than the three or four nights at a time that we get together. But for that half a week the roles are sufficient. No one loses except at poker.

Tonight Arnie's table fan, powered by the battery from his trolling motor, mercifully hums and oscillates in the steamy porch. The six of us have gathered again for cards around the plastic-covered dinner table. There are sticky spots in the corners where players spilled drinks last night.

CHAUTAUQUA

One hundred two degrees officially today in a town north of here, according to our battery powered radio. Record heat. On the side of the house, the rusty thermometer from a long out-of-business car dealership reads in the mid-nineties. We decide to call this year's trip, "Camp Sweat."

We remind each other of an early cottage trip, not to Himmel's but to the small place my family used to own. It was probably college years or just after. It was cold as hell outside, near zero (which is to say in Wisconsin, *not quite up* to zero), and we had to move the card table nearer to the stove. We wore air force parkas indoors. There was a cloud of cigarette smoke in the place so thick you could hear it. We were playing poker, and Himmel set a drink too long on the floor and it froze.

"It's just not funny when you try to tell that story to somebody else," Wes complains years later. "A frozen drink—they think you mean a daiquiri, they think you're a really boring guy."

We *are* really boring guys, all of us. But I've never said that to Wes, or to any of the others: Arnie, Himmel, Blaine, McNally. I only say it to myself.

I remind the other guys, too, of a couple of our recent February trips to Himmel's. One night I clambered down the steps from the bedroom for a three a.m. piss off the front porch into a snow bank. I'm standing out there in my union suit, admiring the blaze of winter stars so bright it seems to hurt. Orion's little dog follows him on the hunt. Castor and Pollux wave from over one shoulder. I turn around to look at that car dealer thermometer. Twenty-three below zero Fahrenheit. If I fell and hit my head, I think, I'd be dead before anyone else would find me— Orion, his dog, the twins, my friends. I like knowing that, like being here at this time and in these conditions. This is my Wisconsin. I take another look at the sky.

This evening, in the heat, the wilderness listens. The drinks are filled and filled again. The insults fly: "You rat's ass," "Hey, shit for brains,"

"Why don't you do something constructive, nimrod, and bring me that ashtray?" I can feel in these invectives an unexpressed affection that takes the simple form of tolerance. None of us here has to be anything other than what we've always been. We don't have a choice, for one thing, and if we would try to be something we're not everyone in the room would know. We're not merely college profs and engineers, New York lawyers and former salesmen, tradesmen and freelance wannabes. We're the sum of our contradictions, laid plain.

Flash forward. By the trip in the year we all turn fifty, Himmel is in management and his wife has long given her blessing to his cottage escapes, McNally has *finished* his Ph.D. and is a college professor, Blaine *has* survived two more bank mergers, Arnie *is back* playing in money making rock and roll bands, Wes's wife has made a small fortune in pharmaceutical sales so that he can stay home with the kids guilt free. I have published several books and the words come now to me easier than they once did.

And I am writing the story of this place, one more time. The more the world changes, the more the story stays the same, each year like all the rest, or so to the best of my memory.

IN WALDEN, THOREAU contends that people, like nations, "must have suitable broad and natural boundaries, even a suitable neutral ground between them." He says how he prefers to talk to a companion standing on the opposite side of the pond. "In my house we were so near that we could not begin to hear."

We're not quite that bad at Pete Lake, though Himmel says that with my teacher voice and the spirited and profane conversation we engage in here, I'm audible a good quarter mile down the trail. The house is a big house, four bedrooms and a porch, and its size is part of its incongruity, set out here in the middle of the woods as far away from the world as you can get in Wisconsin, circa today.

But like old Henry Thoreau, we think of the distance from the cottage to the highway on Himmel's property as an important buffer. If we could get here and be here without a road, like a rope ladder to a second story window that you pulled up behind you, that would be even better. But it would be too much. Some years when we come in winter, we have to walk in the last half mile pulling food and mostly beer on toboggans. Most years we have to hike in with the sleds the whole mile and a quarter from the end of the public dirt road. The first year we did this, we agreed that it was way too much work to make any sense. We also agreed that we'd do the same foolish thing again next winter. Maybe bring less beer and more hard liquor in those sleds, save on weight. This winter trip is the only time we ever hear noise from "neighbors," when the grinding whine from snowmobiles at one a.m. can be heard by anybody taking a leak off the porch. Himmel's Dad gives the machines permission to run over his land, about a half-mile from the house, in exchange for having some of the friendlier riders keep an eye on his house through the winter.

One A.M. is the hour the bars close, this is Wisconsin, the winter nights are still and cold, and so this is when we hear the snowmobiles most clearly. Although we all hate snowmobilers, we don't mind the sound too much, since we don't hear it as much during the day. At night, their whir is almost like a wild sound, something near yet far, and out of our control. We admit, though, that on the two or three snowless winters we've made the trip, the bartime quiet has been a blessing that almost made up for the brown stiffness of the landscape.

Sound: I remember on an early trip here, in summer, when a whippoorwill awakened me at dawn. I was about sixteen. The whippoorwill is a shy bird and before this trip, whenever I'd heard one at sundown or sunrise somewhere in the woods, it was a distant cry, cool and musical. But that morning I had a hangover, and the bird was shrieking right outside my window, as loud as a voice in the next room, only in this case the next room was morning. I listened until the sun was high enough that the bird was satisfied and went away.

Mornings: on one high school era stay at Himmel's cottage, Blaine and Arnie set out early, sporting rotten hangovers, started along the stream away from the lake, cut up a hill to save some steps, made another turn or maybe two. Each thought the other knew where they were and how to get back. "So which way from here?" Blaine asked. "I thought *you* knew," Arnie said, and they wandered through the woods for half a day with no water, finally hitting the highway. They had been lost, and there was enough land and woods for that to be so.

Once or twice in summer when we've been here, some fisherman or hiker has walked up the road, got far enough to see our cars parked in the yard or hear the plastic crack of our whiffle ball bat, or our shouts throwing four Frisbees among four guys at the corners of the house, or doing something else equally stupid for middle-aged men, something we need this solitude to feel free to do. The trespasser has always turned up short and left. Himmel and his father were angry ten years ago when, as part of a statewide effort to put street signs up in rural areas, the road off the main highway was labeled "Pete Lake Road," the usual green and white corner sign planted there like a member of an invasive species.

"People see the sign and naturally wonder where the hell Pete Lake is," Himmel says. And when they follow their curiosity for a few miles, they end up staring into Himmel's front porch.

One winter trip Himmel and I were snowshoeing the quarter mile down from the house to the lake when we saw some footprints coming up from the lake and were impressed that Arnie, a restless sort when he gets into the woods, had been up early for a hike. No, Arnie told us later, he hadn't been out at all. Himmel and I shoed back to the house the way we came and found that the stranger's snowshoe prints came within sight of the house and no farther. He'd apparently had his curiosity satisfied and seeing the place inhabited—how unlikely, in the dead of winter—not ventured closer. But what we couldn't figure: the tracks just stopped. There was no sign of the hiker turning around, which with snowshoes leaves quite a print. It's as if he just stopped in sight of the house and ascended into heaven.

CHAUTAUQUA

The prints came not from the direction of the public dirt road and highway; they came from the lake. Someone must have shoed cross country from the snowmobile trail to get here. One person alone in February. Then, as I said, he vaporized into the crisp air.

"Pete Lake Road," the sign designates. I ask Himmel what the name means. He answers that he's not sure, but guesses the lake is named after somebody called Pete.

I'd guess that Pete was the same guy who came in by himself cross country and left those tracks that stopped cold in the snow. It's not a bad way to go if you think about it—quick and without a trace. Gone the instant you see signs of someone else on your trail. Maybe you learn why winter seems to be the one season that tells the truth. Or does it seem that way only if you grow up in Wisconsin and know to ask the right questions of it?

You disappear in the woods one day and leave a puzzle for someone else to solve. You get a lake named after you. Your name is Pete. Or Henry Thoreau.

MCNALLY IS LUCKY and skillful at poker, paying attention when others aren't. He majored in statistics and has such an analytical mind that his lack of aesthetic judgment and grace make him the butt of the most jokes in our group. No one, for instance, wants to listen to the best-of-the-sixties music he brings to the cottage—Three Dog Night or ZZ Top, or some one hit wonder groups. He leaves his cassette tapes in the car. McNally was an only child, and gets peeved wonderfully when he loses a hand in poker the odds say he should have won. If this happens enough, you can beat him on the night since his money is always fully invested. As with Himmel, his faith is in the logical more than it is in himself. McNally is tall and awkward and ungainly, mismatched features and too many expressions for a face of someone so good at poker. But I have to nudge myself to remember to report these details. I never look at any of these guys, am too busy listening—and talking—to notice what they look like anymore.

Blaine, who looks to me just like a regular guy, is logical in cards and life, like Himmel and McNally, like the rest of us. No one who wasn't logical could win at this table, which is a very good table. While Blaine will not bluff with nothing, he might bet a lot with a mediocre hand to "get the riff raff to drop." I think his college-educated, Minnesota-born parents felt somewhat superior to the working class in provincial Green Bay, Wisconsin. After grad school Blaine moved to a Connecticut suburb of New York, and now has a highly successful and lucrative career in international banking. His poker playing, his occasional bluff, has been subtly classist. But as he's aged, this tendency has mellowed. All our tendencies have.

Blaine's impossible to read when he's drunk, which in this annual game (Blaine lives too far off to make the winter trip) is relatively often. It seems to all of us an appropriate action in this setting and time in our lives, this exception to the rule of the everyday.

Blaine's younger daughter came into the world with birth defects. By age five she'd spent half her life in hospitals. Over the years, I wondered if Blaine used the drinking and hanging out as a way to escape from the pressures first of growing up in a conservative family, then law school, then corporate life in New York, then having to watch, helplessly, the plight of his daughter. We all approve highly of this kind of escape, and use it ourselves. This is Wisconsin, where we grew up, and occasionally drinking too much is common practice, even though it's temporarily out of favor in the larger culture. It may be a bad idea for some, but it's always worked for us.

The test of his daughter's illness made Blaine more spiritual, too, more likely to consider the certainty that life will hand each of us things for which we haven't prepared ourselves. The rest of us can only guess at the exact nature of his contradictory feelings at a given point in time. This, along with the booze, makes him an unpredictable poker player. You have to wait and let him beat himself.

And Arneson: If he wins on Friday he'll lose on Saturday. And probably Sunday and Monday besides. He's not terribly lucky, and he's too nice a guy to push the betting when he's on a streak. As with Blaine, you wait him out.

Once I asked Arnie about the depression medication he takes, asked if, after two years, there are side effects. "It's hard to say," he answers, and I wondered if that were a side effect. A musician myself, I like Arnie's stories about being a guitarist on the road and in Vegas, part of a band that for a few nights was the warm-up act for Frank Sinatra. After the gig, they all hung out, he says, and I ask what it was like partying with the great swinger.

"Fine," Arnie says, "if you could get past his security people."

More than any of us, Arnie plies the trout streams here with his fly rod and hand tied flies. I'm the only other in the group who fishes trout, and do so with some conviction, but Arnie will be up only a few hours after a late night of poker to be on the stream before dawn. It's both spiritual practice and his compensation, I think, for what hasn't seemed to happen in any of our lives, that whatever-it-was.

Or has it happened? Blaine's daughter has done well in recent years, and Arnie's spirits revived and he put the pills away. As I said, our extreme tendencies have seemed to wither away, and not only the best ones. Things have seemed to work out. We've become our own security. We've lived to be fifty.

Knowing this much about each of my friends, over so many years, I should win at cards consistently. Except that we all know this much about each other. I'm not sure what my friends would say about my poker strategy, my lot in life. Maybe they'd say that I second guess myself out of too many big pots. That I bet impulsively, or pay more attention to the players than the cards—Blaine's nervous tick, McNally's hesitation before a raise. That I see extra significance in some things that just are. You shouldn't think too much. Not in cards. In life, you should think even less about anything that won't yield an answer you can take to the bank. You should have learned that much by now.

But I haven't learned, and I think too much about all kinds of things I shouldn't think about if I still expect to be happy. Maybe that's what my friends would say about my nature

I doubt my friends would give me the poker advantage of telling me what they think about the way I play. Maybe that's why over the years I've done only a little better than break even. Maybe that's why we all have, or would claim to. Finally, cards is not a perfect metaphor for our lives. Middle-aged, middle class, and middle-western, we're anything but gamblers. Life is perhaps best compared to a simple table with six chairs around it. You go about the business of your day, and then you sit and talk about what just happened and why. But don't talk too much; that slows down the game.

THIS AGING "COTTAGE" is not really a cottage at all, as I've said. "Cottage" is just a term people in the upper Midwest use for the place you go to that's not your home. It could be a shack in the woods, it could be a cabin on a river, it could be—nowadays, sad to say—a mansion on an overfished walleye lake.

Himmel's place is an old two-story house, built in the 1920s by a guy named Harry who at that time was also in his twenties. It's hard for me to imagine Harry and his friends digging the foundation, hauling the construction materials in over the logging roads by horse cart, putting up the place over months or maybe years. But they finished the house and Harry and his wife moved in, and Harry started the mink farm with which he hoped to earn a living. Then his wife said, "But there's nothing to *do* here." It was that oldest of complaints about solitude, and one that's always dead-on accurate. It's maybe why Thoreau got so much writing done.

So Harry divorced that wife, and his next wife was a schoolteacher—summers off. Eventually, this couple moved to town, spending only June through August at the house near Pete Lake.

By the 1950s, Harry was working for the state highway department, which had hired a young engineer and family man named Himmel, father of my poker pal. By this time Harry had the reputation of a ladies' man. It's unclear, as the story was passed on to Himmel the second, what happened to the schoolteacher. But any time that a construction crew was on the road, in a restaurant or a bar, Harry could find a woman to sleep with, a waitress or maybe the manager's wife, or somebody who just walked in.

With these new interests, Harry's house in the woods fell into disuse. There remained for furniture in the place only one cabinet, the old ice box, an end table cobbled from fallen branches, and two metal bed frames with metal springs. Guys would sleep directly on them, sans mattresses. They used the place only as a deer hunting shack (albeit a four bedroom one). The problem was, and is, that the land around the place was not particularly good for deer hunting, predominantly hardwoods that provide little feed for deer. The forest is too thick for the undergrowth that deer like to eat.

Harry started making noises about selling. My mother claimed that my father answered an ad in the paper for Harry's old house on Pete Lake. But my Dad decided it was too remote for him and his young family to use as a summer cottage. ("It *is* too remote," Himmel says to me now when I tell him my mother's story.) My dad lacked the handyman skills the place would require, so he bought a little place on a lake thirty miles further north. I can't verify that my mother's story is true, but it could be.

Himmel's father, on the other hand, had the skills for maintaining Harry's place. But he didn't have a lot of money in 1960, and he told this to Harry.

Harry asked, "How much money do you have?"

AT SOME EMBARRASSINGLY advanced age, probably college years, after some very empty pony of beer, we took up a late nighttime activity that became a cottage tradition. These were our flashlight wars. We circled the house like post-space age Cowboys and Indians, each with a flashlight that had become a ray gun in the summer dark—all except big Wes, who couldn't keep up with the insane running and so who ambled steadily and declared himself a U.N. observer. The rest of us hid in the passageway to the cellar, in the privy or behind the woodpile; we climbed trees or even to the roof, lying in wait, or we circled the house looking for those lying in wait, men past draft age with fingers on the flash trigger, going, "DOO DOO, DOO DOO," when we fired. Or, "TSH TSH TSH TSH." Or, "BEOW BEOW." And the art of it was the baroque way you found to fall, drunk and laughing straight to the ground.

Sometimes we'd get annoyed and even shoot Wes, trying as always to be neutral, and he would laugh and heavily fall.

We don't do that stuff anymore. Don't do what we did even earlier, on the first trips, which had been undertaken on bicycle and not with beer—too heavy to peddle—but with grain alcohol produced with the basement chemistry set of a bizarre high school classmate. He sold the lightning to us in small vials, one of which per person made for an evening's party. We cut it with grape juice or Wyler's lemonade to make "Arnie Humdingers" or "Himmel Specials," and learned to drink that way until we were dizzy and singing and then passed out laughing on the kitchen floor. More often than not somebody would end the night throwing up in the woods; one time someone in the dark accidentally threw up all over Hal Weston's army backpack, and Wes had to give it a good cleaning the next day with red water from the pump.

We each came through these early benders with our eyesight undamaged.

This trip is twenty years after that winter card game with the frozen drinks, almost thirty since the grain alcohol cocktails, on a day hotter than any day ever in northern Wisconsin. We are again at Himmel's cottage, and the game is five-card draw, jacks or better to open. Wes is the dealer, and he's inquiring about the draw. He's decided that everyone at the table should be named Bill. "How many cards do you want, Bill?...Bill takes three" "And for you, Bill? Bill draws two." And you, Bill?" "And Bill?"

It's a joke that only the six of us understand, the name "Bill" borrowed from an old TV quiz show host who was invariably addressed by name by his panelists: "I'll bid two hundred, Bill." "I'll freeze, Bill." But the larger point has nothing to do with TV. For we don't *need* names here. This is the only place I've ever been in my life, including in my family living room, where I can say everyone there knows me better than I know myself.

And although we don't need names, we assign them liberally. Our annual four-day summer trip has been dubbed TME for "The Main Event"; the shorter winter residence TWIT for "The Winter Ice Trip." Similarly, there are named landmarks on the property. The slough the feeder stream makes before it joins the main stream is called "Arnie Pond" because he's fished there and never caught anything. The spot where Blaine and Arnie, lost in the woods years ago, dropped to their hands and knees to scoop up leaf colored water from a ditch is known, with typical hyperbole, as "The Valley of Death." No one knows where the Valley of Death is, by the way. One deer stand is called the "Kiwanis Club Stand," because it looks like the kind of place where you'd buy a hot dog at a county fair. Another is named after the Rosenbergs because, after a number of beers one day, the wooden bench there reminded me of an electric chair.

A grassy valley surrounded by steep hillsides that as high school kids we thought would make a great venue for a rock concert Himmel used to call "The Amphitheater." Over the years the amphitheater grew over with brush, then poplars, and now has become hard to identify, covered as it is with young white pine taller than we are.

IT'S SURPRISING IT TOOK US so many years back at Himmel's to discover the Weatherwood Inn, an archetypal Wisconsin supper club we drive to on Saturday night of our summer weekend, a few miles on the main highway back toward Green Bay. Since most of us no longer live in Wisconsin, we want one night to have a taste of the supper club culture that we remember growing up with. It's also a break from our own cooking. And after the sojourn to the civilized world, we have the pleasure of retreating again to the semi-wilderness.

Bud's, as we call the place, is famous for old fashioneds, that cocktail mix of brandy and bitters that I've never tasted done right out of my home state. Bud is the owner of this little place, a jammed horseshoe bar and adjacent small dining room, and when he's not concocting drinks behind the bar, he works the room, stopping at each party of patrons to exchange a story or tell a dirty joke.

"Do you want to shake my hand now or after I come out?" he ad libs to our group, at the end of the bar next to the men's room. The year we came the first time we'd ordered a round of the stiff old fashioneds, and then Blaine, on our second round, mimicking the Wisconsin accent we get a kick out of, instructed Bud, "*Put some booze in it dis time now.*"

It was a request I'd heard made once of a bartender at a Wisconsin roadhouse, and it's become a one-liner for us, so typical of good-natured outstaters who want a better buzz.

But Bud took exception. After asking which of us was driving, and making sure that Blaine and I weren't, he filled our fishbowl cocktail glasses to the brim with bar rail brandy. "Do you want sweet or sour?" he asked.

"Sweet," we said.

Bud added to each a dot of mix from the gun, like a telegrapher clicking a short vowel. He had his back to us mixing the grenades, and people across the bar watching him cringed in laughter.

He handed smart ass Blaine and me the drinks, and said, "Goodnight, gentlemen."

The drinks did the trick. We struggled, but managed to keep our foreheads off our plates at dinner. That's because the food at Bud's is good too, and one can get drunk anytime and doesn't want to miss the atmosphere for which one came, that Wisconsin blend of all ages gathering at the country bar. E.g.:

—"Mom, I need another quarter." A blond kid between video games. The machine he's playing is called "Fisherman's Bait: a Bass Challenge."

CHAUTAUQUA

Instead of a ray gun or flippers, the player holds an open bale fishing reel and tries to bag a lunker.

—Bud making the rounds. I can catch parts of jokes: The pro to the woman golfer, "Widen your stance," and "Why does a woman wear a pair of panties but just one bra?"

—"Ohhhhhhhh," intones a balding man in a Packers jacket, putting the whole vowel through his nose in the way they do here, the way we used to do before we moved away.

—Wildlife paintings on the pine-paneled walls. Flying ducks and posing deer. In other frames a white-bearded man holds a husky pup while the dog parents stand benignly in a snowy landscape.

—Bumper sticker humor above the bar: "I didn't vote for Clinton *or* her husband." "Beer: helping men get laid since 1802." "If you don't like the logging industry, wipe your ass with plastic." "24 hours in a day/24 bottles in a case. Coincidence?"

—A thirty-something man seeming more earnest than most around the bar, speaking to a group of three younger women he probably doesn't know well. Pickup line: "Do you know why they don't have interstate highways in Hawaii?" Keep your bait in the water, friend, I think.

"I'M SURPRISED IT'S not even more crowded than this," I say to the red-haired woman managing the bar. She is large-framed, has a presence and a broad putty face, as if she could be cast in a raunchy sit com.
"The crowd comes late on Saturday, so hold onto your shorts."
A pretty young woman behind the bar, a head taller than she, calls her "Mom" and asks nicely for a garnish for her soda, then goes back to her table with her boyfriend. The boss comes around from the other side of the bar.

"How are you doing, Bud?" we ask.

"Well, not too good," he answers. "I'm going to sell out while I'm still alive." He looks drawn and whiter than the last time we were in. Is he kidding again? We wait for the punch line, and he tells us instead he's selling the bar to the red-haired woman with the pretty daughter. So no more Bud at Bud's.

"Are yous ready to order," interrupts an empty-eyed waitress while we're waiting for a table. Our attention is diverted, and then as if to make sure I heard correctly, she addresses us with her second person plural three or four more times while we tell her want we want to eat. Do *yous* want the salad bar. Do *yous* need another drink? Our Wisconsin.

A round of drinks later, we're seated. At a family table next to us, parents ask a boy, maybe four, how many people are sitting with them. There's a long pause.

"Six?" he guesses.

Another, shorter pause.

"Always count yourself first," his father says, "then you won't get confused."

"What kind of fish is that?" they ask the little boy about a mounted trophy above my head.

He looks first at the fish, then at me, then the fish. This time he doesn't hesitate: "Small mouth bass!"

IT'S PAST EVENING into night now, but it's cooled off only a little, and there is no breeze from the lake or through the woods. Arnie's fan hums on the table. Two of us are ahead at poker, two behind, and two close to even. We take a break to piss in the woods. We fight off the dark outside and find the bugs not too bad. Maybe it's still too hot even for mosquitoes. When you're peeing in the woods in the dark, your back to the faint light from the house, you tend to look up, the only direction you can see anything. In the space between the tallest trees, a small patch of night sky.

CHAUTAUQUA

AFTER THE FIRST few trips back here, I decided to write a stage play about a group of friends, forty-two or forty-three years old at that time. They remained close through high school and college, grad school and career, marriage and family, and into the stasis of middle age. But I needed something more in the play, some obvious conflict or action. So I made Blaine into a real estate developer who wants to sell out the cottage from under us (in the play, conveniently for my plot, the place is owned jointly, like a primitive timeshare condo). Blaine wants to play developer and make a quick profit—for all of us, he maintains.

We protest his plan, as we must, and in response he points out that all of us are over forty now, and none of us has a future in our careers that's going to be much different from the immediate past. We're no longer young and promising.

We know he's right. That's the plateau, the tragic recognition of my play.

Then in the last act, someone—probably me—suggests that there's something dishonest about what Blaine is doing, denying the sacred trust of the group so long gathered in this wilderness.

"Dishonest?" Blaine says as he's dealing a game of seven-card stud. Then as he deals each of us the last card which will make or break our poker hands—four card straights and two pair begging full houses—he points out dishonesties and truths each player has failed to face: shady business deals or disappointing children. When he comes to the last player, Arnie, who I call Lefty in the play, Blaine announces that Lefty cheats at cards, that he's been cheating the whole thirty years of our friendship.

We know, the rest of us say. We've known for thirty years and have never said anything. Is this dishonesty? Or is it forgiveness?

"After all," says the character who is based upon me, "there never was much money at stake. And Lefty never came out ahead anyway."

I never finished writing the play. My idea made for a good sounding story, but once I'd figured out how it ended, that the characters were all really failures and liars, I couldn't get interested in writing it down.

The play betrayed our love for the land, that much was right, and the poker element rang true and made a good way for the conflict to work itself out (though no one here ever cheated at nickel and dime poker). Beyond that drama, the play didn't have enough to do with what I wanted to find out about my old friends and our reunions at Himmel's cottage. To research the play, I had for several years brought a notebook on the trip, tried to jot things down in my bedroom between poker sessions and canoe or skiing outings, items that would help reveal the importance of our gatherings. The entries read, "Himmel shoveled a deep path through the snow to the privy," "McNally went out for wood," the most banal and routine of activities. "Good night at poker." "Burned the steaks."

Was I not listening? Avoiding the issue, the revelation that must take place here? Or was there no meaning, just escape and pure experience?

I think neither. But my play had been an attempt to assign easily paraphrasable meaning to the fact that we've known each other for a much longer time in our lives than we haven't. Getting together at Himmel's cottage, we step out of our daily roles and into older, but not better roles. We're each of us a better person now than we were as kids and young men. Yet we want to take up the old roles again, at least for a few days. There is here a drama insufficient for the stage, but truth sufficient for the telling. Something always draws us back to being partly who we used to be. I like to think it's the land that's doing this, that the land is more than just the setting for our foolishness, more vital than that seventh player I compared it too. Maybe the woods are the real and only game.

Coming back loosened up from Bud's two old fashioneds, I remember our early trips to Himmel's cottage when as kids, feeling no pain this way, we'd walk or maybe roll down the short path from the house to the lagoon. A moon and planetary star hung over the part of the horizon above where the lake would be. For some reason, in those days, menthol cigarettes were considered more desirable than regulars, and could be gotten here from your pal in a trade for two regular smokes. Salems or Kools were okay, but Newports, which we dubbed Chryslers, were especially coveted. At the poker table, we parallel parked packs of Chryslers around the cards and chips.

"Hey, give me a Chrysler," someone would say down at the lagoon (or down *by* the lagoon as we say in Wisconsin). We'd light them up, drag deeply, then blow the smoke into the face of a waiting compatriot. It wasn't an insult or sexual come-on. It was the opposite of flashlight aggression. This in our naming obsession we called a "secondhand drag," and the smoke that had been in the lungs of one was taken in smoothly by a second. "It's sweet! It's sweet," the second smoker would say, the menthol and bad stuff in the cigarettes mixed with the air of the woods and the night dampness above the lagoon. Then the second guy would smoke for the first, the process reversed. "Sweet, it's sweet!" he'd proclaim, always the same.

ALZHEIMER'S POKER: What did you say the game was? Who didn't ante? Who *did* ante?

Consider the advantages: Everyone is bluffing, all the time. No night's losings are better or worse than any other.

Do I know you?

Heart attack. Prostate cancer. Car wreck. Massive stroke. There are two of us left. *Thomas Jefferson still lives*, the letter Adams writes, unknowing, when both are to die the same day.

If I am one of the last, I will have wanted all these years to say or ask of my oldest friends things beyond the simply ironic truth. Beyond the simple truth of irony: Does my wife love me? I her? Could you keep your sex life going past fifty? Sixty? Are children the meaning of life, and if so, what of the rest? What is the hardest thing to face, death or regret?

But I will have never gotten past my maleness, my inert Midwestern nature, a human underestimate of the average moment. I drink a beer, I speak in code, there is no key. It's not a bad way to be. It has some truth in it.

At this hour, if I fell and hit my head out here, no one would find me. How much money *do* you have? Gee, isn't it weird. We *are* really boring guys. People naturally wonder where Pete Lake is. Where the tracks just stop cold, and we ascend. Things seem to work out. A simple table with six chairs. Through the trees we can see a moon.

"Time for a break," somebody says in the record heat. "How about a *major* break," Blaine asks and, organized and craving consensus as always, we all agree.

We step outside to talk and stretch and smoke. "Hey, give me a Chrysler," Himmel says to Blaine. Blaine smokes now only on these trips, as does Himmel. I don't smoke at all. Himmel didn't bring any menthol cigarettes along, so Blaine gives him one. Wes provides the light.

"Anybody want to take a walk down the road?" Himmel asks, and some of us say yeah, and another who said nothing comes along, and maybe someone stays back at the house. No one minds because here you can do what you want.

We walk down the road far enough away from the cabin so that we can't see the small light from the Coleman lantern, can't hear the music from the battery driven cassette player somebody left blasting over the poker table, where our money and chips lie in six piles and a pot, like abstract art.

The world around us has changed. Soon the population of America will be double what it was the first time we came to Himmel's cottage. I try to imagine two people every place that I see one now. Except this place won't change. There will be no plots for developments or resorts or hunting preserves, as in my unlikely stage play. Not for a while at least. We're alive.

It's still ungodly hot, a few bugs are out, since we're farther into the woods than we were when standing in the yard, but not nearly so many bugs as there should be on such a muggy summer night. We're too lazy and common sensical to go down to the lagoon; we'd have to walk back up the hill. And we haven't had a flashlight war in twenty years. No one's going to suggest a secondhand drag, older now. So we stand here on the road, and somebody who brought a drink along drinks it, and somebody who didn't, doesn't. Without needing to be told we each shut off our flashlights, so it's perfect dark around us, to match the still and heat. Because of that, through the trees we can see a moon.

Some Long Forgotten Sea Chantey

George Looney

The sky this morning, a dim conspiracy of light,
cumulus and cirrus in cahoots,
makes it harder to ignore this corpse-in-waiting
I call my body, all its usual complaints
more urgent. Weather patterns, I've heard,
are shifting, some Hispanic wind changing
everything but the fact of my deterioration.

It's the nature of all our bodies, even yours, love.

No matter what language we use to record decay,
it's the same, our future. And certain.

The best we can do is practice the art of forgetting,
get good enough we can choose
what to forget, and when. This morning,
the whispered collusion of a sky is more
a reminder than either of us feel comfortable with.

It wants to be an image sung into a poem,
the vehicle in a simile that lets the heart be
understood. It wants desire to be its subject,
and it wants to satiate every reader. Listen,

love, to the sky this morning. *La Niña* sings
some long forgotten sea chantey. Let's work

CHAUTAUQUA

our bodies to its mysterious rhythms,
and in the sweat and the soreness let's forget
the future that waits for us and ignore
this fervent and desperate conspiracy of clouds.

The purpose of our desire to hold one another
is to let us forget. Amnesia, a dance,
calls for two bodies. Memory only needs one.

TO FISHERMEN

Carol Frost

No more savage art: filleting: a deft pressure along the
   backbone

from tail fan to the red gills: fighting mystery with a
   honed blade

through the small bones: salt and scales on face and
   hands:: the Greek God,

as well, found flesh unmysterious, but in anger and
   disappointment:—

seagull cries, your music, are all about you: Apollonian
   but hungrier: nature is hungry::

the brave fish dies the birds swoop for the insides in no
   lovelier spirals.

THE LUNGFISH GASPS IN ITS COCOON OF TEARS: ADAPTATION

Susan Grimm

I.

In that house where I first gazed into a mirror,
where I spoke to an invisible friend (those at the table
requested to pass dishes to the playroom)—was growing up

on Mapledale like living in Cuba? Citizens plan
to escape the regime. Lying on the dining room floor
with dolls, lying to mother, lying in the backwoods

with a joint (not very often).
                                Out in the street
men in their somber colors, spit, shoot
their cuffs. (They have their own magic wands, tell

all one story, while I carry a purse!) The head
idyllic with its pastoral flowers, straw, the feet
moving towards higher heels. Above the waist,

below—a convenient equator—the limbs' tanned
illusions held up by garters, the contradictions
of my white gloves. After girdling, some slips,

eventually I was braless, but the rest of me
stayed tense.

Susan Grimm

II.

       Home, homing in, like the lungfish
who breathes air when the water dries up, who builds

a house from mucous and river bank mud, we do
what we have seen them do. We buy a hammer,
some dishcloths, a rug. We come home to each other,

crack the windows, gather love.
                         Out in the street
men no longer call me honey or open doors
like vertical beds, a little bow to look at the legs.

A serape of age protects me as effectively
as purdah. From my tent of years looking out
the little square (is it getting smaller),

I observe how love runs out, your heart like a sieve.

III.

Sand flying, a flickering cloud. The sky smells
different, wilder. No longer becoming myself,

(was that a bad thing) and longing to leave a puff
of smoke at the end of a jagged trail. Grounded,
the magnet of my brain turned sideways, backwards.

Lost birds circle a continent. Fish remember their wings.

Lake Tahoe Roil

Susan Grimm

My whole edge a tongue licking the rocks, smudging
the shore. My hair grown loopy and long cast
towards willows. Oh, cold cold heart. The lake

is alone no matter what melt water feeds it,
the piddle and splash of its waves. Like fingers
snapping, a head shake. Is this liquid

music? All the blues toyed with and released
each night, refusing reflection. Slosh,
rotate, freckle, wave. The bear and the beaver come

and the hungry duck, the sun projecting light.
Restless non-event—these burdened changes,
the prickly uncertain hills. How to get out

of this bed? Always the band of green
under the froth of white. The fish threading
up from the depths, lipping their flies.

DR. MASON

Lee Gutkind

Excerpted from the essay "WWMG"

One day, about two years into therapy with the psychiatrist I will call Dr. Howard Mason, I was attempting to relate an incident that had occurred when I was thirteen years old, an incident so vivid and frightening that I was unable to remember it all at once. Whenever I started thinking about it—and I found myself re-living snatches once or twice every week—I allowed as much of the memory of that incident to filter back into my mind as I could stand before it became too threatening to endure. I was not haunted by this image, but it was a lingering, unexplored recollection that I could neither eradicate nor confront.

But as I began experiencing the healing that surfaced with the unloading of a lifetime of anxiety on Dr. Mason's shoulders, I noticed that this image was reappearing more frequently, for longer periods, and with sharper resolution of detail. Previously, this memory had returned sporadically and in erratic blurred images, often in black and white. But now I began to visualize swatches of color, blue mostly and yellow—rays from a glaring ball of sun outside a window. The window through which the sun was pouring, I began to see, was in a seventh grade junior high school classroom. I was sitting in this room at my desk. It was homeroom where we all reported in the morning for fifteen minutes of school business before heading to our first class.

But there were unusually few students in the room that day. Most of the people missing were boys. This was my first year at Taylor Allderdice, the largest high school in the city, located in a predominantly Jewish community called Squirrel Hill. Coming here from a small elementary school at the far end of the district, most classmates were strangers.

The neighborhood I lived in, Greenfield, was blue collar, working class, friendly and comfortable, if you were white and Christian, especially Catholic. As I got older, "Kike," "dirty Jew" and "Christ killer" were words and phrases I grew accustomed to hearing; I was ambushed and beaten up by neighborhood kids regularly. My parents' promise and my hope at the time I entered Taylor Allderdice was that I would meet kids my age, many of whom were Jewish like me, with whom I could be friends, kids who would not consider me an outsider.

But I soon realized that a shared faith and culture might not be enough to launch new friendships. I didn't fit, didn't dress right, didn't carry myself in the confident way in which these Jewish kids cruised the hallway, greeting one another with a comfortable familiarity that totally eluded me. Listening to their conversations, I learned that they had relationships outside of school, participated in weekend and summer activities different from my own. These kids had no interest in befriending me, a stranger from the wrong side of the district and, in fact, lumped me in with the Greenfield kids I was hoping to escape.

With the exception of the missing students, this particular morning was just like any other. I was sitting at my desk in homeroom waiting for the day to start, watching out the window for the last few stragglers to run across the lush green lawn and up the spacious front steps of the school, when I felt a change in the atmosphere. No noise—just an electric stillness, like that second of a synapse that precedes the thunder and lightening of a violent storm. Then the missing boys began walking into the room, one at a time, grinning sheepishly and self-consciously to one another. Each wore a loose-fitting, crew-neck sweatshirt, gray with blue lettering, displaying four bold initials WWMG.

When I read the words corresponding to the letters—*work-wisdom-morality-goodness*—I realized that it would be impossible for me to be a part of this in-group. It had been totally unrealistic to entertain the possibility of acceptance. These boys, with their long-standing connections from elementary school, religion or family were now taking steps to define their separateness and close off their circle of intimacy. They had forged a bond, formalized in a fraternity, with a nobility and ethic that I, at thirteen, knew absolutely nothing about. I knew something about work, because I had been sentenced to the prison of my father's shoe store most days after school and on weekends, but the concepts of wisdom, morality, goodness, which these boys had somehow obtained, left me high and dry.

I will never forget my sense of loss and isolation as the boys trooped into the homeroom, the bright rays of the sun streaming through the window, illuminating each of their faces, one after another, like the light from the burning bush on top of Moses' mountain. I found out later that they had planned their dramatic entrance in advance, lining up in the hallway outside the homeroom door to be certain of the class's full attention.

Until now, I had never been able to reconstruct this incident from beginning to end. The exclusion I had experienced was too hurtful, representing a line that was drawn between me and those with whom I assumed a natural connection. Rejected by the kids and families in Greenfield, I had been assured that ultimate acceptance would occur in Squirrel Hill with the Jews, the Chosen people. But I had been immediately rejected by the chosen few—all of them "my" people—the embodiment of that rejection now contained by those initials and the words behind them: WWMG, *work wisdom, morality and goodness*, qualities I had apparently been denied.

Finally able to re-live this incident with Dr. Mason in his office, I suddenly realized that many of my life decisions had been shaped by that moment. My drive in high school to become ultra different, to stop taking my studies seriously, to be rebellious and uncooperative and therefore attract attention to myself, to smoke and drink and become a chronic truant and later to become a hippie, thug motorcyclist and even later to marry two non-Jewish, non-threatening women were all actions in response to these exploding feelings of rejection.

As I sat in Dr. Mason's office and described that incident to him for the second and then a third time, I recalled especially how the sun had spotlighted each boy as he had walked one after another into the room. Suddenly, a familiar face was illuminated in that spotlight, which I instantly freeze-framed. Here was the face of a chubby, curly-haired boy I only vaguely remembered, someone with whom I had never spoken, even though we were in the same graduating class and I had seen him and probably indirectly interacted with him at least once or twice each week throughout high school from seventh to twelfth grade. Although time had slimmed his face of baby fat and his name was inexplicably different, I suddenly realized that I knew the man this boy had become. I *trusted* this man; I had confessed, revealed, more of my true, honest inner self to this man than to anyone else in my entire life.

"You were there," I said, pointing across the shadowed tasteful room at Dr. Howard Mason. "You were one of them! WWMG! Work. Wisdom. Morality. Goodness. You mother fucker," I said to Mason. "You ruined my life."

TRUST WAS THE WATCHWORD in my relationship with Dr. Mason, as it needs to be in any therapeutic setting. I trusted him—I had to trust him with the most intimate secrets of a lifetime. All my life I had felt angry and isolated, alone in a sea of personal subterfuge. I had no friends or confidantes. Keeping my feelings to myself may have made me look strong and independent on the outside, but inside I was fearful and angry. I wanted to know why—and I wanted to release the pressure of my anger. I had hated the WWMG boys from the moment they revealed themselves, and I had taken what had happened—being excluded—quite personally, as if Mason and his Squirrel Hill cronies had planned my humiliation. But they had no reason to hurt me; they had no reason to know who I was, or to know if I was inferior. Which is what I eventually realized, as I tried to process the notion that Dr. Mason was one of those despicable WWMG boys who, as a group, precipitated the worst years of my life. Mason may have been guilty of self-centeredness, but not of malice. After all, he had been an adolescent—no more sensitive or mature than I. And it also dawned on me that he, like me, harbored his own secrets to reveal.

"Why did you change your name?" I demanded at our next session. Instantly, his real name had come back to me; I visualized him the way he had been a quarter of a century before. "You were Mendelssohn—not Mason; you were Jewish, like all of the rest of those bastards in Squirrel Hill who rejected me."

For the first time in our relationship, Mason was visibly upset and uncontrolled. His usually passive pale face flushed with humiliation. "It is a long story, and I don't want to get into it," he said. "Changing my name seemed like the right thing to do at the time . . . I'm not sure if I should have done it, but you never know how things are going to turn out," he added.

Then he lapsed into an awkward silence, and we stared at each other, listening to the clock beside his table click-clicking up until the time for talk was over and I silently jumped to my feet, walked out of the office and out onto the street without saying goodbye. As to whether he really had recognized me all along and had been waiting for this moment of discovery and revelation—or dreading it—I should say that, although it was a very likely possibility, I decided that it didn't matter. I had made my decision to trust someone—a decision that had to do with how much you trust yourself and the people with whom you share intimacies. For whatever reason, I had instinctively put my faith in Dr. Mason/Mendelssohn, who had devoted his time listening to me, and I was not willing to pack my bags and go elsewhere after investing so much of my true innermost self and receiving so much insight in return, even though all the insight gained was mine.

I WAS NOT ANGRY with Dr. Mason. How could I be angry when Dr. Mason, whatever his lapses, helped me unearth a painful, haunting memory. The WWMG story opened the innermost doors to my life, shedding light on who I was—and why I conducted myself the way I did. I trusted Mason, my psychiatrist.

CHAUTAUQUA

DR. MASON HAS come into my life on two occasions since I stopped therapy fifteen years ago. The first time was the morning after Patricia, my second wife, announced her intention of divorcing me.

That morning, I realized that facing my computer and attempting to continue working on my current book project would not be practical or productive so I decided to go to the nearby Starbucks. I would bring my notebook and attempt to jump-start my work there. I could then continue my writing back at my home office later in the morning after I had taken Sam to school and my wife left the house to go to work. I dressed hurriedly and jumped in the car. I arrived just in time for the six A.M. opening and already there was a black Volvo station wagon glinting in the yellow-beamed spotlights of the parking lot. Inside, there was a lone figure hunched over a newspaper at the opposite end of the shop, evidently the owner of the Volvo.

After a while, he got up and walked over to the serving counter and asked for a refill; I could see his reflection in the glass of the front window through which I was peering, but I needn't have looked. I recognized his voice. My heart smashed against the inside wall of my chest, as I was struck by the incredible and undeniable meaning of the coincidence. After fifteen years of silence, Dr. Howard Mason, in some ways a virtual stranger and in other ways the single most important figure of my life, had suddenly reappeared—and at a time I needed him the most. I turned to attract his attention. He came toward me, extending his hand. "I thought I recognized you when you came in," he said.

"Is this your morning hang-out?" I said.

"Two or three times a week," he replied. "How are you doing?" he asked me, softly, with his best seductive intonation. As I paused to allow the sound of his voice and the intensive and intimate warmth of his manner to gush back into me and engulf me with infantile feelings of escape from danger and safety, I realized that this was my moment of reckoning. Dr. Mason had helped me through my last divorce, and now he had magically appeared to help me through my second marital disaster. But after that initial rush of relief and escape, I realized that I didn't need him. His sudden and coincidental appearance there at Starbucks the morning after the disaster of my marriage, actually enhanced my trust of myself. It reminded me of what I had learned—my strength and my inner capacity to deal with the most challenging and trying of circumstances. This is what therapists are supposed to do for their patients, I think—prepare them to be emotionally independent, to not panic when experiencing the familiar and frightening rush of anxiety, to, essentially, learn to "shrink" themselves.

One time when our sessions had been especially intense, and when I began having second thoughts about being able to manage without his help and without regular therapy, he had told me that wherever I was I would be able to hear his voice at times of indecision and crisis. He did not mean that I would actually hear him advising me about what to do, but that I would be able to remember how I had responded in similar difficult situations and, more than that, I would recall that, by acting instinctively and logically, I had survived every major crisis in my life. I had been hurt, but had always been able to rebound in a way that made me proud of myself and had enhanced the shape of my character. I must know and accept the probability, he told me, that I would have more hard times in my life, that I would experience anxiety and depression, but I must learn to trust myself and, just as importantly, trust that if ever I really did need him, he—Dr. Howard Mason—would be available. I don't believe that our coincidental connection at Starbucks was some sort of mystical sign that the great spirits were beaming Mason's energy down toward me, but I felt exceedingly fortunate that it had happened; his presence demonstrated my strength and independence.

"I'm fine, Dr. Mason," I told him, after pausing for a while. "Never better."

meteor
Elaine Terranova

What first he wanted to know, was it
iron or stone or ironstone?

Falling to him, heavy with its own
importance. Mantle and core, it
hadn't burned out, down the hundreds
of millions of years in its descent,
rock dropped into his kitchen
at his feet, into the heart of his life.

It's being there put him in mind
of the great emptiness. Where he sat,
tomatoes in a stiff white soufflé dish.
Tomatoes, seeming to speak to him
frankly. A man. An extra man, at parties,
called into service like an extra chair.

He had read of the end stage of stars,
even the sun, loosening from gravity,
into "the junkyard of the universe."
Red giant, spewing material like the tail
of a comet, to build new stars.

Bow shockwave in front
like a boat moving through water.

Elaine Terranova

Red giant, red as a sting,
wheal and then flare, red on the skin.

And he, released at last from anonymity,
heartbeat, loud as now, slowing to less
than breath, the body's cue,

remembers his mother's insistence
on fresh air, window cracked
to winter. Air coming down to him
as it did then, when he toppled
into sleep, rolling around with the world.

Snow Globe
Maura Stanton

Falling flakes gather on darkening ground
Inside my defective globe. Snowy drifts,
Once white, turn slowly brown as the water
Thickens with bacteria. But Basho's still
Etched into the silver base: "Winter solitude
In a world of one color the sound of wind."
When I push the switch, I hear the wind blow.
A loon cries, and the shaken flakes resettle
Drifting past four bare trees, one a small birch,
That the designer has carefully erected
On the lakeshore, no doubt remembering
Some secret place in a northern forest
Glimpsed in the twilight. When I opened this gift
From my mother, who saw how I'd admired
Her own snow globe, it cheered me up to see
A peaceful scene beyond ordinary weather.
But six months later, the water's all gloom,
And Basho's words now mean something else
That neither he nor the manufacturer intended.
What color is the "world of one color?"
I thought it was just my own rotten luck
To get a damaged globe, but now it seems
My mother's snow is stained and dingy, too,
And my sister, and my sister in law
Report discoloration in their little worlds
Once proudly displayed on mantels and tables.

Maura Stanton

Do we simply throw them out? Or hide them
Behind lamps, or in some messy hall closet?
I touch the smooth glass dome of sky, peer in
At my thin trees, lost in the gathering murk,
And listen hard to the wind, and the loon's cry.

Last Seen, Hank's Grille

Ron MacLean

What can I tell you? Only what I have seen. What I have pieced together from the reports of others and filtered by my own experience. Perceptions which are inadequate and inconclusive. Theories and abstractions about a damaged world, when what everyone wants from me—a witness—is a coherent version of events.

I throw up my hands, befuddled. You will want to punch me.

It's happened already. My snout broken and bloodied for no reason other than I spoke the truth. That I cannot say with any certainty what happened out there.

Becca says that's bullshit. Maybe she's right.

All I know is her brother is missing, and she blames me.

BECCA HAS THEORIES of her own. She is of the opinion that Tom has a head injury, that this explains his decreasing interest in things like paying his bills on time or his willingness to drive cross-country with Fillmore Priest. Although I don't believe it's true, her theory is more plausible than you might think. Tom talked about a fall he took in February, shortly after he moved to Massachusetts, to Ashland. How his front walkway was coated in black ice. How his feet went out from under him and he flew, a tangle of arms and legs, landing ass over teakettle on the walk. He laughed about it later, his introduction to the East coast after nearly a decade in Texas. A concussion, a few hours of jumbled memories, maybe an increased sense of forgetfulness. And while he hasn't had any physical problems since, Becca believes something happened there. That Tom maybe cracked his head on the stone step and the delicate mystery that is the human brain was affected.

Of course, Becca also believes it's my fault that Tom is homosexual. She's determined not to resent Tom for it. Says she's trying to hate the sin, but love the sinner. I want to ask her how she feels about that now, with Tom missing, but my nose is too sore to get hit again.

BECCA IS A BELIEVER. She is able to view the world in discernible shapes and patterns, to form an opinion and stick to it. I've never been able to see things that clearly. The way I see it, none of us humans is intact. We carry a besieged past, inhabit a confused present. What beliefs and values we do pass on are increasingly inadequate to account for the world around us. I believe that the ability to believe has been compromised, maybe irreparably, and that we live in an age where apostasy is necessary: a means of survival, maybe even a source of enlightenment.

This is the shit that drives Becca crazy.

TOM IS BRILLIANT. Though it took him a while to find something he wanted to apply himself to. He worked for the Peace Corps in Indonesia. Got a law degree and stumbled into a job as in-house counsel for a start-up biotech firm. Couple years later went to medical school then transferred, after a year, to study genetics. He looks like a scientist. Thin, intense, a little aloof. That thing with his eyes where even when he's looking right at you, he's looking beyond you. Anyway, he became fascinated by research he'd read on human aging, and the possibility that it could be arrested. It was all about understanding disease in a new way, he said, and using genetics to find treatments. None of us thought Tom would last, but he did; earned his doctorate in cell biology from the Baylor School of Medicine and caught on with a team working to isolate the aging gene. It's not as crazy as it sounds.

A telomere is a cap at the end of a DNA string, which shortens every time a cell divides. When the cap is used up, the DNA is exposed and the cell dies. But if these telomeres could be lengthened, the cell could live longer. Maybe a lot longer. There were scientists who believed in the existence of a telomerase gene, and in the '90s, they found the scientific climate to support them. Funding for their projects. Publicity. Enthusiasm. Tom was one of those scientists. And Fillmore Priest is where he found his money.

"THE FACTS, MAX," Becca says to me. "Just the fucking facts." Becca never says fuck. Her knuckles are still swollen from where she broke my nose. I take perverse satisfaction in my ability to annoy her.

Okay, the facts. Tom and Fillmore Priest and I rented a 1976 Cadillac El Dorado convertible, filled a cooler with ice and Coronas and Priest's baby-shit-brown blend of wheatgrass and carrot juice, and hit the highway. Destination: Nogales Mexico, a little restaurant called the Las Vegas Café that has the best *ropas vieja* that any of us has ever tasted. Crazy as Priest is, I do enjoy his company. And when he and Tom get going, even if two-thirds of what they say sails straight over my head, it makes me smile. It's inspiring. Although I will never taste greatness myself, I do like to be near it, and greatness seems to enjoy my underachieving company. But I digress. Two days into our road trip, near a truck stop outside of Abilene where we'd stopped in search of chili dogs, Tom wandered off. Disappeared. And, although it makes no logical sense when you consider the circumstances, I don't think Tom is missing. I think he left.

I'VE MET SOME odd characters over the years, but none odder than Fillmore Priest, a geophysicist who'd made his fortune finding oil. Could sniff it out like a dog. Priest, now in his seventies, has devoted his later years to a single goal: he wants to be the first person to live to two hundred. "Hell," he told me the first time I met him. "We should be able to do as good as turtles."

I'd gone to visit Tom in Houston in 1995, during the start of his third year at Baylor. He had a work dinner and wanted me to come along. The guy he was meeting was a character, and I would love him.

That night Tom and Priest and I ate steaks and Gulf shrimp and drank martinis, and I first heard Priest's wild thoughts about the "cure" for old age. Priest barely fit at the table—he's an enormous man with a bald skull and a delicate face. Soft skin still tinged baby pink and damn near wrinkle-free.

"I'm having an extremely happy life," he told me, a bubble of steak sauce hanging on his lip. "Why should I have to die?"

Tom raised his eyebrows at me, and ate. He was always hungry then —you couldn't fill him up.

"I have more money than God," Priest said, in a gruff voice too loud for the half-full restaurant. "And yet every year, I grow more terrified of death."

It was one of those places with a cigar room, all brass sconces and mahogany, the musk of serious business deals in the air. The kind of place I never expected to find myself. Priest leaned toward me; his green eyes, framed behind magnifying glass lenses, bored into mine. Our dinner plates were massive. "Do you know how many vitamin pills I take every day?"

I shook my head, "No, sir."

He wore a coral-colored golf shirt nearly the same tint as his skin. There was muscle in his bulk. There seemed no way he could be in his seventies. "Guess."

Tom watched us, intent, his fork in steady rhythm, plate to mouth to plate. Shrimp. Steak. Shrimp.

I shrugged. "Six?"

"Fifty-five." Each syllable punctuated with a poke of his index finger on the table. "Fifty-five god damned vitamins every day. A regimen of karate. And I can't shake the terror of dying. What do you think of that?"

All I could think of was the sight of this enormous perspiring man bowing in a white robe.

"Fillmore has formed a society," Tom said. His angular frame did not fit well in chairs. "The Cure Old Age Right Now God Dammit Society." He cut a piece of steak. Let it absorb the juices. Chewed bread as he spoke. "If you're not careful, Max, he'll recruit you."

"He mocks me." Priest spoke to me, convivial "But we're a team. Joined on a common quest. Because I've given your friend and his cohorts more than a million dollars to make a start."

I concentrated on my meal, eating shrimp to hide my chagrin. I'd never thought about the scads of money that must lie behind serious scientific research. I didn't want to. I wanted only to think of pristine laboratories far from the demands of commerce.

Priest held his fork aloft. "Most of the world suffers from occluded vision," he said. "The inability to see beyond the end of their noses. Tom's gift is he's willing to go into uncharted territory." Priest wrapped an arm around Tom and grinned broadly. "He's a visionary, like me."

Tom put his own arm around Priest's shoulder. The pair of them, intertwined like ceramic monkeys. Tom's face wore a mix of pride and something else. The expression stuck in my mind and later, on the way back to his apartment, I identified it as mischief. Like a child who's getting away with something in plain sight of the adults.

"You don't buy that stuff?" I asked him. "I mean, there's no science there."

It was a warm night in Houston. We wore short sleeve shirts and the flush of good alcohol. Though nearly a head taller than me, Tom slouched when he drank, diminishing the distance between us. He was quiet a minute before answering. "Priest's money can put him at the forefront of scientific development. He's engaged with smart people, exciting work, and that makes him feel alive."

"Sure, he's a good way to get funding." Deep night. The streets were deserted. The city ours.

"In science, the questions we start out asking aren't always the ones that get answered. They may become the engine that drives the work toward some related end." Only when Tom saw my puzzled face did he say more. "We could be two or three years from a major breakthrough, Max. Think about what that means." His eyes doing that thing they do. "To me, this is a religious question. I want to work to end human suffering. Behind suffering is disease, and behind disease is aging."

That was the only answer I ever got. I spent that night—and a good part of the next several weeks—thinking about it all. I decided I was proud of my friend's resourcefulness. How he was able to steer a rich old man's delusions toward enriching human life.

TOM'S SITUATION REMINDS ME of Katie, a woman I knew for a time after college. A bunch of us were working for a market research firm in Brooklyn. Everyone there had something else they "really" did—poets, playwrights, painters—but Katie was maybe the most eclectic of us all. She drifted through her days, trying out everything, tying herself to nothing, and this free-floating quality was essential to her being. Her respiratory system. Two or three guys and as many women got seriously hung up on her, pressed her for constancy. But that wasn't how Katie worked. She was with who she was with for today; tomorrow it might all be different.

We drove to Minneapolis one night on a whim, Katie and Judy and Lori and I, and somewhere in Wisconsin, or maybe Iowa, a few wild horses ran up beside the road, running full tilt, nostrils flaring in the moonlight. They must have run with us for close to a mile and then drifted off, slowed down. None of us saw where they came from, but while we watched them Katie told me about growing up, how she'd never go back to the places she had already lived—Chicago, San Diego, Eugene. That when she left a place, she left it for good. Friends and all. People think big change only happens through some cataclysmic event, some traceable root cause. But Katie just slipped out the back door.

WE HEADED SOUTH through D.C., Virginia. Then on into Kentucky, Missouri, Arkansas. Our own erratic route to Mexico. I hadn't seen

Priest in a couple years, and he was all giddy banter before we settled into the drowsy, quiet rhythm of a long ride. Tom was subdued. His eyes tired. He and I shared the driving.

Outside Bowling Green. Rolling pasture. Herefords grazing in afternoon sun. Priest uncorked a quart bottle of his juice concoction. He had eight more packed in dry ice in the trunk. It was all he would consume until Nogales. I winced at the odor.

"Careful with that. Four cows just keeled over."

Tom's beer-lazy voice from the back seat. "Be glad it's a convertible. He starts to reek."

"Laugh if you want," Priest said, brandishing his bottle, "but this has made me what I am today."

I kept a loose grip on the wheel. "A smelly old fuck who's scared of dying?"

Priest feigned a scowl and sipped at the bottle. He wore a white towel on his head, secured with a leather headband. Wraparound sunglasses with an extra tinted plastic shield tucked into them that covered all the way around past his temples. "Why'nt you boys let me drive?"

"Because you're old and unsteady," I teased. "Because we want to live."

"My ass." Priest delivered a powerful kendo punch toward the dashboard. "I could kick the shit out of both of you." His face wore that grin that is my gift to him. I can amuse, but I don't invest. When things stop being easy, I stop doing them. By the time I recognized this as a character flaw, it was too deep in me to change.

Tom drove all night. He had an open road, a dogged disposition, and a sky full of stars. "Hand me a beer, Max."

Priest dozed in and out. His lips burbled when he slept, then he'd nag at us, a human No-Doz. "Go easy on the cerveza."

Tom watched the road. "Sure thing, boss."

"It's not me I'm thinking of, it's you." Priest leaned against the head rest, spoke toward the back seat. "I've got to take good care of my scientist."

"Fuck you." Tom's face inscrutable in the dashlight.

"He doesn't like it when I get proprietary," Priest said.

"He doesn't like it when you talk about him in the third person," Tom said.

I've wondered sometimes if the two of them were lovers, if that's part of what drew them together. But Tom has long lived like a monk, singularly devoted to his work.

A shadowy tree line interrupted the night sky. Tires hissed beneath us.

"I don't think our friend has ever fully accepted the fact that the real science," Priest raised a finger, "and the publicity–went the other way. Stem cells and all."

Tom adjusted mirrors.

"He and I are the lunatic fringe now." Priest shifted his bulk on the seat. "But he doesn't like that. He wants the big answers and the glory, too. Only it doesn't often work that way."

"We're on vacation." Tom turned up the radio, some generic Seventies pop tune. Priest merely raised his own volume to compensate.

"Did you know our boy has a religious background? He keeps thinking he wants to be a functionary. Tidy little experiments to demonstrate obvious truths. But we know better, don't we Max. If that's what he really wanted, he wouldn't have come home to me."

FOR TWO YEARS, from autumn of 1995 through the summer of '97, Tom and his team worked at isolating a telomerase gene. I'd never seen him happier. He and Priest and I had dinner a few times, even took our first road trip, heading out through west Texas toward Death Valley. I had been skeptical about the marriage of science and commerce, but both Tom and Priest were confident and content. Quirky pals with a shared hobby. "It's a great relationship," Tom told me. "Sure, Priest has an eccentric side. But he respects the science. He knows it's the key to where he wants to go." Then, in August of '97, the research team found a telomerase gene. In the process, though, they had also found evidence—a lot of evidence, Tom told me confidentially—that telomeres were not the whole story on aging. That they didn't know what the rest of the story was, and that even the telomeres part of it could take years to piece together. Tom was inconsolable. But there was more: around the same time, significant work had been done on stem cells, with promising implications for their application to disease treatment. In this, science works like anything else: suddenly the attention, the thinking—and the money that supported the thinking—went into stem cell research. Priest followed the crowd, found a new golden boy. And that was that.

Tom holed up in Houston. From what I could tell, he wasn't even working. Then, last fall, Priest came back into the picture; although the spotlight stayed on stem cell work, Tom moved to Ashland with scads of money, a new lab, and a new sense of purpose. That's when Becca really began to worry.

WE'D PULLED OFF Interstate 20 in Abilene, headed south or maybe east on some state road. Tom and I drank Coronas like water, and Priest sipped at his viscous blend of wheatgrass and carrot juice. We don't like the franchise shops you find at the side of the highway. We prefer to dig a little into the land, find home cooking. We were hungry for chili dogs, like I said. And we all had to piss, what with the beer and juice in all that heat. So we bypassed the Stuckey's and followed the two-lane blacktop out past the municipal airport toward Clyde.

We drove unhurried, top down, A.M. radio playing honest-to-God country music, Priest's bald head covered in a tan cloth hat.

"I can almost taste those dogs," Priest said. "The melted cheese. The congealed grease. The chili seeping into the roll." Not that he would eat one. He'd live vicariously through Tom and I. Bask in the aromas, watch us with the intensity of a hungry pit bull. It was a little off-putting when you first encountered it, him hovering over your food, nose in the air, head dancing sometimes to within inches of your plate, then retreating, a greedy olfactory orbit. But we'd been down this road with Priest before.

"Try not to slobber on Max's shirt this time," Tom called out.

A couple of songs down the road, at a convergence of two truck routes, we found nirvana. Hank's Grille. Burgers. Chili dogs. Hank's wasn't simply a roadside café; it was a complex, a service center, maybe the only real accommodation for miles around. Gas station. Convenience store. Whole outbuilding for rest rooms.

We pulled into the hardpack parking lot, kicked up dust. Tom shifted into park and turned off the engine, and we all took a minute to stretch and otherwise accustom ourselves to the absence of motion.

"My head hurts," Priest said. He removed his hat and rubbed his scalp. He had covered himself with sunblock, SPF 60.

We would go in separate directions. Tom to the convenience store for pretzels and jerky and whatever else looked good for snacking. Priest to the outbuilding for the men's room.

"There'll be one in the café," I told him.

He put the hat on. Adjusted his head under it. "I've had nothing but shit juice for thirty-six hours."

"Right. Take your time. I'll get us a table."

Tom rubbed his eyes. The chili dogs had been his idea.

So we went each to our tasks, expecting to converge in a few minutes. Tom took nothing with him. I sat in the booth—vinyl seats, Formica tabletop—and thumbed through the selections on the individualized juke box, salivating for a chili dog I would never get.

TOM AND BECCA and I grew up together in the suburbs outside Akron. Their family was religious, mine wasn't, but I went to church with them—Southern Baptist—and half lived at their house through my adolescence. Tom drifted from both his faith and his family in college; for a while, I was about the only one he'd talk to. He wanted to believe, and if you could create faith through sheer effort, Tom would have done it. But I guess he couldn't reconcile the church he knew with the world he saw, with his own emerging inclinations. Because college is also when he came out, and his family struggled with that. Especially Becca. She's told me more than once how Tom chose first homosexuality, and then science, over God; but how she believes he has a firm foundation, and that someday he'll come back.

Becca is sure of herself in ways that Tom never was. Maybe that's what happens when you spend your formative years hiding who you are. So it interests me that Tom chose science in the end, as if he, like Becca, had been searching for a system that could supply answers. Becca has speculated that Tom was daunted by the time it would take to piece together an answer; that he left this work, as he'd left so many other things, when he saw that he couldn't make a big impact right away. I'm not denying that's there. Tom had—has—an ego. But I think what discouraged him—if he was discouraged—was the possibility that there were pieces of this puzzle he might never be able to identify. That its boundaries were more expansive than he'd thought, and that therefore he might never know.

THE WAITRESS BROUGHT three waters.

I watched the glasses sweat and thought of Priest fouling the air of the rest room. I fished four quarters from my pocket and picked three songs I didn't know.

Priest came through the door halfway through the second song, a white handkerchief moist on his head, newly clad in a white long-sleeve shirt.

"How could my head get sunburned through a hat?"

I shrugged. "Sun's out. We're in a convertible."

"Through a hat, Max. This is the purpose of hats." He removed the handkerchief. His skull was a touch pink. "I could get skin cancer."

"It's just the heat raising your blood." I touched the top of his head. "Doesn't feel like sunburn."

"It's sunburn, god dammit."

I shrugged. "We'll get some aloe vera."

While Buddy Miller sang "Somewhere Trouble Don't Go," Priest grunted and dug a tube of sunblock out of his pack, rubbed some on his head, then carefully replaced the moist handkerchief. "Shut up."

We waited through the end of the song, sipped water and looked over our menus. The air conditioning an elixir.

"Tom must be overwhelmed by the jerky selection."

I moved to find him. Priest followed a minute later.

We made a circuit of the place and wound up back at the car. No sign of Tom. Keys in the ignition.

"What the fuck?" Priest rearranged the handkerchief on his head, pulled the hat gently on over it. We looked around. The guy at the gas pumps—early twenties, already a few exits along the road to nowhere—sat watching us from a folding chair in the shade.

"We've got to do something about this," Priest said. "Tom's been taken." His voice lacked some of its authority. His face some of its color.

"Tom hasn't been taken."

"He has."

"How?"

"Abducted by aliens. Kidnapped by fucking Zapatistas. How should I know." He rubbed the back of his neck. Touched the top of his head. "How else do you explain this. Where could he have gone?"

He had a point. A hot breeze blew dust at our feet. There were maybe four other cars, a couple rigs parked in the back. Eerie quiet. Lots of nothing, as far as you could see.

"We must have missed him," I said. "Check the men's room. The women's. Maybe he wandered in by mistake. Dozed off."

"He's fucking gone."

I didn't believe it, not for a while, but of course Priest turned out to be right.

We talked to waitresses. The grill man. The guy pumping gas. The only one who'd noticed Tom was the convenience store clerk. And even then all we learned was that he bought a bottle of water and some jerky. Possibly a granola bar.

"We gather a posse," Priest said. Water in one hand, juice in the other. "Look for roving packs of bandits. Wild dogs. Skate punks." He pulled up one sleeve to his elbow. Felt the skin of his forearm. "Stress is not good for me," he said. "These wrinkles. They weren't here an hour ago."

We drove the area. I climbed to the tops of whatever puny hills we passed. We asked anyone we saw.

Priest stood in the passenger seat, sunglasses surveying the endless empty land. One hand gripped the rim of the windshield, the other his hat. Chin thrust out defiantly at the desert that had swallowed Tom. "What do you know about skinheads," he shouted against the wind. "What are their habits? Where do they gather?"

There was nothing out there. Nowhere to go. As far as anyone at Hank's could remember, no cars or trucks had left between the time we pulled in and the time Tom went missing.

"I gotta take my vitamins." Parked on the shoulder of State Route 36. Priest reached into the back seat for a small duffel he kept just for his pill supply, housed in those plastic dispensers where you can pre-arrange your dosages. He had three installments for each day. He swallowed fifteen, twenty pills with water. The process took a while. He tossed the dispenser back into the duffel, the duffel onto the bench seat.

"What the fuck," he said. Between the hat and the sunglasses, Priest's big face was nearly hidden.

We stopped at the airport. The train station in Abilene. The bus depot. No one had seen Tom, no one remembered. We went to the police, but it's hard for them to get worked up over a healthy adult who wandered off only a few hours before.

"Is he mentally ill? Does he have some physical handicap?" The desk sergeant looked young and spindly, baby face and wire-rimmed glasses.

He looked like a high school kid visiting the station on take-your-son-to-work day. He feigned patience with us.

I stood at the desk. Priest muttered and paced behind me on marbled linoleum. "Watch for reports of banditos crossing the border," he said. "A fledgling terrorist group opposed to scientific advancement, fronted by a disenchanted heiress."

The sergeant stared through me at Priest. He looked down at a notepad, then up at me. "As far as you know, did he have a wallet with him? Credit cards? A driver's license?"

I nodded.

Priest had walked to the water fountain; he wet the handkerchief, placed it back on his head. He gestured toward the sergeant. "He's ignoring me. Tell him I hate being ignored."

The desk sergeant kept his eyes on me and shrugged. "People take off." If he gained two hundred pounds, he could be Priest's grandson. The baby face. "We'll monitor the hospitals, see if a body turns up."

"Ask him are there Zapatistas in the area." Priest addressed me. "Are we close to Waco? Are any of those nutballs left alive?" Droplets of water ran down the back of his neck.

NOW THAT BECCA KNOWS a little more about Priest, she thinks he's certifiable. And I can't explain the fact that he and I are friends. Why I find myself defending him to Becca; why I try to make the case that he is at heart a good man, even a religious man. She gets that look in her eyes and raises her index finger at me. "Satan is a religious man," she says. And I know what she means. There may be something ruthless about the way Priest has used Tom's ambition. But that cuts both ways.

WE SPENT THE NIGHT at the Derrick Motel in Clyde, Texas. Checked in with the police the next morning. Drove two-lane roads all day until our vision blurred. Hounded the police again when it got too dark to see. When they had nothing to report—no one matching Tom's description turned up in area hospitals or morgues—we left. I suppose that's the part for which Becca can't forgive me. But what could we do. Tom had money. Credit cards. No bodies had turned up. He knew where we were going. We figured he'd meet up with us if he wanted to.

We drove to Nogales.

"You think we should turn around?" Priest sipped his health juice concoction from a plastic cup. It smelled like sewage.

"And do what?"

Priest drank, and stared into the night.

We took I-20 through the panhandle to I-10, then followed smaller roads whenever we could. I drove, except for short breaks to stretch my legs and doze in the starlight.

It wasn't until Las Cruces and the first signs of daybreak that the question I'd been wanting to ask spilled out.

"What was it made you re-fund the project?"

Priest wedged behind the wheel. He looked at me long enough that I worried we'd leave the road. "It's the nature of science—of anything, really—that today's revelation will look foolish tomorrow. The key to getting anything done—to really making a breakthrough—is to believe enough to push past that." In his cloth hat, long sleeves and giant, wraparound sunglasses, Priest cut a ridiculous figure. Buddha as desert chauffeur. "Stem cell research was going lots of good places, but not where I wanted it to go. Everyone was all hot for the disease-specific possibilities. That's where the real science is headed." A smirk danced on his lips. "But that's the trouble with real science—it lacks vision."

The Las Vegas Café, like everyplace else in the world, had gone upscale. Red tablecloths. A disappointment that might keep us from going back, except that the *ropas* are so damn good. Smoky strings of beef, complex spices so intermingled for so long they finish each other's sentences. We kept a seat open at the table for Tom, the way you're supposed to for Elijah. We almost didn't feel guilty being there. Tom has tasted it. He'd understand. Besides, it seemed as likely as not he'd walk through the door any second.

"I know what you're thinking, Max." Priest's pink face enraptured. "But it's not that simple." The way he rolled the meat on his tongue could get him arrested in some midwestern states. "It's easy to blame me and my money. Cite its corrupting influence." He emitted little moans as he ate—okay, we both did—drawing wary glances from other patrons, who hadn't traveled twenty-seven hundred miles to be there. "But there's no such thing as pure science. Pure anything."

"Wait," I said, but it's hard to stop Priest when he's on a roll.

"I'll tell you what real science is. It's not white lab coats. It's the nutcases out in the wilderness willing to think crazy thoughts, then spend their lives trying to actualize them." He wiped his mouth with warm tortilla. "You want to know what I think, your friend isn't willing to do the hard work."

I didn't want to know what he thought. Didn't want to acknowledge any possibility that serious. "I thought you said aliens."

Priest grinned. My shallowness appeals to him. "Or, it could be aliens."

Across from us, a little girl, maybe three years old, dark curls, ate at a plate of beans while her father, under a straw cowboy hat, watched foot traffic pass by on the sidewalk.

"Not all of us get labs at Harvard or MIT," Priest said. "Some of us have to articulate our vision from the UMass Medical Center."

"You're wrong about Tom," I said, though I spoke more from my heart than from any developed theory.

Priest, head buried in his food, looked at me over the frames of his glasses. "We'll see."

I HAD TO BREAK THE NEWS to Becca, and that's when she broke my nose. The accumulated frustration. The homosexuality. The presence of Fillmore Priest, who sat the whole time in the car. The tainted research. Her brother's fading star. My nose became the target of her anger over all that, maybe more. And we'd driven straight back, thirty-four hours, to tell her.

It's been two weeks now. A short vacation, from one viewpoint. An eternity, from another. Becca is beside herself with worry and anger. She's stopped talking to me altogether. She doesn't feel I'm taking this as seriously as I should. But I don't know what to say to her. I recognize the ugly possibilities—Tom may be hurt or lost or killed; he may have that brain injury Becca fixates on, or have fallen prey to random violence from some West Texas whack job. But I have to be positive about this. I have to.

Priest and I talk daily. He's angry for other reasons. "Karate and vitamins and shit juice are only going to take me so far," he says. "Aging is killing us all. I need my scientist." There was a moment where Priest lost himself, believed that Tom had planned this, had signed on to the revitalized project only to run off with the money; to Priest's credit, he didn't believe this for long.

As for me, I'm convinced Tom is taking care of business.

Here's the thing. If we're going to believe anything in a world where people vanish, we need to leave room for mystery. Be willing to live with what we don't know. We don't know where Tom is. We can't know—despite Becca's insistence—if God is, or what God thinks. Priest can't know if he'll ever find the cure he seeks. And Tom can't know if he's conducting hard science, or simply tilting at windmills with all of his gifts, all of Priest's money, all of our hope. How do we live with that uncertainty. That's the question I hope Tom is asking, the work I trust he's doing, wherever he is.

Canticle for Snow

Gabriel Welsch

Bless the curled edge of it   the hoar frost,
ground mold beneath   the ridge of ice

snow shaved grass blades   drifts of snow mold
water roof-sluiced   until it froze again,

gutters piled with weight,
the roof threatening   a tear or bow,

the terrible weight   of water.
Wonder   at the blessing

of its delay, how it forces
solitude   puts you in the veil

of your own steam   gives you
the moment of focus when the sky

lowers its offering   to us,
its abundance   snow reminds us

how everything floats   how air buoys,
how heat attracts   how snow

stars shift   a galaxy around us,
a reminder of this planet's hurtled floating.

What the Deaf Boy Heard

Gabriel Welsch

White water rumble, cool poplars,
grass green as a promise,
hollow shouts of children
running toward him over a field.
The chime of winter still
an echo, the hospital still a smother
of white, meningitis a word
thick with sound only recalled.
Now, a dump truck's dusty passage,
gravel shifts and shivered leaves,
blue's weight on the sky, the chicory,
and the depth of his own eyes, gazing
back at him from his mother.
She locks on him while her hands
rush before his face, a cloud of clover,
mint, bergamot and sage, nails
worn down each evening in the beds
where she sows what she can
from frailty, from injured stalks,
from old seeds, in the bounty
of rotted black soil.

Casually Vagrant

Elaine Terranova

I barely know the difference between
a sparrow and a wren. So many clutching
at the underside of a winterberry,
red berries exuding a kind of joy.

I'm over where the pond begins.
Branches bend, willow and tamarack.
Their long sleeves dip into the water.
It's a passionate autumn, beauty
dissolving in the heart's bright colors.

On the path, all that's left of criss-crossing life,
one quick snake and, undulant and miniature,
a wooly-bear emerges from the tunnel of a leaf.

These are sparrows, I think, in the winterberry,
having longer tails. They are small and
unglamorous, except maybe to one another.
"Plain" even in the books that feature them.
Gray or brown with whitish streaks so dull
they're referred to as smudges. Nothing to catch the eye.
The books say, "secretive," "casually vagrant."

Sparrows were thought monogamous breeders.
Something—why not?—to be proud of.
Now, though, watching them,

CHAUTAUQUA

omniscient science has discovered
matinee idols even among sparrows.

And it's the female who takes a flier.
To trip some up, scientists accentuate
sexual attraction with a color marker.

Casually vagrant but not a fool,
the female sparrow holds onto her steady branch,
the dull provider with parenting skills
and keeps to herself who the real father is.

Because beauty is a trait even sparrows
express. Because a species can survive on it.

TO THE NIGHTS
Richard Lehnert

Why name your bright brothers
and not you who half the year
are more tall and strong
you we fear more whose breath
we once thought could kill
we who fill our holy books
with lists of fears but not
the seven unnamed names of
you who make difficult
what we do by days
except what we then need
resting close in you to share
what heat days leave us
as you take us in
your great cool mouths

I can name a few of you
night I was born
night I will die or
night of that day
night I met the woman
I share with each of you
night wet snow snapped trees
night that leaves as it arrives
the longest night
night of soaking rain

CHAUTAUQUA

night we slam down windows
on waddling stink of skunk
night I woke into from dream
after dream of night
night I did not sleep but
through all of you met your gaze
your dark face stately in repose
night that already this summer morning
you draw far back into yourself

but when these bluff days
exhaust themselves with bragging
how beautiful they are and follow
around the round world's corners
the echoes of their braying
you will come back to us
not falling but rising through
the earth the stones and forests
the sands and each named sea
the deep lawns of the suburbs
where all along you rest
and now lift through each of us
and when with your long fingers
you touch the stars and planets
to clear their eyes of day
it is only then we see how far
you reach beyond us all

melon man

David Lazar

I remember the melon man in terms so impossibly caricatured that his image is indelible. In childhood, not yet jaundiced by experience, its visual taste buds not yet dulled, we see with a clarity that seems exaggerated to the older, larger, more worldly self. In "Such Such Were the Joys," George Orwell tells us that if he went back to his old school how small it and its inhabitants would seem. Yes, if we were to go back our heroes might shrink, our demons de-demonize, our confusions fade into the depressing process of understanding and categorizing, depressing in the potential of reducing our personal myths with our fears and confusions. How to keep both, how to use memory to enlarge and not dismiss? For one thing: realize what we have lost, acknowledge that we have forgotten even what we seem to remember. Which brings me, for many reasons, to the melon man.

The melon man lived a scant block away, his house on the corner lot of Ocean Parkway and Manhattan Court. In some ways his appearance matched the house perfectly: the front yard was overgrown, unkempt in its creeping vines, rotting leaves, fruit trees half lush and half dead, completely shaded. The house was large ugly brick and wood slanting in on itself, a fairy tale melange of aesthetic misdirection: a *bric-a-brac* house, brick and Braque. In memory it is uniformly dark and colorless. Surrounded by an old half-height chain link fence, the yard would engulf all balls that bounced into its dominion, too scary for even the dared rescue. Our Spalding rubber balls were elastic Grails, one of the most familiar items of my childhood, and yet each almost instantly assumed its own character, its own color, displaying the provenance of its bounces and ricochets, and the relative firmness of its uses: stickball, punchball, stoopball, boxball....

The balls that bounced into the melon man's yard were sacrificed, yielded to a surreal landscape of rotting peaches, creepers, and the other detritus that washes up on lots and lawns.

The melon man was very old, bent. Before I knew him as the melon man, a genial name which his appearance belied, he was the old man who lived in the scary house, a dour rubber-featured entity, always in shabby black suit—the old country look that second-generationers such as myself had lost connection with—stained and faded white shirt buttoned to the top with no tie, floppy big black shoes that seemed never to have strolled, each foot lifted and stamped when he would apparently mimic what the rest of us called walking. He had the largest nose I had, or have, ever seen. It was multidirectional: it sloped and bulged and had a knot at the top and a wart or mole on the side. He was crescent-bald, gray splayed hair spraying out the sides, down the back, at different lengths. He must have been sixty-five or so. He was scary, larger than life, yet I could nevertheless perceive something pathetic in his physical demeanor that didn't rankle with his status as goblin, Golem. Children are open-mindedly fanciful, but astute.

There he was in my kitchen, smiling semi-toothlessly and nodding his head as I came in. "David, this is Mr." and there followed a Polish name, all consonants, that second-generation or beyond children are genetically incapable of pronouncing, or in trying to pronounce turn into bizarrely generic utterances such as "bush-mish-nish," trailing off into a whisper. They were sitting at the table eating cantaloupes. I could pronounce cantaloupe, so I joined them, the three of us making awkward squishy sounds with our spoons for a few minutes, sounds that seemed to mimic the melon man's name.

As taught, I started excavating the rind, shovelling the spoon over the small ridges of fruit until all traces of opaque green yielded to white. As the child of depression-era parents I was instructed to eat everything edible, even if only hypothetically so, on my plate. Gristle, fat, bones sucked dry. And one more scant generation removed from turn of the century pogroms and shtetls, we ate foods that make some of my friends go white in holy gastronomic terror: marrow bones, intestines, brains, lots of liver, salvers of chicken fat the genteel do regard as poisonous, for me a legacy of eat the whole animal, but also, in truth delicacies I haven't had in years, and dream about.

The melon man was horrified; he stumbled over his blubbery lips to ask what I was doing, less gentle than solicitous, more gentle than admonishing. With uncharacteristic simplicity (when at all threatened by a question, which was virtually always, I could invoke a streak of baroque circumlocution from a strangely early age) I replied, "Eating it all."

"Only eat the fruit, the good part, the sweet part," he said. "I brought your mama these nice melons. Look, there's plenty. You want another piece, have another piece, okay? It's so sweet. Eat what's sweet."

I was suspicious. Adults were not supposed to counsel abandon, even melon-abandon, and that's what this seemed like. What to do with this counter-propaganda? Of course, part of me was immediately attracted by the idea. Visions of cornucopias, biblical melon-scenes (Were there any? Probably *Song of Solomon*). But all children have their supererogatory superegos, family House Un-American Activity Committees, deeply institutionalized, which questions all foreign-seeming practices. The depth of the threat is in direct proportion to the strength of the stultifying injunction it is challenging.

"No thanks, I've had enough. I'm going around the corner now." HUAC adjourned in the face of a standoff.

Since it was July, and the pure enticements of pleasure made so much sense, I decided to cut my conscience to fit this summer's fashion. I didn't realize then that revelations can come full force over what seem like trivial issues, moments. But I felt tremendously upset by the wisdom of the melon man's call to melon-hedonism. What if pleasure, symbolically located in melon-colored pulp, in green sweetness, were a more ubiquitous rule of spoon, what if I had been denying simple and available gifts? What if my father had a mean streak? A moist scent of supple, and not at all subtle, appreciations threatened to beckon a monsoon that could overrun the superego sweeping regulations planted like bulwarks in my desire. In short, what if the pleasure principle was the big one, the Godhead of motivations, and denial the dark temptation. The world, as I knew it, would be turned on its head, all because of the forbidden fruit dispensed by a dishevelled man.

The melon man started coming by regularly. Always in shabby white and black with a crumpled bag of fruit, mostly melons, but the occasional crop of cherries. He would say "luscious cherries," sloppily sibilanting every chance he got, as though watery lispings of language were thoughtlessly sensual enterprises, a fricative fricassee. His pronunciation was recognizably first generation American, though I suspect he was not born here. It had the slight formality, the accent-less accent of the professional who struggled hard through mediocre schools and exhausted his achievement when a higher status was in sight, as though being a lawyer were the goal and not the means to improvement. In other words, his diction was proper, but uninteresting unless considered as a specific exemplar of what he was. You know the type of speech, I'm sure: "That is exactly the situation I was discussing previously"; "It was a very amusing experience, all things considered"; "I cannot say I had completely comprehended what the gentleman meant."

Of course, this is all hindsight. My feelings about the melon man continued to explore the narrow ground between unease and discomfort, even after I had settled into my full belief in his position on watching the rind, as opposed to choking on it. I didn't like having this new creature around so much. It seemed as though every time I turned around—no, came in, since he always seemed to have appeared in my absences—every time I flung open the screened storm door, a quick two step masquerading as wiping my feet, rushing into the house (one returns home as an adult, throws oneself into one's house as a child, supposing the house a desirable place to have returned to) there he was, black crow bending over fruit plate, a slight nod hello with hint of rubbery smile: somewhere between genial and indifferent. We had the kind of nervous stalemate that gives adolescents nervous tics. I had only one way of looking at this Polish blackbird. He had dispensed, apparently, in the one tiny torrent of megabytes, his one Gnostic truth. So I barely slowed my pace on the way past the kitchen, distinguished from the dining room only by a stroke of the imagination in the kind of arrangements that make rowhouses geographical wonderlands of the Eastern European order: want to call this Hungary and this Czechoslovakia for awhile? Presto change-o, this is this and that is that, because we have said so, and come to think so. Alice in Brooklynland. Alice through the shtetlglass.

As I think back, I find I was quite oblivious to my mother's reactions to the melon man. Since I resented his presence in our dining room, a resentment based on unarticulated mistrust and focused on physiognomy, a resentment, I might add, which would probably have greeted any new human variable in the kitchen, thanks to our almost morbidly nuclear household, I believe I was at pains to give my mother a hard time about the violation of the inner sanctum, and wondered, in a diffuse way, why she was entertaining this tiresome, if clumsily exotic man. Surely we weren't hurting for fruit-money. Twice, three times a week, we would go to the fruit stall in Sheepshead Bay, its awning proclaiming, "I MAY NOT BE A POET, BUT WHEN IT COMES TO FRUITS AND VEGETABLES I KNOW IT." Whatever unfulfilled dreams of ripe Rilkean elegies lay behind the summer squash, or crisp visions of sonnets hidden in the bins holding kale, I merely thought it a non-sequitur, but gave it points as an oddity.

In any case, I cast a cold eye at my mother, assuming that she merely hadn't the heart to get rid of him. My mother could be easily imposed upon as long as my father, my brother and I were not being overtly inconvenienced. And I had no convincing argument to put forth concerning my objections. Discomfort in the kitchen, the truth, apparently never came to mind, perhaps because any "new" adult made me uncomfortable, and I was casually seeking specific objections. He was more an annoyance than a threat, however, so my response stayed short of critical mass, instead took the form of mildly sardonic asides: "Are melons always in season?" Or, "If there were a parallel universe would we eat can-elopes and honey-don'ts?" Such scorn seemed a proper fate for minor prophets and their accidental impresarios, once the wisdom was exhausted. I simply wasn't quite sure if the melon man was being tolerated out of kindness, a bit sickening but respectable, a lack of assertiveness, despicable in myself and disappointing in my mother, or appreciation, perhaps of some attention or even a whiff of the old country for a young woman with dead parents: incomprehensible to me at the time, but not impossible. The chances are it was a combination of the three, which may seem a safe adjudication, but I have learned not to chase the motivations of my own dead parent beyond psychological necessity. It is bad enough to chase one's own tail without chasing the tail of a ghost; it can disappear most inopportunely.

Around the melon man, then, swirled a certain minor current of uneasiness: my psychological rejection of the father's canonical law, confusion about my mother allowing me to stave off derision, and a near-revulsion at this bearer of fruit which exceeded comprehension. Not to mention a growing aversion to anything containing vitamin C.

Then he stopping coming. I noticed the pattern of his absence, not suddenly, since he would appear frequently, but not constantly. I asked my mother what had happened, why he no longer came around. She said, "He was coming over too often, so I had to tell him to stop." I was puzzled, but didn't understand why I was puzzled. It seemed simple enough, and to boot I had an admirable backbone-affirmation to plug into my image of my mother, which should have relieved some psychic congestion. Like a narrative Vicks VapoRub. So what was the rub?

The rub was tone. There was an unseasonable mist of dissimulation covering her version of the melon man's departure, as though, close as we had come to autumn, he had not faded into the mellow fruitfulness of eccentric family hangers-on, but had somehow turned bad. That was as close as I got: something not quite right, and not to be pursued. I knew, even then, to let things slide when the open-hearted turned away from further explanation.

Orwell says of his school years that he could have remembered them with a finer, more accurate sense of detail, if he had written of them sooner, closer to the experience and his earlier self, somewhere between his current middle age and childhood. However, he says, "It can also happen that one's memories grow sharper after a long lapse of time, because one is looking at the past with fresh eyes and can isolate and, as it were, notice facts which previously existed undifferentiated among a mass of others." He speaks of details that "lay unnoticed in my memory." And it occurs to me that unnoticed in my memory was the turning away of my mother, and what that meant. For some reason I know now that the melon man had made a pass at her, perhaps even an aggressive one, and that this was terribly embarrassing, probably because it implied an error of judgement on her part of whom to entertain, to let into the house. I know this; it is not at all a matter of speculation.

The weeds in the melon man's yard grew more tangled, the vines more twisted, if demystified. Which is not to say some mystery didn't remain, dwarfed as it nonetheless was by the restoration of equilibrium: the kitchen liberated. Subsequently, the old man who had apparently wanted to play knick knack with my mother must have made the occasional cameo appearances—non-speaking walk-ons—in the theater of my childhood; I seem to remember him walking past me, bent and muttering, a few times. I place a paper bag in his hand. I dress him in the same shabby black and white. And then he disappears. And the house on the corner disappears, replaced by newer one-family rowhouses.

I wonder if my mother ever mentioned the episode to my father. I would guess not, knowing as I do that any conflict, which is to say anything that ever went wrong, never served a higher goal, a greater good, no matter how blameless the one who introduced it, or its irrelevance to other family members. Resolution meant the fight had stopped, someone was no longer mad at someone. I get exhausted just thinking about it, which makes how much I think about it seem somewhat perverse. But I know that in the way my mother turned, she was saying she had something to say which she could not say to anyone. She had no really close friends at the time. My parents did not live hungrily off friendships the way I and much of my generation seem to. Of course a sentimentalist could argue that she is talking to me now, the communication merely slowed by the space-time continuums of memory and mortality. I am drawn to the idea that we communicate in stages, sometimes decades apart, as gestures coalesce if they haven't congealed, that something said today might light up in twenty years like the light reaching us from distant stars. The lyrical turns elegiac, however, when we consider that the star may no longer exist.

These days I eat my melon to the rind sometimes, partly as a gesture to an old superego who has seen better days, lurking like a cranky beggar rather than a stern schoolmaster, partly in that search for the last sweet spot, the gastronomical diamond that requires mining, but is always something of a disappointment since one knows that's it, that's all there is, and another piece would be redundant. "Gilding the lily," my mother used to say.

East of the Garden

Mary Gilliland

No redstart slips from the woods to wrangle blue jay.
The bright fruit is missing. The peace of this summer:
colorless, motionless, lawnmower-droneless.

I steal into the mummified brambles,
half-clothed, half-woken, waiting for dewpoint,
waiting to scold, clap my hands.

Leafhoppers cover what hangs on the stem.
Dragonflies multiply. Locusts glint green.

Drought has burnt half the canes orange,
sucked dozens of four-foot stickers to sticks
nobbed with sickly wizened changelings.

Daddy longlegs crossing my palm
lifts its moist feet: the absence of blackberries.

AFTER SCHOOL
Bruce Bennett

"You have poetry in you,"
he pronounces,
as he leafs through
my efforts.

"This is a skimpy one.
Here"—my eyes
follow his finger—
"you almost get it.
You could do more
with this."

Outside,
the clash of helmets
yells and commands

mean nothing to me,

intent
on that faint hallowing
from farther fields,

the scrimmage
that goes on and on.

DEAD RECKONING

Margaret Gibson

Rain suspended on a branch yet to bloom,
the sweep and glide of swallows in the dusk—
the beech tree whose husks of last year's leaves
stay on, and on, and are silver—

you think I'm the ghosted voice of these?

You stand at the edge of the glade
where shadows brindle and the deep woods begin,
the Dipper above you, upside down, north.
A cry—you hear a cry out there, so forlorn
you think, *wind through the fissure of a skull.*

And you're right: this is a swift dead reckoning.

The dust I was comes through the spit of rain
and thunder. The dust I was is a compact pinch of mud
you can put beneath your tongue. As you suck it,
recall how sternly Siddhartha's mother

peered into her toddler's mouth. She thought him
an odd child, wandering off to sit beneath
the rain-laden bougainvillea, in the rain-lit quiet
eating mud. She was checking for mud
when she opened his mouth and looked in—and saw

the whole universe spinning within the dark interior of his throat.

CHAUTAUQUA

From the depth of that luminous dark, he spoke.
You must find your way. Look within.
It is that intimate. More birds fly through.
The branch blossoms. It is that close to you. That close.

BUTTERFLIES

Anthony Doerr

Between 1995 and 2005, because of graduate school, jobs, wanderlust, and love, I moved sixteen times. Always by car, always in summer. The drive I made most often was between Idaho and Ohio, in both directions, sometimes alone, sometimes with my dog, once with a goldfish named Fran riding shotgun in a one-gallon water jug. Eastward, westward, the great unspooling latticework of American interstates—for that decade, my summers were about movement, the sun-baked juniper flats of Southern Idaho, the incandescent canyons of Utah, the rambling prairies of Nebraska, the deep, heavy damp of Iowa in August.

In the span of a single hour, on those trips, I could see our country at its worst—the shrapnel of shredded tires, the crumpled chassis of an eighteen-wheeler, hundreds of drivers hurrying past—and at its most transcendent—moonlight over a thousand acres of wheat, a lone lamppost rising gracefully, uselessly, from the flooded Mississippi.

There were plenty of lonely moments, when there'd be nothing on the radio but static, and it'd be getting dark, and a few rain drops would spatter the windshield, and I'd see no other headlights in any direction, and no motels for miles. But there were also peaceful, near-perfect moments, hurtling through a warm dusk with the smell of wet corn blowing through the vents, when a baseball game would come cleanly through the speakers, play-by-play out of Cleveland, say, or Kansas City, and I'd watch the sunset fade and lightning flare on the horizon and listen to the roar of some distant crowd as a ball sailed through the lights.

It was on one of these drives that I saw one of the most marvelous things I've ever seen. I was crossing the western half of Wyoming, my car shuddering in a crosswind, big rafts of cumulus cruising above the highway. Everything seemed stripped clean by the wind and light; there was hardly any traffic, only a long-hauler now and then plying along in the right lane. Up ahead, the air suddenly grew darker, a thick band of gray, as if a long, opaque ribbon was being pulled along above the road.

I slowed as I drew closer, but the light was already noticeably dimmer, and butterflies were exploding across the windshield. The air was thick with them; they lodged themselves in the grille, pieces of their wings caught and vibrated in the wipers. For maybe a minute, at forty miles an hour, this kept up, thousands of butterflies breaking over the front of the car. Sometimes their bodies seemed to simply pulverize—as if there were no liquid to the creatures at all, just a wash of gray powder across the glass.

When I was through the band, I pulled onto the shoulder and got out and walked back up the road. I was maybe 1,400 miles from where I started the day before and nearing that strange long-distance daze I sometimes would slip into, when I'd feel as though my brain was trailing miles behind my body.

Butterflies: a long, shimmering curtain. Millions of them. They were smaller than monarchs, with orange and black panels on their wings and white dots fringing the edges. I felt as if some secret had torn free from the Earth and I was witnessing something very private and old, something much larger than myself. It was the same sensation I once had watching a fisherman reach over the stern of a boat and seize the thrashing bill of a marlin with a gloved hand, feeling the sleek, hard flank of the fish strike the underside of the boat: a feeling like the world possessed quantities of power I would never understand.

The butterflies coursed onward, some landing on fence posts, on the blacktop, on the roof of my car. A few landed on my sleeve and beat their wings carefully, thoughtfully, their bodies seeming to quiver, as if panting.

Every now and then a truck barreled past, its wipers smearing back and forth, and a wreckage of insects tumbled in its wake. I stood on the shoulder of I-80 for maybe fifteen minutes, waiting for the tail end of the swarm, staring up into a river of insects, staring up into the limits of my own understanding.

Some butterflies, I'd read later, migrate thousands of miles every year. In the fall, nearly every monarch in the United States east of the Rockies will attempt to fly to central Mexico. After particularly rainy winters, painted lady butterflies migrate up from Mexico into California in the billions.

The desire for something sweet to eat, the chemical compulsion to move: Who can't relate?

This year, as the leaves of summer unfurl, it's as if the cells in my body start leaning forward, careening off of one another, pleading with me: sell the furniture, scrub out the refrigerator, call in sick.

The heart contains, always, two opposing desires: the urge to stay versus the urge to leave. One day, home feels peaceful and snug; the next, it feels ordinary and stifling. We travel for the thrill of seeing new things, of course, but we also travel to renew our understanding of the places and people we've left behind. We travel to break open the habitual, lift away the film that builds up over our lives, our eyes, our hearts. Sometimes, I think, we have to leave home so that we can feel our attachment to it that much more keenly.

I still think about those butterflies, resting for a moment on my sleeve, one brief respite along their merciless journey. In all of my trips across the country, there was no sweeter feeling than the one that would come at the end, in the last miles, as I'd ease off the highway, the windshield grimed with heat and fingerprints, the grille caked with dust and insects—the feeling that in a few more minutes, this time, I might be lucky enough to settle down.

CONTRIBUTORS' NOTES

COVER ARTIST

STEPHEN WESTFALL was born in 1953 and received his MFA from the University of California, Santa Barbara. His work has been exhibited regularly in the United States and abroad and has been widely reviewed, most recently in *The New York Times* and *Art in America*. He is represented by Lennon, Weinberg Gallery in New York, Galerie Wilma Locke in Switzerland, Galerie Zurcher in Paris, and Galerie Paal in Munich. Westfall was recently awarded the Guggenheim Foundation Fellowship and the Nancy Graves Foundation Grant. His work is included in the collections of the Louisiana Museum of Modern Art in Denmark, the Albertina Museum in Vienna, the Baltimore Museum of Art, and the University Art Museum, Santa Barbara. He teaches in the MFA program at Bard College, New York and Rutgers University, New Jersey. Westfall is a critic as well as a painter. His articles appear in *Art in America*, *Flash Art*, and other publications. He currently lives and works in New York City.

WRITERS

MARILYN ABILDSKOV is the author of the memoir *The Men In My Country*. Her short stories, essays, and poems have appeared in such literary journals as *Puerto del Sol*, *Quarterly West*, *Bellingham Review*, *Alaska Quarterly Review*, and *Southern Review*. She teaches in the MFA program at Saint Mary's College of California.

FAITH ADIELE is author of the travel/spiritual memoir *Meeting Faith* (Norton), which won the PEN Beyond Margins Award for Biography/Memoir; writer/subject/narrator of *My Journey Home* (PBS), a documentary based on her Nigerian/Nordic/American heritage; and co-editor of *Coming of Age Around the World: A Multicultural Anthology* (The New Press). Her essays and travel writings have appeared in numerous magazines, journals and anthologies. A frequent contributor to O and *Essence* magazines, she has been awarded seventeen residences in five countries and taught in summer programs at Chautauqua Institution, the Iowa Summer Writing Fest, the Geneva Writers Conference

Contributors' Notes

and Voices of Our Nations Foundation. A graduate of Harvard College and the Iowa Writers' Workshop, Adiele is currently assistant Professor of Creative nonfiction at the University of Pittsburgh.

Kathleen Aguero's most recent book of poetry, *Daughter Of*, is published by Cedar Hill Books. She is the author of two previous books of poetry, *Thirsty Day* (Alice James Books) and *The Real Weather* (Hanging Loose Press). She has edited three volumes of multicultural literature published by the University of Georgia Press and has an essay in the anthology, *Why I'm Still Married*. She is a Professor of English at Pine Manor College in Chestnut Hill, MA, teaching in their low-residency MFA and undergraduate programs and has been a Poet-in-Residence at The Writers' Center of Chautauqua.

Maggie Anderson is the author of four books of poems, most recently *Windfall: New and Selected Poems* published by the University of Pittsburgh Press in 2000. She is the co-editor, with David Hassler, of *After the Bell: Contemporary American Prose about School*, the companion volume to their award-winning anthology *Learning By Heart: Contemporary American Poetry about School* (University of Iowa Press). Anderson is also the editor of the new and selected poems of Louise McNeill and co-editor of *A Gathering of Poets*. She was a workshop leader for the Chautauqua Writers' Center in June 2007 and Poet-in-Residence at the Chautauqua Writers' Festival in June 2006. Currently, she is the director and a member of the faculty in the Northeast Ohio MFA program at Kent State University, where she directs the Wick Poetry Center and edits the Wick Poetry Series of the Kent State University Press.

Emily Barton is the author of the novels *The Testament of Yves Gundron* (Farrar, Straus, and Giroux 2000) and *Brookland* (FSG 2006), which was a 2007 selection of the Chautauqua Literary and Scientific Circle. She currently serves as Distinguished Visiting Writer at Bard College and has also taught writing and literature at the New School.

Jan Beatty is the author of three books of poetry: *Red Sugar* (2008), *Boneshaker* (2002) and *Mad River* (1994 Agnes Lynch Starrett Prize) published by the University of Pittsburgh Press. She is host and producer of *Prosody*, a public radio show on NPR affiliate WYEP-FM, and teaches the Madwomen in the

Attic Writing Workshop and in the MFA Program at Carlow University, where she also directs the Undergraduate Writing Program. She taught a week-long poetry class and gave a guest lecture at the Chautauqua Writers' Center in August 2005.

ROBIN BECKER's six collections of poems include *Domain of Perfect Affection* (2006), *The Horse Fair* (2000), *All-American Girl* (1996) and *Giacometti's Dog* (1990), all with the University of Pittsburgh Press. In 2001, The Frick Art & Historical Center (Pittsburgh) published *Venetian Blue*, a limited-edition chapbook of Becker's poems on graphic art. Professor of English at The Pennsylvania State University, Becker has received individual fellowships from The Bunting Institute, The Massachusetts Cultural Council, and the National Endowment for the Arts. In 2000, she won the Atherton Award for Excellence in Teaching from Penn State. Becker's book reviews, essays and poems appear in journals including *The American Poetry Review, The Georgia Review, O: The Oprah Magazine, Poetry*, and *Prairie Schooner*. She has served as judge for numerous national poetry competitions including the *John Ciardi Book Award, New Letters Poetry Prize, The Prairie Schooner Book*, the *Benjamin Saltman Prize* from Red Hen Press and *The Idaho Prize* from Lost Horse Press. Becker writes a column on poetry, "Field Notes," for *The Women's Review of Books* where she serves as Contributing and Poetry Editor. She is delighted to join the Chautauqua community in 2008.

BRUCE BENNETT is the author of seven full-length books of poetry and more than twenty poetry chapbooks. His *New and Selected Poems, Navigating The Distances* (Orchises Press), was chosen by *Booklist* as "One Of The Top Ten Poetry Books Of 1999." He co-founded and served as an editor of *Field: Contemporary Poetry and Poetics* and *Ploughshares*, and was an Associate Editor at Judith Kitchen's State Street Press. He has reviewed contemporary poetry books in publications including *The New York Times Book Review, The Nation, Harvard Review* and his poems have appeared in literary journals, textbooks, and anthologies. He is currently Professor and Chair of English and Director of Creative Writing at Wells College in Aurora, New York. He has taught Poetry Workshops at the Chautauqua Writers' Center, most recently in 2004.

Contributors' Notes

DAVID BOUCHIER is an award-winning essayist for National Public Radio affiliates in Fairfield, Connecticut. For ten years he contributed a regular humor column called "Out of Order" for the Long Island section of the Sunday *New York Times* and has published fiction and nonfiction in many literary and political magazines. He is a regular workshop leader at the University of Iowa Summer Writing Festival and has taught prose workshops in humor and essay writing at Chautauqua since 1990 (most recently in 2007). His latest book of essays, *A Few Well Chosen Words*, was published in 2007. Other recent books include a collection of essays about life in America, *The Song Of Suburbia*, published in 2002 (reprinted 2007); stories of life in a French village, *The Cats and the Water Bottles*, also published in 2002; and *Writer at Work* (2005), a semi-autobiographical compendium of advice and philosophical reflections.

PHILIP BRADY's next book is *By Heart: Reflections of a Rust-Belt Bard*, forthcoming from University of Tennessee Press. He is the author of three books of poems and a memoir. His work has been awarded five Ohio Arts Council Fellowships, a Snyder Prize from Ashland Poetry Press, a Thayer Fellowship, and residencies at Yaddo, Ragdale, Hawthornden Castle and Fundacion Valparaiso. He directs the Youngstown State University Poetry Center and Etruscan Press, and plays in the New-Celtic band, Brady's Leap.

JANE CIABATTARI is the author of the critically acclaimed short-story collection, *Stealing the Fire*. Her short stories have been published in *KBG Bar Lit*, *VerbSap*, *Ms. Magazine*, *The North American Review*, *Denver Quarterly*, *Hampton Shorts*, *The East Hampton Star*, *Blueline*, *Caprice* and *Redbook*. Her story "How I Left Onandaga County," which originated during her time at Chautauqua in 2005, appears in the anthology *The Best Underground Fiction* (Stolen Time Press, 2006). She has been nominated for the Pushcart Prize, the O. Henry Award, and a National Magazine Award; she has won an Editors' Choice STUBBY Award. She has been honored with fiction fellowships from the New York Foundation for the Arts, The MacDowell Colony and the Virginia Center for the Creative Arts. She has been a prose writer-in-residence at Chautauqua during summers 2003, 2005 and 2008. She also is a book critic, a vice president of the National Book Critics Circle, and a regular contributor to the NBCC blog, *Critical Mass*.

GERALDINE CONNOLLY is the author of the chapbook, *The Red Room*, as well as two full-length collections of poetry, *Food for the Winter* and *Province of Fire*. A new book, *Hand of the Wind*, is forthcoming from Iris Press in 2008. Her poems, reviews and essays have appeared in *Chelsea, The Gettysburg Review, Poetry, Shenandoah, The Georgia Review* and *The Washington Post*. She has been awarded two NEA fellowships, a Maryland Arts Council fellowship and the Margaret Bridgman fellowship of the Bread Loaf Writers Conference. She has taught for four summers at the Chautauqua Writers' Center. She divides her time between Montana and Arizona.

JOAN CONNOR is a full professor and the Director of Creative Writing at Ohio University and a professor in the University of Southern Maine's Stonecoast MFA program. She is a recipient of the John Gilgun award, a Pushcart Prize, an Ohio Arts Council fellowship in fiction, the *Ohio Writer* award in fiction and nonfiction, and the AWP award for her short story collection, *History Lessons*. Her two earlier collections are: *We Who Live Apart* and *Here on Old Route 7*. Her collection of essays, *The World Before Mirrors*, recently won the *River Teeth* award and was published by University of Nebraska Press. Her work has appeared in: *Glimmer Train, Shenandoah, The Southern Review, The Kenyon Review, Chelsea, Manoa, The Gettysburg Review, TriQuarterly, The Journal of Arts and Letters,* and *Black Warrior*, among others. She lives in Athens, Ohio, and Belmont, Vermont.

ROBERT CORDING teaches English and creative writing at College of the Holy Cross. He has published five collections of poems: *Life-list*, which won the Ohio State University Press/Journal award, in 1987; *What Binds Us To This World* (Copper Beech Press, 1991); *Heavy Grace*, (Alice James, 1996); *Against Consolation* (CavanKerry Press, 2002); and most recently, *Common Life*, from CavanKerry (2006).

STEPHEN COREY's ten poetry collections include *There Is No Finished World* (White Pine Press, 2003), *All These Lands You Call One Country* (University of Missouri Press, 1992), *Synchronized Swimming* (1985), and *The Last Magician* (1981). Individually, his poems, essays, and reviews have appeared in numerous periodicals over the past thirty years. Born in Buffalo and reared in Jamestown, fifteen miles down the lake from the Chautauqua Institution, Corey had the

Contributors' Notes

thrill and honor of having his Jamestown High School graduation ceremony in the Chautauqua Amphitheater. During the summer of 1969, he was the Chautauqua correspondent/reviewer for the *Jamestown Post-Journal*. Since 1992 Corey has served on the faculty of the Chautauqua Writers' Center an overflowing handful of times, mostly teaching poetry but sometimes essays.

JIM DANIELS's recent publications include *Revolt of the Crash-Test Dummies*, winner of the Blue Lynx Poetry Prize, Eastern Washington University Press, *Mr. Pleasant*, short fiction, Michigan State University Press, and *In Line for the Exterminator*, Wayne State University Press. He is the Baker Professor of English at Carnegie Mellon University. He first taught at the Chautauqua Writers' Center in 1992 and has returned a number of times since then, either as a writer or as a spouse tagging along while his wife, Kristin Kovacic, taught. Their children have grown up there, going up the Irion's stairs to either the second or third floor apartment, first as children, now as teenagers. Mary Jean and Paul Irion represent the spirit of Chautauqua—their open-minded engagement with the world, their compassion and thoughtfulness, will always be an inspiration to him as a writer and teacher, and as a human being.

TODD DAVIS teaches creative writing, environmental studies, and American literature at Penn State University's Altoona College. His poems have been nominated for the Pushcart Prize, have won the Gwendolyn Brooks Poetry Prize, and have appeared or are forthcoming in such journals and magazines as *The North American Review*, *The Iowa Review*, *West Branch*, *River Styx*, *Arts & Letters*, *Indiana Review*, *Quarterly West*, *Green Mountains Review*, *Poetry East*, and *Image*. He is the author of two books of poems, *Ripe* (Bottom Dog Press, 2002) and *Some Heaven* (Michigan State University Press, 2007). Poems from *Some Heaven* have been featured on Garrison Keillor's *The Writer's Almanac* and in Ted Kooser's *American Life in Poetry*. During summer 2008, he will lead a workshop at the Chautauqua Writers' Center with a focus upon the body and its relationship to the writing of poems.

MARK DeFOE is Professor of English at West Virginia Wesleyan College. He has published seven chapbooks, the most recent *Mark DeFoe's Greatest Hits* (Pudding House 2004) and *The Rock and the Pebble* (Pringle Tree 2006). His new book, *Weekend Update*, will come out in the spring of 2008. DeFoe's poetry has appeared widely in journals, anthologies, college texts, and Internet e-zines in the U.S., Canada, and Great Britain. He has shared his expertise with writers of all ages and has conducted workshops at colleges, libraries and arts centers. In 1998 and 2003, he was awarded West Virginia Commission on the Arts Fellowships in Literature.

CARL DENNIS was a member of the Chautauqua Writers' Festival in the summer of 2007. In 2004, he gave a solo reading there. His most recent book of poems is *Unknown Friends*, published by Penguin in 2007.

ANTHONY DOERR is the author of three books, *The Shell Collector*, *About Grace*, and *Four Seasons in Rome*. *The Shell Collector*, a volume of eight short stories, was published in 2002 and won the Barnes & Noble Discover Prize, two O. Henry Prizes, the Rome Prize, and the Ohioana Book Award. It was a *New York Times* Notable Book and an American Library Association Book of the Year. His novel, *About Grace*, was named a Best Book of 2004 by the Washington Post, won the Ohioana Book Award again, and was a finalist for the PEN USA fiction award. In 2007, *Granta* placed Doerr on its list of 21 Best Young American novelists. Doerr lives in Boise, Idaho with his wife and two sons.

GREGORY DONOVAN teaches at Virginia Commonwealth University where he is Senior Editor for *Blackbird*, the online journal of literature and the arts. His poetry collection, *Calling His Children Home*, won the Devins Award, and his poetry has been several times anthologized, most recently in *Commonwealth: Contemporary Poets of Virginia*, published by the University of Virginia Press. His poems have appeared in *The Kenyon Review*, *New England Review*, *The Southern Review*, *Hayden's Ferry Review*, *CutBank*, *Poet Lore*, *Alaska Quarterly Review*, and other journals. Recently he has taught in a summer program that takes writers to the highlands of Peru, and he has often served as poet-in-residence for the Chautauqua Writers' Center.

ALICE B. FOGEL's most recent poetry collection is *Be That Empty*. Her poems have appeared in the *Best American Poetry* series, Robert Hass's *Poet's Choice*, and *The Bedside Guide To No-Tell Motel*, among other anthologies and journals. Recipient of an Individual Artist's Fellowship from the NEA, she teaches writing and other arts and, in a different vein, creates clothing primarily out

Contributors' Notes

of "reprised" materials (LyricCouture.com). She has led poetry seminars at Chautauqua, including the "entering the realm of poetry" class for those who don't "get" poetry, and a workshop for teens.

PETER FORTUNATO is the author of two books of poetry, *A Bell or a Hook* and *Letters to Tiohero*. He taught at the Chautauqua Writers' Center in the late 20th Century, when he visited with his wife, the poet Mary Gilliland, who was also teaching a creative writing workshop. Peter has lived in Ithaca, New York, for most of his life and taught writing at Cornell and Ithaca College for many years. Since 2005 he has been in the Middle East, teaching writing and literature in the pre-medical Program of Weill Cornell Medical College in Qatar. Recently with artist Annemarie Zwack he published his first illustrated book for children, *Color Me Earth* (Heartland Studios, Spencer, New York.)

CAROL FROST's first book, *The Salt Lesson*, was published in 1976 by Graywolf Press. Since then, nine collections of her poems have appeared in print, including *I Will Say Beauty* (2003, Northwestern University Press) and *The Queen's Desertion* (2006, Northwestern University Press). She is the recipient of two fellowships from the National Endowment for the Arts, three Pushcart Prizes, and magazine prizes from *Ploughshares* and *Prairie Schooner*. Her poems and essays appear in such places as *The Paris Review, Kenyon Review, The New York Times, New England Review, Atlantic Monthly, TriQuarterly, Shenandoah, The Southern Review*, and have been read on *The Writer's Almanac*. She has taught for the Master of Fine Arts programs at Washington University, Wichita State University, and the low residency program at Warren Wilson and been on the faculty for the Bread Loaf Writers' Conference, the Sewanee Writers' Conference, and the Vermont Studio Center, and the Chautauqua Writers' Center. Currently, she teaches at Hartwick College.

RICHARD FROST is the author of three poetry collections: *The Circus Villains, Getting Drunk with the Birds*, and *Neighbor Blood*. His poems have appeared in *Paris Review, Poetry, The Southern Review, The Gettysburg Review*, and many other magazines. He has held a CAPS fellowship, a Breadloaf Fellowship, and a NEA creative writing fellowship. He has taught poetry and prose writing workshops at Chautauqua Writers' Center. He is a working jazz drummer and is Professor of English at the State University College, Oneonta, New York.

DIANA HUME GEORGE, Professor of English Emerita at Penn State University, teaches nonfiction in the MFA writing program at Goucher College. She is the author or editor of many books of nonfiction, poetry, and literary criticism, including *The Lonely Other*. Her family traditions at Chautauqua extend through several generations, and she has taught workshops at The Chautauqua Writers' Center for many years. George also co-directs The Chautauqua Writers' Festival. Of her essay in this anthology, Diana says, "This essay is the opening chapter of *White Girl/Living with the Senecas*, a memoir-in-progress. I have changed everyone's name. The dead cannot give permission to reveal their identities, and I know that the living don't want to be identified."

MARGARET GIBSON is the author of nine books of poetry and one prose memoir. Louisiana State University Press has published the poetry, most recently *One Body* (2007). Other titles, all from Louisiana State University Press, include: *Long Walks in the Afternoon*, the Lamont Selection, 1982; *Memories of the Future, The Daybooks of Tina Modotti*, the Melville Cane Award given by the Poetry Society of America, 1986-7; *The Vigil*, a Finalist in 1993 for the National Book Award; *Earth Elegy, New and Selected Poems*, 1997; and *Icon and Evidence* (2001) and *Autumn Grasses* (2003), Finalists for the Connecticut Center for the Book Award in Poetry in 2002 and 2004. Her memoir, *The Prodigal Daughter, Reclaiming an Unfinished Childhood*, will be published by University of Missouri Press in March, 2008. Gibson has been awarded a National Endowment for the Arts Grant, a Lila Wallace/Reader's Digest Fellowship, and grants from the Connecticut Commission on the Arts. She has been awarded two Pushcart Prizes and the James Boatright Poetry Prize. She is Professor Emerita, University of Connecticut, and has taught poetry workshops at the Chautauqua Writers' Center for over twelve summers. She lives in Preston, Connecticut.

MARY GILLILAND lives in Ithaca. Recent and forthcoming poetry can be found in *Notre Dame Review*, *Passages North*, *Seneca Review*, and *Stand*. Awards include the Stanley Kunitz Fellowship at the Fine Arts Work Center in Provincetown and an Ann Stanford Prize. She was Poet in Residence at Chautauqua for a week in 1999.

Contributors' Notes

DAVID VALDES GREENWOOD is the author of two memoirs, *A Little Fruitcake: A Childhood in Holidays* and *Homo Domesticus: Notes from a Same-Sex Marriage*. As a playwright, Valdes Greenwood's work has been staged across the US and in the UK, including at the Humana Festival and New York International Fringe Festival. As an essayist, his columns have appeared in *Boston Globe Magazine* and *the Boston Phoenix*.

SUSAN GRIMM is a native of Cleveland, Ohio. Her poems have appeared in *West Branch*, *Poetry East*, *Rattapallax*, *The Journal*, and other publications. In 1996, she was awarded an Individual Artists Fellowship from the Ohio Arts Council. Her chapbook, *Almost Home*, was published by the Cleveland State University Poetry Center in 1997. In 1999, she was named Ohio Poet of the Year by the Ohio Poetry Day Association. Her book of poems, *Lake Erie Blue*, was published by BkMk Press in 2004. She edited *Ordering the Storm: How to Put Together a Book of Poems*, which was published by Cleveland State University Poetry Center in 2006.

LEE GUTKIND is known as the Godfather of Creative Non-Fiction. His latest book is *Almost Human: Making Robots Think* (2007). He is the author of *The Art of Creative Nonfiction* and *Forever Fat: Essays by the Godfather*. He is the founder and editor of the journal *Creative Nonfiction*.

JEFFREY HARRISON is the author of four full-length books of poetry—most recently *Incomplete Knowledge* (Four Way Books, 2006)—as well as of *The Names of Things: New and Selected Poems*, published in England by The Waywiser Press. Of his experience at Chautauqua, he writes, "In my teaching for the Writers' Center, I have found Chautauqua to be a unique place in its combination of relaxation, stimulation, and sense of history. I have also felt an affinity with the lake setting because I have spent part of every summer of my life on a lake in the Adirondacks."

WILLIAM HEYEN lives in Brockport, New York. His *Shoah Train: Poems* (Etruscan Press) was a Finalist for the 2004 National Book Award. MAMMOTH Books has recently published his *Home: Autobiographies*, *The Hummingbird*

Corporation: Stories, and *To William Merwin: A Poem*. Etruscan Press will publish his *A Poetics of Hiroshima & Other Poems* in 2009. He has led poetry workshops at Chautauqua.

RICK HILLES's book, *Brother Salvage*, won the 2005 Agnes Lynch Starrett Prize (Pitt Poetry Series, 2006) and was named 2006 Poetry Book of the Year by ForeWord Magazine. His work has appeared in *Harper's, The Nation, The New Republic, Poetry, Ploughshares*. He was the Amy Lowell Poetry Traveling Scholar for 2002-2003 and has received fellowships from the Stegner Program at Stanford and the Institute for Creative Writing at the University of Wisconsin in Madison. He grew up in northeastern Ohio, was educated at the Columbus College of Art & Design, Kent State, Columbia and the University of Houston, and is now an Assistant Professor in the English Department at Vanderbilt University. He leads workshops at the Chautauqua Writers' Center.

RICHARD HOFFMAN is author of *Half the House: a Memoir*, and the poetry collections, *Without Paradise* and *Gold Star Road*, winner of the Barrow Street Press Poetry Prize. His work has appeared in *Agni, Ascent, Harvard Review, Hudson Review, Poetry, Witness* and other magazines. He has been awarded several fellowships and prizes, most recently a Massachusetts Cultural Council Fellowship in fiction, and The Literary Review's Charles Angoff Prize for the essay.

ANN HOOD is the author of eight novels, including *Somewhere off the Coast of Maine* and, most recently, *The Knitting Circle*; a collection of short stories, *An Ornithologist's Guide to Life*; a young adult novel, *How I Saved My Father's Life and Ruined Everything Else*; and two memoirs, *Do Not Go Gentle* and *Comfort*. Her short stories and essays have appeared in *The New York Times, Bon Appetit, Traveler, Food and Wine, Good Housekeeping*, and *Ladies Home Journal*. She has won two Pushcart Prizes, the Paul Bowles Prize for Short Fiction, and a Best American Spiritual Writing Award. Ann has taught fiction and nonfiction at Chautauqua since 2002.

JOHN HOPPENTHALER's poetry has recently appeared or is forthcoming in *Barrow Street, The Laurel Review, Tar River Poetry, Inkwell, ABZ, The Potomac*, the anthologies *Blooming through the Ashes* (Rutgers UP) and *Poetry Calendar*

Contributors' Notes

(Alhambra Publishing, 2008), and elsewhere. His books of poetry are *Lives of Water* (2003) and *Anticipate the Coming Reservoir* (2008), both titles from Carnegie Mellon University Press. He teaches at East Carolina University.

Laura Kasischke has taught at Chautauqua during several summer sessions. She has published seven collections of poetry—most recently *Lilies Without* (Ausable Press)—and four novels, including *The Life Before her Eyes*, which was made into a movie in 2008, starring Uma Thurman. She lives in Chelsea, Michigan, and teaches at the University of Michigan.

Susan Kinsolving's three books of poems are *The White Eyelash*, *Dailies & Rushes*, a finalist for The National Book Critics Circle Award, and *Among Flowers*. Before joining the Core Faculty of The Bennington Writing Seminars, Kinsolving taught poetry at University of Connecticut, Southampton College, Chautauqua Institution, Willard-Cybulski Mens' Prison, and California Institute of the Arts. As a librettist, her works have been performed by Glimmerglass Opera and the Baroque Choral Guild in the Netherlands, Italy, New York, and California. A recipient of several international fellowships, she was the poetry fellow at The Camargo Foundation of France, 2007. She will be a 2008 fellow at the Bogliasco Foundation in Italy and at Hawthornden Castle in Scotland.

Kristin Kovacic is the editor, along with Lynne Barrett, of *Birth: A Literary Companion* (University of Iowa Press) and a forthcoming, follow-up companion about parenting adolescents. She is widely published in many genres, including poetry, fiction, and nonfiction, recently winning a Pushcart Prize and a Pennsylvania Council on the Arts fellowship for her work. Since 1999, she has taught poetry writing at the Pittsburgh High School for the Creative and Performing Arts. She has taught at the Chautauqua Writers' Center since the son in the poem in this anthology was an infant. She began thinking about writing about parenthood at Chautauqua and began talking about her ideas in lectures at the Writers' Center and in classes. About the Writers' Center, she says, "Chautauqua has truly 'mothered' my career."

Greg Kuzma was born in Rome, New York, and wrote many of his earliest poems about the Adirondack Mountains. A recent collection, *McKeever Bridge*, collects most of the Adirondacks poems. Mary Jean Irion invited him to teach poetry workshops at Chautauqua some years ago, and he has served three summers on the grounds. Kuzma teaches poetry writing at the University of Nebraska, Lincoln, where he has taught since 1969. Over the past few years he has been trying to teach himself to write screenplays. His work in progress is a film about Virginia and Leonard Woolf called *Blooms-Berries*.

DAVID LAZAR's books include *The Body of Brooklyn* (Iowa), *Michael Powell: Interviews* (Mississippi), *Conversations with M.F.K. Fisher* (Mississippi) and a forthcoming anthology, *Truth in Nonfiction* (Iowa), and a book of prose poems, *Powder Town* (Pecan Grove). His essays and prose poem have appeared in *The Southwest Review*, *The Ohio Review*, *Gulf Coast*, *Pleiades*, *Arts & Letters*, *Best of the Prose Poem*, *Sentence*, *Denver Quarterly*, *Southern Humanities Review*, and other journals and magazines. Four of his essays have been named Notable Essays of the Year by *Best American Essays*. He is currently the Director of the nonfiction program at Columbia College Chicago, before which he taught at Ohio University, where he created one of five doctoral programs in the country in creative nonfiction. He is the founding editor of the literary magazine *Hotel Amerika*. In the summer of 2008, he will teach prose writers at the Chautauqua Institution for the third time.

RICHARD LEHNERT was Poet in Residence for the final week of the Chautauqua Institution's 2006 season. His first book, *A Short History of the Usual*, was published in 2003 by The Backwaters Press. His second book, *The Only Empty Place*, is forthcoming from a press as yet unknown. He and his wife, Susannah, live in Santa Fe, New Mexico, where they try to do as little as possible. They fail.

GEORGE LOONEY's third collection of poems *The Precarious Rhetoric of Angels* won the 2005 White Pine Press Poetry Prize and was published by White Pine Press. His novella *Hymn of Ash* won the 2007 Elixir Press Fiction Chapbook Award and was published by Elixir Press in the spring of 2008. He is chair of the BFA in Creative Writing Program at Penn State Erie where he is editor-in-chief of the international literary journal *Lake Effect* and translation editor

Contributors' Notes

of *Mid-American Review*. Along with Philip Terman, he is a founding director of The Chautauqua Writers' Festival, and he has taught a one-week poetry workshop during Chautauqua's summer season.

Ron MacLean's fiction has appeared in *GQ, Greensboro Review, Prism International, Night Train* and other quarterlies. He is a recipient of the Frederick Exley Award for Short Fiction and a Pushcart Prize nominee, and author of the novel *Blue Winnetka Skies*. *Why the Long Face*, a collection of stories, will be published in fall 2008. He is excited to be back teaching at Chautauqua in summer '08 after a delightful fiction residency in summer '06.

Dan Masterson spent his early years in Buffalo, New York, involved in back-street drumming, and boxing. He resides in Rockland County, New York, with his wife, Janet. During his four residencies at Chautauqua, he and his wife, Janet, have bonded so deeply with the place they call Camelot that they spent a week there as paying guests in celebration of their 45th anniversary. He was elected to membership in Pen International in 1986, and is the recipient of two Pushcart Prizes, the Bullis, Borestone, and Fels awards, and is an AWP Award Series honoree, as well as the founding editor of *The Enskyment Poetry Anthology*, online. His *New and Selected, All Things, Seen and Unseen* was released by The University of Arkansas Press in 1997. His work has appeared in an eclectic array of publications including *Poetry, Esquire, Poetry Now, Hotel Amerika, Shenandoah, The New Yorker, Esquire,* and *The London Magazine*, as well as *The Ontario, Sewanee, Paris, Hudson, Gettysburg, Massachusetts, Yale, New Orleans,* and *Georgia Reviews*.

Jane McCafferty teaches at Carnegie Mellon University and has enjoyed teaching prose writing at Chautauqua twice. She is the author of three books of fiction: *Director of The World, Thank You For The Music,* and *One Heart*. She is the winner of The Drue Heinz prize, an NEA, and two Pushcarts for fiction and nonfiction; her stories and essays have appeared in journals and anthologies. She currently works with the photographer Charlee Brodsky in verbal-visual mediums and is writing both fiction and nonfiction.

Michael McFee has published thirteen books of poetry and prose, most recently *Shinemaster* (Carnegie Mellon University Press), *The Napkin Manuscripts:*

CHAUTAUQUA

Selected Essays and an Interview (University of Tennessee Press), and *The Smallest Talk: One-Line Poems* (Bull City Press). He taught at Cornell in the late 1980s, and he now teaches poetry writing at UNC-Chapel Hill. In the summers of 1992 and 1995, he had the pleasure of leading week-long poetry workshops at Chautauqua. Mary Jean Irion and the Writers' Center were wonderful, and he greatly enjoyed the class, the Poetry Symposium, and the Reading on the Porch; but the real gift of Chautauqua was all the unfettered time he could spend with his wife and young son in such a beautiful cultural and intellectual refuge. He'll always be grateful for their time there.

DINTY W. MOORE was born and raised in Erie, Pennsylvania, and spent his formative years fishing for bluegill, riding a bike with a banana seat, and dodging the Sisters of St. Joseph. He earned a BA in writing from the University of Pittsburgh and went on to earn an MFA in fiction writing from Louisiana State University. A National Endowment for the Arts fellowship recipient, Moore has guest taught creative nonfiction seminars across the United States and in Europe. In addition to editing the Internet journal, *Brevity*, he is on the editorial board of Creative Nonfiction and is coordinating editor for the anthology *Best Creative Nonfiction* (W.W. Norton). Moore teaches writing at Ohio University and serves on the Board of Directors of The Association of Writers & Writing Programs.

KIRK NESSET is author of two books of short stories, *Paradise Road* (University of Pittsburgh Press, 2007) and *Mr. Agreeable* (forthcoming), as well as a nonfiction study, *The Stories of Raymond Carver* (Ohio University Press, 1995). His books of poems and translations are also forthcoming: *St. X* (Lewis Clark Press) and *Alphabet of the World* (University of Oklahoma Press). He was awarded the Drue Heinz literature award in 2007 and has received a Pushcart Prize and numerous grants from the Pennsylvania Council on the Arts. His stories, poems and translations have appeared in *The Paris Review, Ploughshares, The Southern Review, The Kenyon Review, Agni, The Gettysburg Review, Iowa Review, The Sun, Fiction, Prairie Schooner* and elsewhere. He teaches creative writing and literature at Allegheny College, and has taught as fiction-writer-in-residence at the Chautauqua Writers' Center numerous summers (experiences he considers especially rewarding).

Contributors' Notes

Ann Pancake's newest book is *Strange as This Weather Has Been* (October 2007). Her earlier novel, *Given Ground*, was the 2001 winner of the Bakeless Literary Publication Prize in Fiction. She has also been awarded a National Endowment of the Arts Fellowship, the Thomas Wolfe Fiction Prize, a Pushcart Prize, the Glasgow Prize, and the 2003 Whiting Writers Award. Her short stories have appeared in *Glimmer Train*, *Shenandoah* and *Virginia Quarterly*. She teaches at Pacific Lutheran University.

Alan Michael Parker's fifth book of poems, *Elephants & Butterflies*, will be published in June by BOA Editions. He teaches at Davidson College, where he directs the program in creative writing, and as a core faculty member in the Queens University low-residency MFA program. His essays and reviews appear in journals including *The Believer*, *The New Yorker*, and *The San Francisco Chronicle*. He shares this memory of Chautauqua: "I remember clearly the moment my three-year-old son got on the bus in Chautauqua to go to Dance Camp, and I walked across the grounds to teach a workshop at the Writers' Center that included Coleridge's poem, 'Frost at Midnight,' about his own son. The students couldn't have been more deeply engaged, which I found profoundly rewarding. From family to poetry and back again, Chautauqua remains with me, and for the best reasons."

Stanley Plumly's latest book, *Old Heart*, has been nominated for the National Book Award. His collections of poetry also include *Now That My Father Lies Down Beside Me: New and Selected Poems 1970–2000*, *The Marriage in the Trees* (1998), *Boy on the Step: Poems* (1989), *Summer Celestial-Poems* (1983), *Out-of-the-Body Travel* (1978), *Giraffe* (1974), and *In the Outer Dark: Poems* (1970). His book of essays on poetry and art, *Argument & Song: Sources and Silences in Poetry*, came out in 2003. Plumly has been nominated for the National Book Critics Circle Award, the William Carlos Williams Award, and the Academy of American Poets' Lenore Marshall Poetry Prize. He has won the Delmore Schwartz Memorial Award. Plumly teaches at the University of Maryland.

Sara Rath has taught both fiction and nonfiction at Chautauqua Writers' Center since 1992. Her fourth and most recent visit was in August, 2005. Rath was awarded an MFA in Writing from Vermont College and has received fellowships to The MacDowell Colony and The Ucross Foundation. For her first novel, *Star Lake Saloon & Housekeeping Cottages* (University of Wisconsin Press, 2005) she was awarded a Wisconsin Arts Board Individual Artist Grant. Her eleventh book, *Night Sisters*, a novel, will be published in autumn 2008. Meanwhile, she is completing a biography of the 19th century Vermont spiritualist Achsa W. Sprague.

NANCY REISMAN is the author of the novel *The First Desire* (Pantheon), a 2004 *New York Times* Notable Book, and the story collection *House Fires*, which won the Iowa Short Fiction Award (University of Iowa Press, 1999). Her fiction has appeared in many anthologies and magazines, including *2005 O.Henry Award Stories*, *2001 Best American Short Stories*, *Tin House*, *New England Review*, *Kenyon Review*, and other journals. She grew up in Western New York and for many years has visited Chautauqua; in 2006, she joined the Chautauqua Special Studies faculty. She now lives in Nashville and teaches at Vanderbilt University.

LIZ ROSENBERG, a professor at Binghamton University, is the author of fiction, nonfiction, award-winning childrens books, and four books of poetry, most recently *Demon Love* (MAMMOTH Press) and *The Lily Poems* (Bright Hills). She has taught poetry, micro essays, and fiction at Chautauqua, a place her whole family adores. She is at work on her first novel for adults.

LESLIE RUBINKOWSKI is the author of *Impersonating Elvis*. A journalist, feature writer and entertainment critic, her work has appeared in *Harper's*, *Creative Nonfiction*, and *River Teeth*. She has also worked for six newspapers, most recently the *Pittsburgh Post-Gazette*. She was director of the news-editorial department at West Virginia University and has lectured at the Poynter Institute. Her essay "In the Woods" was named a Notable Essay in *Best American Essays, 2001*.

MAURA STANTON's poems have appeared recently, or are forthcoming, in *Cincinnati Review*, *32 Poems*, *Barrow Street*, *Mid-American Review*, *Denver Quarterly* and *Harpur Palate*. Her new book of poetry, *Immortal Sofa*, is forthcoming from the University of Illinois Press. She led a workshop at the 2007 Chautauqua Writers' Festival and currently teaches at Indiana University in Bloomington.

Contributors' Notes

PHILIP TERMAN is the author of three collections of poetry: *The House Of Sages* (MAMMOTH Books, 1998), *Book of the Unbroken Days* (MAMMOTH Books, 2005) and *Rabbis of the Air* (Autumn House Press, 2007). Recent poems have appeared in *The Georgia Review*, *Prairie Schooner*, and *Blood to Remember: Poets Respond to the Holocaust*. He teaches English at Clarion University and co-directs the Chautauqua Writers' Festival.

ELAINE TERRANOVA's most recent book is *Not to: New and Selected Poems*. She has been a Pew Fellow, recipient of an NEA, and winner of a Walt Whitman Award. She has been a fan and supporter of the Chautauqua Writers' Center since it was barely a gleam in Mary Jean Irion's eye. She was poet in residence first in 1992 and then four times since, as well as a member of the advisory board for several years when they met annually over bagel breakfasts at the House of the Redeemer, a Fifth Avenue mansion turned mission.

RICHARD TERRILL, a Chautauqua faculty member in 2007, is the author of a collection of poems, *Coming Late to Rachmaninoff*, winner of the Minnesota Book Award, and two books of creative nonfiction, *Fakebook: Improvisations on a Journey Back to Jazz* and *Saturday Night in Baoding: A China Memoir*, winner of the Associated Writing Programs Award for nonfiction. He has been awarded fellowships from the National Endowment for the Arts, the Wisconsin and Minnesota State Arts Boards, the Jerome Foundation, and the Bread Loaf Writers' Conference. He has taught as a Fulbright professor in China, Korea, and Poland, and currently teaches creative nonfiction and poetry writing in the MFA program at Minnesota State University, Mankato.

MICHAEL WATERS's eight books of poetry include *Darling Vulgarity* (2006—finalist for the Los Angeles Times Book Prize), *Parthenopi: New and Selected Poems* (2001), *Green Ash, Red Maple, Black Gum* (1997) from BOA Editions, *Bountiful* (1992), *The Burden Lifters* (1989), and *Anniversary of the Air* (1985) from Carnegie Mellon UP. His several edited volumes include *Contemporary American Poetry* (Houghton Mifflin, 2006) and *Perfect in Their Art: Poems on Boxing from Homer to Ali* (Southern Illinois UP, 2003). In 2004, he chaired the poetry panel for the National Book Award. The recipient of fellowships from the National Endowment for the Arts and the Fulbright Foundation, Individual Artist Awards from the Maryland State Arts Council, and four Pushcart Prizes, he teaches at Salisbury University in Maryland and in the New England College MFA Program.

GABRIEL WELSCH is the author of the poetry collection, *Dirt and All Its Dense Labor*. His poems, stories, essays and reviews appear in journals including *Georgia Review*, *New Letters*, *Other Voices*, *Mid-American Review*, *Ascent*, *Missouri Review*, *Isotope*, *Harvard Review*, and others. The poems in this issue mark Welsch's third appearance in *Chautauqua*; Richard Foerster solicited his work for the inaugural issue and his story "My Enemy" appeared in 2006. Welsch also taught a poetry workshop at the Chautauqua Writers' Center in the 2006 season. Welsch works as assistant vice president of marketing at Juniata College and lives with his family in Huntingdon, Pennsylvania.

SARAH WILLIS'S first two novels take place in Mayville, New York. *Some Things that Stay*, about a family that moves into the farmlands of Chautauqua in 1954, was a *New York Times* Notable Book of the Year, won the Stephen Crane Award for First Fiction 2000 and The Cleveland Arts Prize in Literature 2000, and was made into a movie. *The Rehearsal*, set in 1971, is a story about a group of actors trying to "live" *Of Mice and Men* at the director's family farm. She chose this setting, the woods of Chautauqua, because her father was an actor who worked at the Chautauqua Institution during the summer. She still has a family home in Chautauqua County. Her other novels are *A Good Distance* and *The Sound of Us*. She writes short stories, essays, poetry and book reviews. She is presently writing her fifth novel. Willis has taught creative writing classes at Hiram College, John Carroll University, The Imagination Conference at CSU, The Chautauqua Writers' Center, and the Maui Writers Retreat.

acknowledgements

Some of the poems, stories, and essays first appeared, often in partial or slightly different form, in the following publications:

Maggie Anderson. "Art in America," "The Artist," and "Small Citizens." From *Cold Comfort*, University of Pittsburgh Press, 1986. Reprinted by permission of the University of Pittsburgh Press.

Emily Barton. "Eli Miller's Seltzer Delivery Service." From *Brooklyn Was Mine*. Eds. Chris Knutsen and Valerie Steiker, Riverhead Books, 2008. Used with Permission.

Jan Beatty. "Long White Sky" and "Procession." From *Red Sugar*, University of Pittsburgh Press, 2008. Reprinted by permission of the University of Pittsburgh Press.

Robin Becker. "The New Egypt." From *Domain of Perfect Affection*, University of Pittsburgh Press, 2006. Reprinted by permission of the University of Pittsburgh Press.

Bruce Bennett. "Calligraphy." From *Were I to Tell You*, Wells College Press, 2004. Used with permission.

Bruce Bennett. "After School." From *Navigating the Distances*, Orchises Press, 1999. Used with permission.

David Bouchier. "The Plastic Horse of Troy." From *National Public Radio*, Stations WSHU and WSUF, 18 June 2007. Used with permission.

Philip Brady. "Gilt." From *Fathom*, Word Press, 2007. Used with permission.

Joan Ciabattari. "Mama Godot." From *VerbSap.com*, Fall 2007. Used with permission.

Gregory Donovan. "Sarah Henry, Phantom Wife: 1775." From *Calling His Children Home*, University of Missouri Press, 1993. Used with permission.

Carol Frost. "To Fishermen" and "Man of War." From *Poetry*, March 2005. Used with permission.

Richard Frost. "Drummer Goes to Hear Harry James." From *Brilliant Corners*, Winter 2006. Used with permission.

Richard Frost. "Drummer Young." From *The Southern Review*, Spring 2001; reprinted in *Brilliant Corners*, Winter 2006. Used with permission.

Richard Frost. "Cereal." From *The Gettysburg Review*, Spring 1996. Used with permission.

Lee Gutkind. "WWMG." Reprinted from *Forever Fat: Essays by the Godfather,* available wherever books are sold or from the University of Nebraska Press 800.526.2617 and on the web at nebraskapress.unl.edu. © 2003 by Lee Gutkind.

Jeffrey Harrison. "Household Spirits." From *The Names of Things*, The Waywiser Press, London, 2006. All rights reserved. Used with permission.

Jeffrey Harrison. "Visitation." From *Incomplete Knowledge*, Four Way Books, 2006. All rights reserved. Used with permission.

Acknowledgements

Rick Hilles. "The Last Blue Light." From *Brother Salvage*. Pittsburgh: University of Pittsburgh Press, 2006. Reprinted by permission of the University of Pittsburgh Press.

Richard Hoffman. "The Wave." From *Madonna Muse*, Madonna University, Spring 2008. Used with permission.

Ann Hood. "Comfort Food." From *Alimentum*, Summer 2006. Reprinted in *Comfort*, Norton, 2008. Used with permission.

Greg Kuzma. "Childhood." From *Virginia Quarterly Review*, Summer 1987. Used with permission.

Ron MacLean. "Last Seen, Hank's Grille." From *Night Train*, Winter 2006. Used with permission.

Dan Masterson. "Clown with Trained Duck." From *That Which Is Seen: Poems Based Exclusively on Artwork*. Used with permission.

Dan Masterson. "By the Sea, By the Sea." *Hotel Amerika*, Fall 2003. Used with permission.

Nancy Reisman. "Another Kiss." From *Subtropics*, Fall 2007. Used with permission.

Michael Waters. "Man in Black." From *The Gettysburg Review*. Used with permission.

Michael Waters. "Epistle Sonatas." From *The Mississippi Review*. Used with permission.

Chautauqua Institution

DONATIONS to the Chautauqua Writers' Center
and *Chautauqua* are tax-deductible
through the Chautauqua Fund.

CHAUTAUQUA is open to submissions year-round from any writer. The editors welcome original, previously unpublished works of poetry, fiction, and creative nonfiction, particularly those pieces that embody the vision of Chautauqua, as much a philosophy and an aesthetic as a physical place whose soul lies in the American passion for self-improvement—the drive to enrich oneself culturally, artistically, morally, and intellectually.

Book reviews, interviews, and profiles are by invitation only; please query the editor before submitting. General submissions and other business should be addressed to the Editors, *Chautauqua*, Department of Creative Writing, University of North Carolina Wilmington, 601 South College Road, Wilmington, NC 28403. Please include a self-addressed, stamped envelope for notification. Manuscripts will not be returned. Other queries may be addressed to clj@uncw.edu.